An Introduction to

SCANDINAVIAN
LITERATURE

An Introduction to

SCANDINAVIAN LITERATURE

FROM THE EARLIEST TIME TO OUR DAY

By

Elias Bredsdorff, M.A.	*Brita Mortensen, M. A.*	*Ronald Popperwell, B.A.*
Lecturer in Danish in the University of Cambridge	Lecturer in Swedish in the University of Cambridge	Department of Scandinavian Studies in the University of Cambridge

GREENWOOD PRESS, PUBLISHERS
WESTPORT, CONNECTICUT

ACKNOWLEDGEMENTS

For permission to make use of copyright material the following acknow-
ledgements are due: — for the Danish chapters to Andr. Fred. Høst & Søn,
Copenhagen, for extracts from Mr. R. P. Keigwin's translations of poems by
H. A. Brorson, Johannes Ewald, Jens Baggesen, N. F. S. Grundtvig, B. S.
Ingemann, St. St. Blicher, Christian Winther, Ludvig Bødtcher, Holger
Drachmann and Jeppe Aakjær (from *In Denmark I was born* ..., 2nd
edition, Copenhagen, 1950); to the Editor of *The Norseman*, London, for
Mr. Keigwin's translation of a poem by Wessel; to the Editor of *Gads danske Magasin*, Copenhagen, for Mr. Keigwin's translation of a poem by Ambrosius Stub and one of Aarestrup's "Ritournelles"; to Flensteds Forlag,
Odense, for quotations from Mr. Keigwin's version of *Hans Christian Andersen: Fairy Tales*, I-II, Odense 1950; to the American-Scandinavian Foundation for the translation by S. Foster Damon of a poem by Carsten Hauch,
and for an extract of R. S. Hillyer's translation of Oehlenschläger's "Guldhornene" (from *A Book of Danish Verse*, New York, 1922) and for the translation of a Danish ballad by Miss E. M. Smith-Dampier (from *A Book of
Danish Ballads*, Princeton; New York, 1939); to Mr. Mark Baker for an
extract of his version of a poem by Fr. Paludan-Müller; and to Mr. R. P.
Keigwin for the translation of two of Aarestrup's "Ritournelles", published
here for the first time; — for the Swedish chapters to George Allen & Unwin
Ltd. for extracts from *Frithiof's Saga* by E. Tegnér in the translation of
C. D. Locock, and for extracts from *Modern Swedish Poetry* by C. D. Locock:
— for the Old Norse and Norwegian chapters to the Viking Club for translations from Hávamál and Skirnismál by Olive Bray; to Everyman's Library
for an extract of Sir G. Dasent's translation of Njál's Saga; and to Messrs.
Gyldendal, Oslo, and Hodder & Stoughton, London, for poems by Wergeland, translated by G. M. Gathorne-Hardy, Jethro Bithell and I. Grøndahl.

CONTENTS

PREFACE

The purpose of this book is to provide a short introduction to the history of Danish, Norwegian, and Swedish literature for readers in the English-speaking world. Neither Modern Icelandic, Finnish, nor Finnish-Swedish literature has been touched; for the geographical definition of Scandinavia can only doubtfully be stretched to include these fields.

It is the word "Introduction" that we would wish our readers to take as operative. We have tried to give an account of the main lines in the development of Scandinavian literature, and therefore only the more important writers and works have been mentioned. We have n o t wanted to load the text with all the names and data and biographical details which one may legitimately expect to find in an encyclopædia article. In fact, to quote Professor Alexander Gray's Preface to *The Development of Economic Doctrine,* we have "proceeded by a process of selection and concentration, ruthlessly casting overboard people of quite considerable importance ... like other frail vessels, an introductory text-book also has a Plimsoll-line ..."

We have laid the main emphasis on the periods and authors that may be expected to have the greatest interest for readers outside Scandinavia, more especially on the writers of the 19th and 20th centuries.

The chapter on *Old Norse Literature* (I) and those on

Norwegian Literature (VII and X), are by Mr. Popperwell, those on *Danish Literature* (IIa, III, V, and VIII) by Mr. Bredsdorff, and those on *Swedish Literature* (IIb, IV, VI, and IX) by Miss Mortensen.

Titles of works are normally given (in italics) in English translation, followed by the original title in brackets. Only when titles are simply proper names, or when they absolutely defy translation, is the original alone given. When the original work has actually been rendered into English, and is known by a title quite distinct from the Scandinavian form, this English title is given in a bracket.

Extracts from Scandinavian prose and poetry have occasionally been quoted, where it has been possible to find or provide *suitable* translations. Lack of space has unfortunately very sharply limited such illustrative material, and we can only hope that our readers will themselves find their way to the original texts. That they should be impelled to look for these is, after all, the main object of this book.

Cambridge, April 1951.

E. B., B. M., R. P.

CHAPTER I

OLD NORSE LITERATURE

The Earliest Literature.

Runic inscriptions scratched on stone are the earliest communications preserved to us from the fathers of the Norwegian people. Most of them consist of short and rather dull statements of fact, with a noteworthy exception in the inscription on the stone, found at Eggjum in the district of Sogn in Western Norway, which gives information about the runes themselves and the magical properties the ancient Norsemen generally supposed that they possessed. It is thought to date from about the year 700 and is the longest and most enlightening runic inscription found in Norway. There can, however, be no talk of a literature in Norway until after the introduction of Christianity. This brought foreign clerics and the Latin of the church in its wake and for some time Latin remained the only written language. In the course of time native-born priests were trained and soon turned their hand to the task of adapting the current language, which we call Old Norse, to the Latin alphabet. Their efforts were well-rewarded, for the instrument they provided was to be used in the writing down of a literature which, in some respects, stands supreme in the field of early Germanic literature. Much of it had come into being at an earlier period and had been preserved by oral tradition, particularly in Iceland, which the Norwegians had begun to colonize in the years before 900, and it was in Iceland that most of the writing down was

to be done. This was partly due to the fact that Iceland
was already a literary centre and partly due to the circumstance that when writing began to flourish, about 1100,
the cultured classes in Norway were soon to be greatly
weakened by internecine strife, occasioned by the civil wars
which raged for about 100 years after 1130. So it was
then that the Icelanders became predominantly the authors
and custodians of this remarkable corpus of Old Norse
literature, and it was not until the 17th century that the
outside world got any inkling of the treasures stored in
that remote isle.

In the year 1643, the bishop of Skálholt in Iceland,
Brynjólfur Sveinsson, discovered an ancient manuscript
containing a collection of lays about the old Scandinavian
gods and heroes which he called the *Elder Edda*. This
manuscript was, however, only one of the many the bishop
had collected, but like most of his fellow collectors in Iceland he kept his treasures for himself, scarcely permitting
them to be copied, in spite of repeated requests from Professor Ole Worm in Copenhagen, who was the moving spirit
in 17th century research into the Nordic Middle Ages.
Fortunately for scholarship, family considerations weighed
even more heavily with the bishop than his manuscripts.
His only daughter had been compromised by a young parson, but Icelandic law laid many difficulties in the way of
the satisfaction both bishop and daughter desired. He
therefore applied to the Danish King Frederik III, backing
his supplications to that monarch, an ardent bibliophile,
with the gift of all his manuscripts which besides the *Edda*
included *Njáls Saga, Flatey Book* and many others of importance. His sacrifice was not in vain, his daughter
received the satisfaction desired.

The *Elder Edda* manuscript dates from ca. 1270, but its
content shows that it belongs to pre-Christian Norway and
is largely based on legends which are the common property

of the Germanic peoples. Most remarkable are *The Sooth Saying of the Vala* ("Voluspá") and *The Words of Odin the High One* ("Hávamál"). The first relates a visit made by Odin to the oracle and the account she gives of the origins of the world, its present state (possibly in Erik Blood-Axe's time) and her prophecy of the end of the world *The Twilight of the Gods* ("Ragnarok"), and the new world which is to emerge to replace the old. *Hávamál* contains a long account of the moral code of the Norsemen and their social conventions and is largely didactic in purpose. Some of the advice given indicates a certain prosiness on the part of the author and moderation is the virtue most highly praised; in other places a high moral tone prevails. Most important, we learn, is to pass out of the world with a good reputation, for whilst:

"Cattle die and kinsmen die,
thyself too soon must die,
but one thing never, I ween, will die,
fair fame of one who has earned."

Other parts of *Edda* show the gods as less lofty beings, afflicted with human failings and weaknesses, *The Lay of Thrym* ("Þrymskviða"), for example, tells of the fun Thor had in getting back his hammer. In *The Story of Skirnir* ("Skírnismál"), the god Frey gazes out over all the worlds and looks into Jötunheim. There he beholds a fair maiden going from her father's hall to her bower, and at the sight of her he is seized with a great sickness of heart. His servant Skirnir woos the maiden on his master's behalf; she is not unwilling but lays down a waiting period of nine days. On learning this the god sighs:

"Long is one night, — long are two nights —
how shall I live through three!
Shorter a month has seemed to me oft
than waiting this half night here".

The heroic lays in the *Elder Edda* mainly concern the hero Sigurd, (the slayer of the dragon Fafnir). Here again we are on common Germanic ground, Sigurd is the Siegfried of the *Nibelungenlied*, although the *Edda* version belongs to an earlier period and is more realistic. In it passion and suffering are on a monumental scale and the tone is dark and tragic. It gives a clear insight into the psychology of the Norsemen and their struggles to create a philosophy of life suitable to the violent times they lived in.

The Scalds.

Whilst a great deal of the literature of the period we are dealing with is from unknown hands, certain of the poets and their works are known. Most of these scalds, as these combined composers and reciters of poems were called, were Icelanders who had settled down at the court of one or other Norwegian king. Their art was highly thought of and they often exercised much influence with their royal patrons. Even the kings themselves were not above poetizing. King Olav (the Holy) had considerable talent as a scald and Harald Hardrade was noted both as a connoisseur of the scaldic art and as a skilled practitioner in it. Some of these poems provide us with valuable historical evidence regarding persons and events, but few people would read them with any pleasure to-day. One of the main reasons for this is that as time went on technical skill in writing verse became the main thing admired. This led to scalds making their poems as complicated as possible and the most banal preciosity was often the result. One of the most celebrated of them was Torbjörn Hornklove. He sang the praises of Harald the Fairhaired and his victory at Havsfjord in *Hrafnsmál* ("Haraldskvæði", the Lay of Harald). Another scald of repute was Eyvind Finnsson; called Skaldaspillir by his contemporaries because of his habit of making use of earlier lays and thereby (in their eyes) spoiling them. His best known poem is *Hákonarmál*, the lay of the death of Hákon the Good. Greatest of all the scalds was perhaps EGIL SKALLAGRÍMSSON. He was a man of independent nature and far too fond of going his own way to take service as a court poet; further he was not averse to making public what he thought of important personages. On one occasion, it was in England as it happens, he saved his life, after having fallen into the hands of Erik Blood-Axe, (whom he had earlier unmercifully lampooned) by composing and reciting a poem of great technical skill lauding that monarch's bravery as a warrior. His best piece of work is called *Sonatorrek*, inspired by the loss of his son Bodvar who was drowned in a fjord in Iceland.

The Family Sagas.

Early Norse society was a society in which the family was the most important unit and it was the family's interest, honour and prosperity which had first claim on the allegiance of its members. The history of the family and in particular the exploits and travels of its members was a treasure piously preserved and added to by succeeding generations and in Iceland the histories of the most prominent families were common knowledge. Those family histories or sagas which eventually received written form and have been preserved to us tell of a society rough and violent, where a fanatically sensitive conception of family honour prevailed and where destructive blood feuds between family and family took heavy toll. Most famous of them is *Njáls Saga*, which largely concerns Njál and his sons and Gunnar of Hliðarendi whose wife Hallgerda is the evil genius of the mutually destructive strife which eventually destroys both families. The saga is written with great skill and the characterization of the leading persons

in it is masterly. Most memorable and sublime are Gunnar's last defence of his home at Hliðarendi and the bur-
ning-in of Njál. Gunnar has been outlawed and on his
way down to the ship that is to take him from Iceland his
horse stumbles so that he catches sight of his home once
more. "Fair is the Lithe (the valley)", he says, "so fair
that it has never seemed to me so fair; the corn fields are
white to harvest, and the home mead is mown; and now
I will ride back home, and not fare abroad at all". This
he does although he knows it will lead to his death. When
his house is later besieged by his enemies he asks his wife
Hallgerda for two locks of her hair to restring his bow.
"Well", she says, "now I will call to thy mind that slap on
the face which thou gavest me; and I care never a whit
whether thou holdest out a long while or a short". Later
Njál and his family are surrounded by enemies intent on
burning them in. When Njál realises that further resistance is useless, he and his wife lie down with a grandson
between them to await the end: "So there they lay down
both of them in their bed, and put the boy between them.
Then they signed themselves and the boy with the cross,
and gave over their souls into God's hand, and that was
the last word that men heard them utter." In *The Laks-
dale Saga* bloody strife plays a much smaller part. The
main story in it is concerned with Kjartan and his foster-
brother Bolle and their love for the brazen, sensuous yet
vital and integrated Guðrún. In *Gunnlaug's Saga* a complete contrast to Guðrún is to be found in Helga the Fair.
The story of her love for Gunnlaug is one of the most
beautiful and touching in the whole of the saga literature.
Artistically too it is a masterpiece, simple, direct and with
a deep understanding of human nature. Some of the sagas
tell of the scalds, chief amongst them *Egil Skallagrimsson's
Saga*, the greater part of which takes place outside Iceland.
Also of a different type from the family sagas is the *Saga*

of Grettir the Strong, the story of the outlawed Grettir.
Other sagas deal with the Norwegian colonies, *Orkneyinga-
saga* tells of the history of the Orkney earls, *Færeyingasaga*
with the Faeroes and particularly with Sigmund Brestesson,
who was responsible for the introduction of Christianity
into the Faeroes. *Erik the Red's Saga* and *Leif Eirikssons
Saga* tell of the discovery of Greenland and Vinland (North
America).

It will be clear from what has been said about the late
introduction of writing into Norway and Iceland that a
long time elapsed before the sagas were written down and
this inevitably, in spite of the importance attached to main-
taining the accuracy of the oral tradition, led to error and
confusion in the recording of events, and the historical
accuracy of much in the sagas is open to serious doubt. It
is not, however, proposed to enter into this question here,
but whatever their historical accuracy it will be obvious
that the sagas do give a remarkable picture of the life and
philosophy of the Norsemen.

Fornaldarsögur or Sagas of Olden Time..

This is the title given to a group of sagas which have
little or no historical basis and were intended purely as
entertainment. Many of them are based on old legends
and folk-tales. Most important is the *Völsunga Saga,* much
of which is based on the *Elder Edda,* and perhaps most
famous of this group of sagas is the *Saga of Friðthjóf the
Bold,* which is set in the district of Sogn in Norway. This
has become very well known through the poetic version
of it written by the 19th century Swedish poet Esaias Tegnér
(see p. 119).

Historical Writing.

In this field as in others it was in Iceland that most of the work was done. Attempts were made at an early stage in the settlement of Iceland to write down its history. SÆMUND, who died in 1133, is said to have been a very learned man and to have written a history in Latin of the Norwegian kings, but this has been lost. From the pen of ARI (died 1148) who, like Sæmund, was surnamed "the Wise", we have an *Íslendingabók* which is a short account of Iceland from the time of its settlement up to 1120. Ari was a reliable and conscientious historian and his work provided a good example and a reliable basis for later historians. From the hand of an unknown writer we have an account of those who first settled in Iceland called *Landnámabók*. Many Icelanders took service with the Norwegian kings and some took a particular interest in the history of Norway and wrote down all they could find out about it. Amongst them was Abbot KARL JÓNSSON, whose history of King Sverre's reign was written largely at the dictation of Sverre himself, and it is regarded as a good piece of work. Other odds and ends of historical writing about the Norwegian kings are collected together in manuscripts called *Ágrip,* probably the work of a Norwegian, *Morkinskinna* (rotten skin), so called because of its dilapidated condition, and *Fagrskinna* (fair skin), so called from the elegant binding of one of the two copies which existed in the 17th century. *Fagrskinna* is the most important of these manuscripts. Most celebrated of the Icelandic historians was SNORRI STURLUSON, who was born in 1178. As a child he was adopted by Jón Loptsson, the most powerful man in Iceland at the time, whose home at Oddi was the centre of Icelandic culture and learning. Snorri's history of the Norwegian kings from earliest times to the Battle of Re in 1177, called *Heimskringla*, is his chief work and has become a sort of national treasure to the Norwegians and a constant reminder of former national greatness.   Snorri's historical accuracy has in recent times been severely challenged, but there seems, all the same, no doubt that his method was critical.   His use of conversation made it necessary for him to have recourse to his imagination, but the result is a wonderfully lively and vivid picture of the times and personalities he depicts.   Snorri was not only a historian, but was active in politics, a distinguished lawyer, and skilled in the art of verse.   In this last connexion he wrote what was intended as a text-book in the art of scaldship, usually called the *Younger Edda*.   The first part of it gives an account of the legends about the old Gods and heroes which Snorri says must be the stock-in-trade of any aspiring scald;   many of the legends related here are to be found in the *Elder Edda* but Snorre presents them in a better arrangement.   The second part contains a long description of poetic words and phrases and the third part consists of a poem to Hákon Hákonarson and Duke Skúli, where Snorri gives a virtuoso display of the use of all the different verse forms.

Snorri's successor in the historical field was his nephew STURLA THÓRÐARSON (born 1214, died 1284). His chief work is the *Íslendinga Saga,* which forms the major part of the *Sturlunga Saga.*   It tells of Snorri and his times and is remarkable for its objectivity, wealth of detail and accuracy. Besides this Sturla wrote the *Saga of Hákon Hákonarson* and *Magnús Lagabætir,* the latter (which for the most part has been lost) was written under the supervision of the king himself.   Here, as in the *Sturlunga Saga,* Sturla shows great precision and objectivity, but he lacks the artistry and the power vividly to recreate history which mark the work of his uncle.

The Mirror of the King ("Konungs Skuggsjá").

This is one of the most remarkable works of Old Norse literature and is of completely Norwegian origin. It was written about 1270 and consists of a series of conversations between father and son, in which the latter asks advice and guidance from his father concerning the life of the merchant and courtier. The merchant, the father says, must have a good knowledge of navigation and geography; Ireland, Iceland and Greenland are particularly mentioned and described and he must know foreign languages, especially French and Latin. The second part deals with the life of the courtier and tells of the etiquette to be observed at court and the duties of the courtier in war and peace. The father is obviously a man of wide experience and much travelled who favours the middle way in all things. He has a good knowledge of astronomy and can prove that the world is round! He is very religious, with an ecclesiastical background and is fond of moralizing, quoting extensively from the Bible. The work is also marked by the ideals of chivalry which had begun to penetrate from the South, and bears witness to wide reading.

Religious Literature.

The coming of Christianity to Norway and Iceland did not make any immediate impression on the literature of the period. Only exceptionally can it be noticed that the sagas from heathen times were written down after the introduction of Christianity. Nevertheless, in the course of time a purely religious literature did grow up, to which the death of King Olav in 1030 and his subsequent canonization gave great impetus. One of the first works of this kind was the poem *The Ray of Sun* ("Geisli"), i. e. Saint Olav, by EINARR SKÚLASON. It is entirely Catholic in its conception and symbolism and owes nothing to Northern mythology. Most remarkable of this early religious literature is, perhaps *Sólarljóð*, written by an unknown Icelander around 1200. One part of it is reminiscent of *Hávamál*, but its terms are the terms of Christianity, in another a father reveals himself to his son and tells him of what he has experienced beyond the grave; the whole is marked by a terror of the tortures of hell. A medieval treasure not known to scholarship until the 19th century, when it was discovered and written down by M. B. Landstad, is *Draumkvæde*. It belongs, probably, to the period around 1200 and seems to be older than *Sólarljóð* and tells of Olav Åsteson who remains asleep from Christmas Eve to Twelfth-day and awakes just as people are going to church. He rides to church himself, sits down in the church-door and tells of what he has dreamt. He has experienced purgatory, hell and heaven.

The fourteenth century brought a marked decline in literary productivity both in Iceland and in Norway. As far as Norway was concerned literature had, on the whole, long been regarded as mainly the province of the Icelander, and the 14th century, with the disintegrating effects of the Black Death and the unions with Sweden and Denmark, marked the beginning of a long period of decline both politically and culturally in Norway, and the only thing of importance to be produced at this time was the religious lay *Lilja,* written by the monk, EYSTEIN ÁSGRÍMSSON. It is a remarkable piece of work, marked by the vivid personality of the writer and by great originality.

From about the middle of the 14th to the middle of the 16th century nothing which can be dignified with the name of literature was written in Norway. During this period the life of the country became completely subordinate to Denmark. Danish administrators, lawyers and parsons ruled in the land; the country's oversea's trade passed into alien

2*

hands and the old Catholicism was replaced by the Lutheranism of Copenhagen; the old Norse language had decayed, and only survived, split into many dialects, as the language of the peasantry: the language of the educated Norwegian had become Danish. Indigenous culture was only to be found amongst the peasantry in the form of popular ballads and folk-tales which were kept alive by oral tradition, and it was not until the 19th century that they were written down. Many of them are based on themes to be found in many other European and Oriental countries, modified, however, by local conditions and outlook. It is difficult to lay down the exact period when these ballads came into being; the content of many of them seems to suggest the 13th and 14th centuries. Some are clearly marked by Catholic doctrines, others deal with trolls, some with historical personages and some are clearly modelled on French ballads of knightly courtship. In addition to these *Folkeviser* as they are called, there are *Folkesagn* and *Folkeeventyr*. It is difficult to draw a hard and fast line between the last two. In general, the former deals, or is supposed to deal, with actual occurrences and real personages — the story of Per Gynt, which Ibsen uses in his play of that name, comes into this category — but in many cases the imagination has had free play. The *Folkeeventyr* was understood to be entirely a product of the imagination and deals often with giants, trolls and other supernatural beings; animals talk and the hero, usually called Askeladden or Tyrihans, is the personification of the Good which eventually triumphs over Evil, and he is rewarded by a princess and half the kingdom.

CHAPTER II

DANISH AND SWEDISH LITERATURE BEFORE 1700

A. *Danish Literature before 1700.*

Denmark's first literature is hewn in stone or carved on metal. Runic inscriptions were used in Denmark from about 300 A.D., but most of those preserved date from the period 800—1100. They are mainly epitaphs of kings, warriors and priests, and they are brief, factual, and precise. They tell stories of battles, but not of love, they tell stories of Viking raids and of great leadership, and in some cases the carver was a poet whose short, unrhymed, alliterative verses reflect the virile Viking spirit. "A brave warrior" was the highest praise the living could give the dead. Some of the inscriptions towards the end of the runic period reflect the conflict between Nordic paganism and the newly introduced Christianity. An invocation to Thor was superseded by an invocation to Christ, but the pagan and Christian symbols remained side by side.

With the introduction of Christianity a new European culture was brought to Denmark, and its language was Latin. Danish medieval literature became therefore to a great extent latinized; only very slowly did the mother-tongue regain its position. Literature was now considered the business of learned men, and these were either monks or priests, or in some other way closely connected with the Church. ANDREAS SUNESØN (1160—1228) wrote an impressive Latin poem, *Hexaëmeron,* in which he described the Creation and the ecclesiastical dogmas in more than 8,000

Latin hexameters. This great poem, together with two poems of mourning and despair, of unknown origin, are Denmark's most important contributions to medieval Latin poetry. A number of biographies of saints were also written in Latin, and a brief outline of Danish history before 1185, *Historia Regum Daniæ compendiosa,* by SVEND AGGE-SØN, but the only single work of world importance in Danish medieval literature in Latin is the Danish chronicle by SAXO GRAMMATICUS (12th — 13th century).

Of Saxo himself hardly anything is known, but we do know that his great work, *Gesta Danorum,* i. e. *The Deeds of the Danes,* must have been written between 1185 and 1222. It is indeed a life's work. Saxo's Danish history consists of sixteen books, of which the first nine cover the whole period of prehistoric Danish antiquity. Christianity was now so firmly established in Denmark that even a member of the clergy (as Saxo presumably was) could afford to record these pagan legends and heroic poems, which had been passed down by word of mouth from generation to generation. Some of these legends date back, e. g. the legend of Uffe (or Offa, as he became known in England when the Vikings brought the legend there) to the 4th century, and those about the Danish *skjoldunger,* i. e. the first Danish legendary kings, to the 7th — 11th centuries. Almost identical names appear in the Anglo-Saxon poem *Beowulf,* the scene of which is laid among the "Sea-Danes". One of the stories in Saxo's chronicle is the legend of Amleth, which came to England via France, and the theme of which Shakespeare used in *Hamlet.* The first nine books of Saxo have little historical value, but are unique in their highly dramatic quality — rendered in eloquent Latin which must often have contrasted unfavourably with the brief, saga-like style in which Saxo presumably heard the legends told.

In Saxo's chronicle three heroic poems stand out. In

these, behind the Latin hexameters, it is sometimes possible to discern the originals, the oldest known poetry of Denmark, probably dating from the 10th and 11th centuries. *Bjarkemaalet* is an incitement to war, meant to be recited before a battle; *Ingjaldskvadet* is in praise of the old warlike spirit, and a warning against effeminate luxurious tendencies; and the poem *Hagbard and Signe* is a tragic, but unsentimental, love story against a background of family feuds.

Saxo had a definite purpose in mind when he wrote his Danish history covering a period of two thousand years. He wanted to demonstrate to the world that Denmark was an ancient country with old traditions, and he was inspired with a feeling of patriotism, centred on the king as the symbol of national unity. His history is Denmark's first important contribution to world literature.

Danish medieval literature in the mother-tongue includes a number of edifying books, hymns, and various provincial laws: the *Law of Scania*, two *Zealandish Laws,* and the *Law of Jutland.* The latter was the only one which had any legal force; it was accepted by the rulers of the kingdom at Vordingborg Castle in 1241. Its introduction, beginning with the words: "With law shall the land be built —", is famous for its statement of the reasons for the necessity of a legal system, and for its complete independence of Roman Law.

Other important Danish literary and linguistic treasures from the Middle Ages are PEDER LAALE's collection of old Danish proverbs (14th century), some medical books, e. g. HENRIK HARPESTRÆNG's book on medical herbs (13th century), and — towards the end of the Middle Ages — *Lucidarius,* a Danish adaptation of a medieval "encyclopædia", reflecting medieval man's conception of theology, astronomy, geography and physics. The first tendencies away from the Church, in which Danish drama had its origin in mysteries, miracles and moralities, did not appear till the very end of the Middle Ages.

Denmark's most important literary contribution during the Middle Ages, however, was not actually written down until later. The *medieval ballads* were sung as an accompaniment to the round dance and the chain dance which, coming from the south, mainly from France, became fashionable in Denmark towards the end of the 12th century and remained in vogue for the next four centuries. With the possible exception of Scotland, no other country possesses such a rich treasure of ballads as Denmark. Altogether 539 Danish ballads exist in more than 3,000 variations.

The Ballad was usually introduced by a lyrical stanza indicating its general character and mood, and the refrain has a similar lyrical quality.   Otherwise, the ballads are mainly epic in form, for they are concerned only with the telling of a dramatic story.   It is a mistake to look on them as folk poetry, for they were in fact the poetry of the nobility, and it is the atmosphere and adventures of the knighthood and kings which are reflected in them.

The warrior ballads form a link with ancient Danish legends and heroic poetry, and with Old Norse mythology, but they are few in number. The ballads of magic reflect a long period of development.   In the early Middle Ages the dangerous powers of Nature had supernatural significance.   Later, the supernatural elements had become mere literary symbols, deprived of their original menace.   Among the historical ballads three different cycles are of particular interest: the ballads about King Valdemar I, his Queen Sophia and his mistress Tove;   the ballads about King Valdemar II's two Queens, Dagmar and Bengerd;   and the ballads about the regicide of 1286 and the outlawing of Marsk Stig.   Of the latter group one ballad only takes the side of the murdered King Erik Glipping, while the others maintain that King Erik was himself to blame for his tragic fate, having seduced Marsk Stig's wife. Among the historical ballads that about Niels Ebbesøn and his murder of the German Count Gert in 1340, is outstanding. By far the largest group is that of the ballads of chivalry. One of the earliest is probably *Torben's Daughter*. Sir Torben is killed in a blood-feud while ploughing his field, and the avengers then ride on to his home where his daughter stands outside:

> She stood there as slim as a willow-wand,
> with a goblet of gold in either hand.

> In mirth and sport with wine-cup flowing
> she pledged the slayer, all unknowing.

> "Now had I guessed thee so mild of mood
> ne'er would I have spilt thy father's blood."

> "And if my father thou hast slain,
> then I must dree full bitter pain."

> "Have I done ill to thee thereby,
> thou shalt fare hereafter as well as I."

> He set her on his steed so true,
> he wrapped her in his cloak of blue.

> They rode away o'er the darksome heather,
> (On the lea)
> nevermore did she see her father.
> The day it dawneth and the dew it driveth so free.

> *Ude stod hans Datter, saa smal som en Vaand,*
> *med et Guldkar paa hver sin Haand.*

> *Hun skænked deri med Lyst og Spil,*
> *hun drak først sin Faders Banemand til.*

"Havde jeg vidst, du havde været saa god,
aldrig skulde jeg set din Faders Hjerteblod."

"Og har I slaget min Fader til Død,
da har I gjort mig saa stor en Nød."

"Har jeg nu ikke gjort vel mod dig,
da skal du herefter have saa godt som jeg."

Han satte hende paa Ganger graa,
saa slog han over hende Kaaben blaa.

Saa red han over de sorte Heder,
— under Lide —
aldrig saa hun sin Fader mere.
Der Dagen han dages, og Duggen den driver saa vide.

A great variety of subject is covered in the ballads of chivalry, but love is the predominant theme. Sometimes it is a tragic love story, as in *Ebbe Skammelsøn,* in which the sinister inevitability is reminiscent of Greek tragedy; at other times the atmosphere is gay, as in *Lave og Jon,* where a similar story is treated with fun and laughter. The ballads of chivalry give us a whole poetic picture of Danish knighthood in the Middle Ages, of its social life, its feelings and its sympathies.

Towards the end of the Middle Ages, and shortly after, some new forms of ballad were introduced, a more deliberately artistic form, as in the allegorical *Ballad of the Eagle* ("Ørnevisen"), and a coarser, often indecent, satirical form.

In the 16th century the nobility lost interest in the ballad, which became the fashion among the lower classes; and many of the most valuable Danish ballads might easily have been forgotten — or have been recorded much later in a less true form — but for the fact that it became the fashion for ladies of the nobility to write them down in their poetry books. The first printed edition of Danish ballads appeared in 1591. Denmark was now beginning to realise that she possessed one of the finest collections of ballads in the world, and from the end of the 18th century the Danish medieval ballads have been a frequent source of inspiration for generations of Danish poets.

*

The first printing press was established in Denmark in 1482, and the first book printed in Danish was *The Rhymed Chronicle* ("Rimkrøniken", 1495), a versified history in which each of the Danish kings tells his own story.

In 1536 the Reformation came to Denmark, and this marks the end of the Middle Ages. The beginning of the 16th century is characterized by its many polemic religious pamphlets, for or against the Roman Catholic Church. This inaugurated a new literature in the mother-tongue. European Humanism and the Renaissance made their influence felt also in Denmark, where CHRISTIERN PEDERSEN (died 1554) ranks as the most prominent among the Humanists who supported the Reformation. His editions of Saxo's *Gesta Danorum* (1514) and of Peder Laale's *Proverbs*, his translation of the New Testament, and his Danish adaptations of Luther's pamphlets, are valuable evidence of his genuinely humanistic spirit. But his greatest contribution is his participation in the translation of the Bible, published in 1550 as *Christian III's Bible,* an important milestone in the history of the Danish language. In polemic literature PAUL HELGESEN (ca. 1485 — ca. 1535) was the most gifted opponent of the Reformation, whereas HANS TAUSEN (1494 —1561) was its most talented spokesman. PEDER PALLADIUS (1503—60), the new Protestant Bishop of Zealand, kept a private notebook containing the speeches he delivered when he went on visitation. In addition to its historical value the *Visitation Book* ("Visitatsbogen") is a charming literary work. With its vivid, unrestrained style its author has won fame as a master of the Danish language. The bulk of 16th century Danish poetry is either religious or polemical, the main lyrical contributions are some fine hymns. ANDERS SØRENSEN VEDEL (1542—1616) translated Saxo into Danish and edited the first collection of ballads; ARILD HUITFELDT (1546—1609) wrote a ten volume *History of the Danish Kingdom* ("Danmarks Riges Krønike"), and in the field of Natural Sciences the Danish astronomer TYCHO BRAHE (1546—1601) acquired European fame.

In the 17th century the literary Renaissance Movement reached Denmark, which led in Danish literature to a strict adherence to classical patterns, often with disastrous effects on the poetry of that century. It was an age of orthodoxy and blind belief in authority, whether in political, religious, or literary matters. The chief exponent of religious orthodoxy in the latter half of the 16th century, NIELS HEMMINGSEN (ca. 1511—1600), had himself fallen a victim to the heresy hunt, and the dogmatic theologians were now firmly established. Latin dogmatics, pious sermons reflecting a new Protestant mysticism, edifying leaflets, and a host of pamphlets reflecting the superstitions of the century, now dominated the picture.

Medicine and Natural Sciences, however, broke away from the Church, and many great Danish scholars made their names known all over Europe, e. g. CASPAR BARTHOLIN (1585—1629) and his son, THOMAS BARTHOLIN (1616—80), anatomists, NIELS STEENSEN (1638—86), anatomist and geologist, OLE RØMER (1644—1710), physicist, SIMON PAULLI (1603—80), botanist and anatomist, and OLE WORM (1588—1654), antiquarian. TORMOD TORFÆUS and ARNE MAGNUSSEN introduced the scholarly study of Old Norse literature, and PEDER SYV (1631—1702) introduced linguistic study of the Danish language.

The most important Danish prose work of the 17th century is *Jammers Minde,* the memoirs of Christian IV's daughter LEONORA CHRISTINA (1621—98), written during her twenty years' imprisonment in the Blue Tower of Copenhagen. It is a fascinating human document of high literary quality, brilliantly written in a vivid style, yet full of genuine pathos.

Danish poetry in the 17th century tends to follow the Classics slavishly, thus the favourite metres are the hexameter, the alexandrine and the sonnet. Simplicity is deliberately avoided, the style is precious, allegories and euphemisms and metaphors abound, and there are continuous references to Roman mythology. ANDERS ARREBO (1587—1637) translated the Psalms and wrote — mainly in alexandrines — *Hexaëmeron* (1661), a religious epic. The 17th century was rich in occasional poetry celebrating weddings and birthdays, or mourning for a deceased paragon of virtue. Didactic poems and pastoral poems were also frequent in this age of artificiality. ANDERS BORDING (1619—77) was an interesting exponent of Danish baroque poetry. He also founded the first Danish newspaper, *The Danish Mercury* ("Danske Mercurius", from 1666), in which the news appeared in rhymed alexandrines.

Only one 17th century poet was really great, THOMAS KINGO (1634—1703), a clergyman of Scottish descent who became Bishop of Odense. He was a supreme master in almost every field, and the greatest exponent of Danish baroque poetry, superb in his best hymns which reflect a violent, passionate character. He was worldly and deeply religious at the same time, a man trying to tear himself away from what he knew was nothing but vanity. "His genius is a cherub: a bull's body with angels' wings," has been said of him. Among all the queer instruments of the 17th century Kingo alone sounds like a whole orchestra.

B. Swedish Literature before 1700.

The year 1000 is an arbitrary date in the history of Sweden, and scholars seeking for definite facts concerning the country at this stage of its development, when it was still in a primitive condition, have, up to now, had little positive success. Sweden, indeed, hardly existed as an entity at this time, though it is probable that by about the beginning of the 11th century the scattered kingdoms from which the bold and greedy Swedish Vikings set out on their marauding expeditions to the Continent had been roughly united under the rule of Olof Skötkonung. The country was by no means entirely Christian, even though Olof himself had embraced the new faith, and in spite of the missionary activities of Ansgar, who visited Sweden in the 9th century, and of other, later, foreign monks, especially English, German and French. The resistance offered by paganism was tough, and, not least for geographical reasons, the conversion of Sweden proved a more difficult proposition than, for example, that of Denmark. We know that Uppsala, the most renowned place of pagan sacrifice in Sweden, persisted in its bloody rites until about the end of the 11th century, when a Christian church was erected on the foundations of the old shrine: later it became the seat of an archbishopric. It is interesting that, so early in its history, Uppsala should have played this rôle of a "home of lost causes", which it has on many occasions shared with Oxford in the history of ideas.

The tremendous cultural importance of Christianity in the development of Sweden can hardly be exaggerated, yet the influence of the new religion made itself felt only gradually, and there is no doubt that pagan rites and superstitions continued to flourish, beneath the surface, well into the Middle Ages. Arts and crafts, especially in the form of jewellery and weapons, had been more appreciated

by the Swedish Vikings than had literature, and the only
remnants of the native writings of this early period are to
be found in the Runic inscriptions, which commemorate
the lineage and deeds of notable men in artless but sometimes moving simplicity. Yet how naive these epitaphs,
written in the 11th century, seem, when one compares
them with similar inscriptions from the Greece of, say, the
fifth century B. C! That an early Swedish literature, in
the manner of that of Iceland, had existed, probably only
in oral form, has been argued by various scholars: but,
failing any evidence concerning its character or even its
existence, it seems useless to speculate about it here. Certain it is that not before 1200 had Christian influences so
penetrated and stimulated Swedish life as to make possible
the beginnings of a Swedish medieval culture, and by that
time the original, virtually one-class, society of primitive
times had been replaced by a more complex social fabric,
increasingly dominated by the two rising classes of the
nobility and the clergy. These two sections of society were
to be respectively patrons and providers of literature during
the Middle Ages, the writings of which accordingly manifested a religious and aristocratic character, and often a
political inspiration: they reflected, in fact, the main trends
of contemporary Western literature. For Sweden, through
her links with the Catholic Church, had now become part
of European civilisation, and here as elsewhere it was largely
in the monasteries and convents founded by the various
international religious orders that European and native
culture was studied and developed. Latin was, of course,
the linguistic medium, parchment, and later paper, replaced
the primitive Runic stones.

Latin, then, came to overshadow the vernacular as a literary language, and this fact helps to explain the essentially
derivative nature of medieval Swedish literature, exposed
as it was also to the impact of French knightly codes and

French scholasticism, and later to German influences, which often reached Sweden via Denmark: for throughout the Middle Ages, with the bitter struggles for power between Swedish, Danish, and later on German princes, the cultural links between Denmark and Sweden, and also between Sweden and Norway, appear to have been close. It is significant for the whole later development of Swedish literature that so many foreign influences should have been brought to bear on it so early. Many later Swedish writers and thinkers, including Strindberg, have uttered warnings — and with good reason — against the Swedish cult of "the foreign" at the expense of the native product, yet, in spite of this habitual aping of models from abroad, Swedish national characteristics, in nearly every age, have managed to assert themselves with a curious, healthy, truculence. This conflict between the foreign and the native may in fact be picked out as the leitmotiv in Swedish literature as a whole.

All these factors appear essential to an understanding of the genesis and development of Swedish letters, and it is for this reason that I have dwelt on them here.

With this concentration on Latin as a written language and with the tainting of the spoken Swedish tongue by German, especially Low German, expressions, it is not surprising that Old Swedish (Fornsvenska), as a medium for literature, developed slowly and uncertainly, and permitted its users little chance of stamping their own individuality on their style, so that a strange anonymity makes itself felt in so much of the work that has survived. Nevertheless the first period of medieval Swedish literature (approximately 1200–1363, coinciding with the rule of the Folkunga kings) saw the creation of a number of literary masterpieces in the vernacular, in the shape of the legal codes written down in the various provinces for the use of the local "lagman." Of those which survive, *The Law of Västergötland* ("Västgötalagen"), going back to 1220, is the oldest, *The Law of Gothland* ("Gutalagen") rivals it in age, while *The Law of Uppland* ("Upplandslagen") of 1296 differs from these in being an officially inspired lawbook, whereas the earlier collections had simply been records, privately noted down, of the statutes then current. All these manuscripts, however, testify to an apparently deep respect for the law, such as prevailed even then in Sweden, and even in their divergencies they bear witness to a spirit of endeavour which underlay the achievements of the age and helped to overcome its material and economic difficulties. Judged as literature, these writings owe their interest and quality to their pregnant, forceful, almost brusque style. The prose is full of concrete images, and possesses a solemn rhythm, often relying on alliteration to impress its decisiveness on the reader. These laws crystallise an earlier, oral, tradition, are closely connected with proverbial wisdom, and thus provide a valuable link with that earlier, lost, literature which was mentioned above. The crowning effort in this work of legal codification is to be found in King Magnus Eriksson's *Common Law of the Realm* ("Landslag"), of approximately 1350, the combined work, probably, of a number of clerics and nobles of Magnus' court, which reflects both Christian European learning and the native tradition of self-reliance.

Overwhelmingly practical considerations had inspired the laws. *Belles-lettres* in the stricter sense of the word are, at this period, of much slighter intrinsic merit, so far as we can judge by the surviving evidence. The poetry of chivalry which had flourished in France and Germany around 1200 had been exported to Sweden too, with the usual time-lag, but the native products inspired by these knightly ideals are little more than free, often almost unrecognizable, adaptations of the foreign originals. Of these, the so-called *Songs of Euphemia* ("Eufemiavisorna"), three verse romances anonymously translated, perhaps by order of Queen Eufemia of Norway, between 1303 and 1312, possess the greatest interest, in that they reflect, however dimly, some of the psychological subtlety of their French models. The verse form used is rhymed doggerel, borrowed, probably, from Germany, where it then had such a vogue, uncouth but convenient. With the exception of some earlier, rather weaker religious poems, *The Songs of Euphemia* provide the first surviving examples of the new metric system. The old alliterative schemes, based on syllables, had now been ousted.

Doggerel occurs again in the chronicle romance *The Chronicle of Eric* ("Erikskrönikan"), which records the shifting fortunes of the Swedish Kings between the years 1220 and 1320, and was probably written down fairly soon after the latter date: however, neither the exact date nor the authorship is known to us. Chronicle, epic, romance, this curious hybrid work has both force and imagination, and may rank as the most powerful single poem in medieval Swedish literature. In it, too, religious and political ideas are interwoven, together with the ideals of chivalry which the unknown but evidently aristocratic author venerates.

It is really only in the sphere of religious writings that, at this time, the anonymity of the individual author is occasionally discarded, and that one encounters strong personalities — a not unexpected phenomenon when one considers how, during the Middle Ages, religion dominated every sphere of life, and how the Catholic faith, with its ascetic other-worldliness and its yearning for mysticism, was bound to shape and kindle all the potentially creative personalities of the time. Even so, the discipline of doctrine and word subdued originality, and the personalities, of whom one catches a glimpse behind the word and whom one knows by their achievements, often appear more vital and appealing than the word itself, whether it be in Latin

or Swedish. The Latin hymns of BRYNOLF ALGOTSSON
(ca. 1250–1317) do not reveal the energy and intelligence of the zealous bishop, who had acquired his learning
in Paris. More vividly does the character of the Dominican
monk PETRUS DE DACIA emerge, and that of his spiritual
love for the holy Christina of Stommeln, in the account of
her life entitled *Vita benedictae virginis Christi Christinae*,
and in the letters he exchanged with her until his death.
Petrus (ca. 1235–1289) had met the young woman in
Cologne, where he studied in a seminary, and much of his
account is a record of her strange visions and religious
experiences, which in themselves do not essentially differ
from many other contemporary European legends. Even
Peter's love is expressed in the conventional mystical terms
of his age. Nevertheless, the intensity of underlying emotion makes the monk a living character.

Petrus in his turn is overshadowed by SAINT BIRGITTA
(1303–1373), the strongest personality in medieval Swedish history, and the only one, really, who has left an imprint on Western civilisation. This ambitious, energetic,
arrogant noblewoman, who, after bearing eight children,
went on a pilgrimage to Rome and Jerusalem, after having
reproved the Pope, and planned a religious order for her
own country, has tempted many authors, including Strindberg and Heidenstam, to portray her, but her complex
character defies successful evocation, even though the facts
of her life, and her achievements, are known. The range
of her own interests, her boldness and almost vicious sever-
ity, are reflected in the nine volumes of her *Revelationes*,
in which she communed with God, took the Folkunga kings
to task, foretold their downfall, and laid down rules for
the members of her order. The original Swedish text —
for Birgitta wrote or dictated in that tongue — has been
lost: only the contemporary Latin translations, and some

3*

Norwegian versions, survive, yet even in the Latin translations the racy outspokenness of the writer prevails.

Birgitta's life spanned that period of Swedish history which witnessed the flowering of the country's medieval culture: by her death this was already in decline. The complicated feuds of the so-called Union period, and the insecurity they brought with them, had on the whole an adverse effect on literature. One may say that the second period of medieval Swedish literature coincides with this political epoch (ca. 1370–1526), which is initiated by the pre-Union reign of Albert of Mecklenburg and German domination. Yet in cultural life Birgitta's character continued to make itself felt, after her canonization, not only in Sweden, but also in the other Scandinavian countries, through the religious foundations established by her order, and the work carried on in them. It is, then, fitting that one of the most beautiful of the country's medieval Latin hymns, *Rosa rorans bonitatem,* by NICOLAUS HERMANNI (1326–1391), should have been written in her honour.

Though the creative forces appear to have decreased, translations and adaptations multiplied, as the reading public grew: these ranged from versions of certain books of the Bible to romances in doggerel (such as that of King Alexander), allegorical short stories, e. g. *Seven Wise Masters* ("Sju vise Mästare"), and *The Game of Chess* ("Schacktavelslek"), an allegorical poem in doggerel (about 1465) with political intent. Political polemics, too, inspired the rhymed chronicles which continued the tradition of *The Chronicle of Eric,* that is, *The Chronicle of Karl* ("Karlskrönikan"), and *The Chronicle of the Stures* ("Sturekrönikan"), the latter reviewing events up to 1496, and the so-called *The Little Rhymed Chronicle* ("Lilla Rimkrönikan"), which, with additions, took the story up to 1520.

Political passion also animated the lyrical poetry written in Swedish by Bishop THOMAS SIMONSSON (ca. 1380–

1443). His two surviving poems, *The Song of Freedom* ("Frihetsvisan"), and *The Song of Loyalty* ("Trohetsvisan"), have earned him the name of the first Swedish national poet, yet if the good bishop had merely been concerned with the fate of Engelbrekt (the people's hero and defender of popular rights who was assassinated in 1436) or with the immediate political circumstances inspiring *The Song of Loyalty*, it is improbable that these two poems, the first of which, especially, is a masterpiece, would have possessed any wide or lasting appeal. The fact that Thomas sounded a universal note in his cry for freedom, freedom, that is, from oppression, and expressed his anguish in skilful rhythms and inspired phrases, has made his verses live. Here is the fountain-head, however unpretentious, of that lyricism which has proved to be the richest vein in Swedish literature.

This lyrical consciousness, coupled with a grasp of the epic in its simplest form, asserted itself also in the "folkvisor" (ballads and folksongs) which were sung and danced to at medieval courts, and then, as they became more popular, enlivened the festivities of ordinary folk, and so were handed down from one generation to another by oral tradition. Not until much later, in some instances in the 16th and 17th centuries, sometimes not until well into the 19th century, were they transcribed, and it is, therefore, almost impossible to decide exactly when a particular ballad was composed, even when internal evidence, such as political background, provides a clue. They may, on the other hand, be classified in groups such as warrior ballads, historical and legendary ballads, burlesques, and so on. The Swedish ballads, it is clear, are often derived from Danish or Norwegian prototypes, Denmark, of all the Scandinavian countries, possessing the richest store of poetry of this kind: these models in their turn had often been inspired by English or Romance originals. (See above pp.

24—27). Despite this hybrid ancestry the Swedish folksongs often possess an appealing simplicity and a lilting rhythm or refrain, such as "The dew drifts, the hoar falls"[1], in *Sir Olof and the Elves* ("Herr Olof och älvorna"), which goes far to explain their survival.

Such literature, together with folk-tales and legends, nourished popular imagination, and survived, as we have seen, notwithstanding the coming of the Reformation — which ushered in the modern period — and in spite of the more rational religious orthodoxy which ensued. The Reformation in Sweden did not correspond to any popular demand, but was imposed from above for political reasons, long before the common people were ready for it, by King GUSTAV VASA (who reigned from 1523 till 1560) in his anxiety to get control of the wealth of the Catholic Church, so that he might settle the national debts which had been incurred in driving the Danes out of the country. The cleric OLAUS PETRI (1493—1552), a sincere follower of Luther and a former student at Wittenberg, acted at first as Gustav's instrument, but was too independent a person not to oppose his royal master and take him to task for what he considered his arrogance and materialism. These two individualities dominate their time, Gustav typifying the new style Renaissance autocrat on the throne, Olaus the Protestant theologian, with his practical, realistic approach to religion. Neither of them had the smallest interest in literature for its own sake. Gustav's proclamations and letters reveal him as a master of direct and forceful Swedish prose, Olaus' didactic tendencies drove him to prepare books of sermons and a catechism, to assist in translating and writing hymns, even, perhaps, to compose a biblical drama, *Tobie Comedia* (1550), attributed, though without certainty, to him: this is the oldest surviving Swedish play. With the same didactic intentions he produced *A Swedish*

[1] "driver dagg, faller rim."

Chronicle ("En Swensk Crönika"), an account of historical
events up to the beginning of Gustav Vasa's reign, which
the king disliked for its truthfulness, but which, with its
critical attitude to the national past, was particularly valuable. Olaus Petri would have no truck with the theory of
"göticism", which the medieval chroniclers had sponsored,
and which was taken up again by the Catholic prelate
JOHANNES MAGNUS in his *Historia de omnibus Gothorum
Suenomumque regibus* (published 1560). This legend,
which has repeatedly been taken up in Swedish literature,
relates that Sweden had been the cradle of Western civilisation, and that the Goths had carried its culture to the West.
     The most important part of Olaus Petri's literary work,
however, was his connexion with the Swedish translation
of the Bible — and here his interests and Gustav Vasa's met
in happy communion. The translation of the New Testament appeared in 1526, that of the whole Bible in 1541.
Even now the exact extent of Olaus' contribution has not
been ascertained, and it is known that a number of scholars
were concerned with the work, including Laurentius An-
dreae and Olaus' own brother Laurentius. Yet Olaus Petri
was certainly the moving spirit in the whole undertaking,
and his influence can be distinguished in the style. Thanks
to the introduction of the printing press into the country,
the translations of the scriptures became accessible to an increasing number of persons, even though the mass of the
people were still illiterate.
     The purity and beauty of the language in these versions
were to prove a literary treasure which enriched the imagination and style of subsequent writers. The effects took
some time, however, in making themselves felt. In other
respects Gustav's rule did not foster the arts: in fact, by
plundering and destroying Catholic foundations the king
actually harmed them. Money was too tight at the Court
to permit of the patronage of art, and even Uppsala, then

the only university, founded in 1477 and closed owing to political strife in 1517, was not reopened. Not until towards the end of the 16th century were serious attempts made to get it going again, and it was Gustav Adolf (ruled 1611—1632) who turned it into a university in the modern sense of the term. Thus under Gustav Vasa cultural dependence on Germany (which, as we have seen, had already corrupted the Swedish language during the Middle Ages) increased, and Swedish students were driven to study at the, narrowly orthodox, German Protestant colleges such as Rostock. The cultural breach with Denmark, resulting from Gustav's unification of Sweden in opposition to the Danes, also had pernicious consequences in the sphere of the arts.

The Reformation in Sweden was not then, as in so much of Western Europe, associated with the full flood of Renaissance Humanism. That current reached Sweden belatedly, when conditions at home became more favourable. Under Gustav Adolf the task of developing education, not only at the university, but in the schools, was taken seriously, and that zealous prelate Johannes Rudbeckius (1581—1646), famous preacher and controversialist, distinguished himself in this field. As a result of the Swedish intervention in the Thirty Years' War contacts with the Continent were increased and widened, and it became common for both peasants and noblemen to have done that century's equivalent of the "grand tour". One result was, naturally, a renewed and more general appreciation of the arts, and a gradual growth in both the quantity and quality of Swedish literature. It is typical of this period's poets, such as LARS WIVALLIUS (1605—1669), the most remarkable of them, that they can compose poems to order — celebrating marriages, funerals, and so forth — in Latin, German, and even French, and that they have picked up many of the complicated rhyme schemes that had become popular in Italy and France.

The figure of Wivallius, vagrant, adventurer, unscrupulous lawyer, who wrote his best and most spontaneous poems under the pressure of his prison experiences in Kajaneborg, is characteristic of this transition stage in Swedish letters. Wivallius was of low social standing, had no sense of responsibility, and was unaware of the value of his own poetry and of his position as writer: yet in his naive, attractive feeling for nature, and the spontaneity of his emotions, he carries the Swedish lyrical tradition a stage further than it had reached hitherto. Moreover, rascal though he was, he clung, in the face of death, to the simple piety of his fathers, and this element of religious orthodoxy in poetic inspiration was to continue, almost unchallenged, in all literature until the end of the 17th century, even after pagan currents from the Continent had set in; for the power of the Church was backed, save in Kristina's reign, by the Crown, while the Crown, in turn, was supported by the Church.

The marked national self-confidence, the consciousness of being a great European power, whose actions affected the fate of nations, was, however, the greatest inspirational force behind the literature of Sweden from 1650 onwards, so that, just when cultural contacts extended not only to Germany, Holland, France, and England, but also to Italy and Spain, as well as the New World and the Orient, when Swedes studied at Leyden, Rome, and elsewhere, and one might, therefore, have expected national characteristics to be submerged in the tide of new impressions and foreign fashions,[1] Swedish literature enters, in actual fact, on its maturity and asserts itself with an arrogance which is no doubt naive, but certainly also forceful. This development

[1] Queen Kristina, for instance, brought in French poets to her Court, and even persuaded Descartes to settle in Stockholm.

was much affected by the improved position of the nobility, now enriched by the campaigns abroad and rewarded for their services by estates at home. Thus, just as in England and France, Sweden could now produce wealthy noblemen as patrons of the arts, as for example Magnus de la Gardie. It was natural that at this epoch the theme of "göticism" should be taken up again, this time by OLAUS RUDBECKIUS (1630—1702), son of the bishop, in his weighty work *Atlantica*. This had a great vogue and probably exerted the deepest influence of all the published works of its sort. Translated into Latin, it was designed to make known internationally the ideas of "göticism", but it was composed in Swedish in order to prove to contemporaries how excellently suited this language was to serious scientific purposes. Yet prose still was of less importance than verse as an instrument in the 17th century, notwithstanding the diaries and letters of ERIK DAHLBERG, URBAN HIÄRNE, and others, and in spite of the nascent technical interest in the language as such, manifested for instance by the pseudonymous SKOGEKÄR BERGBO, in his work *The Plaint of the Swedish Language* ("Thet Swenska språketz klagemål, at thet som sigh borde, icke ährat blifwer", 1658), and by SAMUEL COLUMBUS (1642—1679), pupil and friend of GEORG STIERNHIELM (1598—1672), and by various Uppsala scholars. The most powerful prose of the time is to be found in the sermons; but the medium of prose at its most interesting and flexible occurs in Columbus' collection of anecdotes *Table Talk* ("Målroo eller Roo-mål"), which offers charming vignettes of Stiernhielm, of the poet LASSE LUCIDOR (1638—1674), and of other contemporary writers.

Not primarily by virtue of his prose, then, does Rudbeck stand out, but rather as a remarkably versatile individual, whose many-sidedness earns him the title of a "Renaissance" man. Anatomist, botanist, philologist, architect, University Rector of inexhaustible energy and ingenuity, he virtually

ran Uppsala for many years, and was the first to apply
practical principles of pedagogy to the sciences.

Such a Humanist, too, was Urban Hiärne (1641—1724),
poet, doctor, novelist, and dramatist, whose tragedy *Rosimunda*, acted in 1665 at Uppsala castle before the young
Charles XI, by Hiärne himself and a troupe of fellow-
students, is one of the few noteworthy phenomena in the
earlier Swedish drama. For the drama was, in Sweden, one
of the most backward of literary genres, economic and
material conditions being such that no regular theatre was
opened until 1686 (at Lejonkulan in Stockholm), and this
venture actually failed after a few years. The years between
Tobie Comedia and Hiärne's work had offered little:
ASTEROPHERUS' tragedy *Tisbe*, acted in 1610, some formless
dramas by MESSENIUS (ca. 1579—1636), one or two naive
comedies, and then Stiernhielm's masques, which are essentially elegant versions of French texts. Not that *Rosimunda*
can be called an original piece of work: yet it was a
"respectable", actable attempt at tragedy, in the Senecan
manner. To modern readers its interest — like that of the
repertoire produced at Lejonkulan — is historical: they
constitute steps in the search for a native dramatic tradition.

Some of the main figures of "Stormaktstiden" have already been treated, and this has carried us ahead towards
the end of the 17th century. The most important literary personality has, however, been deliberately left to the
last, namely Georg Stiernhielm, whose name has already
occurred in various connexions, and who actually belongs
to an earlier generation than Hiärne or Columbus. Stiernhielm, *par excellence*, deserves the epithet "Renaissance":
he was court poet, civil servant, lawyer, researcher into the
old language of his country, by training a philosopher and
astronomer, and so on, but above all else a p o e t. Thanks
to the dignity and worth of his own person, he raised the
value of that profession in the eyes of the populace, who

had generally associated rhyme-making with begging. His ardent love of poetry, his high standards, and his achievements, were to point the way to many subsequent writers. It was his happy combination of classical learning, familiarity with contemporary European letters, and native skill and feeling that made him, in Atterbom's phrase, "the father of the Swedish art of poetry." He wrote lyrics, idylls, sonnets, possibly (though this is not certain) the masterly *Reminiscences of Wedding Cares* ("Bröllopsbeswärs Ihugkommelse"), but he is known above all for his didactic epic *Hercules,* written in hexameters, which treats of the hero's choice between virtue and vice. Stiernhielm, in this respect almost the sole exception to the general rule, does not take the orthodox Protestant point of view. His morality is, rather, based on antique stoicism, just as it is the ancient Classics to which he especially looks up in poetry, but it is fresh, *actuel,* for he is writing with the problems of his own vigorous generation in view. Poetry, in various manners, was the heritage that "Stormaktstiden" bequeathed to subsequent ages, and much, though not all, of it was learned from this master, or stimulated by him:[1] for example, the tender notes in Columbus' *Odae Sveticae,* and the majestic hymns by SPEGEL and SWEDBERG which were included in the new and influential hymnbook of 1695. Hymn-writing, it is to be observed, continued to occupy many leading poets. Only Lasse Lucidor stands apart, closer in many respects to Wivallius, whose careless improvising he repeats, and whose reckless vagrancy — Lucidor was killed in a tavern brawl — he also followed in his life. His poems, published posthumously as *Helicon's*

---

[1] Skogekär Bergbo's sonnet cycle *Wenerid,* though not published till 1680, was, according to the complete title, written more than 30 years earlier, and there is no evidence that, at that time, the pseudonymous author knew Stiernhielm's work. He professed to have been inspired by the sonnets of Petrarch.

Posy ("Helicons Blomster"), seem to have survived by chance. Yet Lucidor was widely travelled, very well read, and could write poems in Latin, French, even English. More sophisticated in a sense than Wivallius, and with less apparent feeling for nature, he reveals in his most spontaneous poems the two dominating but contradictory emotions of his time; the passionate yet realistic enjoyment of life and physical experiences, and the fear of death, with the religious awe accompanying it. This poignant dualism makes Lucidor a memorable poet, and his: "Should I mourn, then I would be mad"[1] may serve to sum up the principal impulses and moods of the 17th century.

[1] "Skulle jag sörja, då wore jag tokot."

CHAPTER III

DANISH LITERATURE IN THE 18TH CENTURY

Two contrasting tendencies are characteristic of Danish literature in the 18th century. One is critical, based on reason, mainly influenced by French and English literature and philosophy; the other is emotional, introspective, often with a tinge of religious mysticism, and in its origin essentially a German movement. In the first half of the century Ludvig Holberg and H. A. Brorson are the two most important exponents of these two tendencies.

Ludvig Holberg (1684–1754) was born in Norway, the son of a Lieutenant-Colonel of peasant stock. In 1702 he came to Copenhagen to matriculate, and after a few short stays in Norway settled permanently in Denmark. Of four European tours Holberg made between 1704 and 1716, those to Holland and Germany were of little importance, but a long visit to England (1706–08), most of which time he spent in Oxford, working in the Bodleian Library, and a journey to Paris and Rome (1714–16), were both of the utmost importance to him, since they involved a meeting with modern European ideas, especially French critical philosophy and literature.

In 1711 Holberg published his first work, *An Introduction to the History of the European Kingdoms* ("Introduktion til de europæiske Rigers Historie"), and three years later he was appointed "professor designate" of Copenhagen University, and so began his academic career. In 1717 he became professor of Metaphysics — a subject he detested and later ridiculed in his writings — and it was not until 1730 that he became professor of History, his real interest; by then he had already made a name as a creative writer. Holberg's literary career began with some satirical poems, among which is the great mock-heroic poem *Peder Paars* (1719—20). In this, in alexandrines, with a wealth of learned paraphernalia, mythological allusions, footnotes referring to existing or imaginary books, etc., Holberg tells the tale of a common-or-garden Danish Aeneas, a very ordinary citizen indeed, a paragon of respectability, who travels across the water from Zealand to Jutland in order to visit his fiancée; but the Gods and Goddesses of Love, Envy, Rumour, Disagreement, etc., interfere in his plans and make it a journey worthy of a Ulysses. The satire was mainly aimed at the current imitations of classical heroic epic poetry, but it was also directed at social conditions, especially that part of the poem in which Peder Paars and his men have been beached on the small island of Anholt in the Kattegat. The description of social conditions on this island was no doubt meant as a satire on conditions in contemporary Denmark. It was taken as such in its own time, and *Peder Paars* only just escaped being publicly burnt for poking fun at Danish institutions and traditions.

When the first Danish theatre was established in Copenhagen in 1722 it was natural that its leading men should appeal to Ludvig Holberg to write for them; for although *Peder Paars* had appeared under the *nom de plume* of Hans Mikkelsen, it was generally known that Ludvig Holberg — then a distinguished professor of Latin Rhetoric — was its real author. For this theatre, which opened on September 23, 1722, Holberg wrote 32 comedies, of which the first 15 — written in as many months — are comedies of character. The other main group is 11 comedies of manner, written between 1723 and 1727. In his old age he wrote a small number of plays — mainly moral allegories — greatly inferior to his earlier work.

Among Holberg's comedies there are such masterpieces as *The Political Tinker* ("Den politiske Kandestøber"), *Jean de France , Jeppe of the Hill* ("Jeppe paa Bjerget"), *Jacob von Thyboe, The Fussy Man* ("Den Stundesløse"), and *Erasmus Montanus*. In most of them the play is centred on a main character who personifies some human folly. *The Political Tinker* thus ridicules ignorant know-alls who regard themselves as great potential statesmen; *Jean de France* exposes the foolish snobbery in the use of the French language and French manners in Denmark; *Jacob von Thyboe* pokes fun at boasting and stupid officers; *The Fussy Man* is a satire on people who are so busy that they have no time to do anything at all; and in *Erasmus Montanus* the satire is directed at academic superiority, its main character being a Danish undergraduate who has become a latinized academic pedant, lost in the technique of formalistic logic discussion, and stripped of the human quality which Holberg admired most of all — common sense. One of these early plays, *Jeppe of the Hill*, is a superb character study of a Danish peasant, an ignorant and bibulous serf, a henpecked cuckold, but in all his humiliation and pitiable lowliness a wise philosopher, full of human charm. Jeppe, found dead drunk on the manure heap, is carried to the manor-house, where he wakes up in a beautiful four-poster bed, and is made to believe that he is the Lord of the Manor. When he gets drunk again he is taken back to the manure heap, and he is made the victim of a mock-trial. The moral given at the end of this extravagant play is, that it is dangerous to make sudden changes in a man's life; but the moral has very little to do with the play, which is one of the wittiest and most charming comedies in Danish literature.

In writing his first comedies Holberg's aim was to create

a modern Danish literature on European lines, and to entertain by making people laugh at their own follies.

Among Holberg's comedies of manner the best known are *Henry and Pernilla* ("Henrik og Pernille"), *Masquerades* ("Maskarade"), *The Masked Ladies* ("De Usynlige"), *The Pawned Peasant Boy* ("Den pantsatte Bondedreng") and *Christmas Games* ("Julestuen"). In all these, Holberg has employed a number of stock characters: Leander, the young lover who loves Leonora; Henry and Pernilla, their sly and ingenious servants, who are always responsible for the plot through which a happy ending is brought about; Jeronimus, an elderly morose and reactionary gentleman, who disapproves of the foolishness of young people; his friend Leonard, who is more broadminded and takes the side of the young; Arv, an ignorant and superstitious peasant servant, and so on. In these later plays Holberg is less concerned with moralizing than with entertaining.

The importance of Holberg's comedies can scarcely be overrated. With them he literally put Denmark on the map and made Danish literature part and parcel of contemporary European literature. He is probably one of the twenty greatest dramatists in the world. Like so many other great playwrights he did not hesitate to take the framework of his plays from a variety of different sources; he borrowed freely from Aristophanes, from the Romans, from the Italian *commedia dell'arte,* and from Molière, whom more than anyone else he resembles; but this does not affect his dramatic originality, and there is the important difference between Holberg and Molière that the latter was a court dramatist, whereas the former wrote his plays for and about the ordinary people of his day: officers, artisans, peasants and respectable small town citizens.

In addition to the comedies, Holberg also contributed in many other ways to the creation of a modern Danish literature. His satirical novel, *Niels Klim's Subterranean*

Travels (originally written in Latin, 1741) was modelled on
Swift's *Gulliver's Travels* and Montesquieu's *Lettres Per-
sanes;* it is a witty narrative of fantastic journeys into strange
countries which are either Holbergian Utopias or caricatures of Denmark as Holberg saw it. His *Moral Thoughts*
("Moralske Tanker", 1744) and his nearly 500 *Epistles*
("Epistler", 1748—54) are the finest examples of 18th century Danish essays. The latter are written in the form of
letters to an imaginary correspondent, and reflect Holberg's attitude to almost everything in the world: dogs
and cats, life in the country and life in the town, marriage,
women's gossip, religion, the Devil, scientific and philosophic and historic matters — a Danish *Spectator* literature
which gives us an excellent picture of the critical and
sceptical old bachelor professor, who was led by reason in
all matters, and always preferred to follow a middle course.
His *Memoirs,* written in the form of three letters in Latin
(between 1727 and 1745), are equally fascinating;   their
object was to demonstrate to the world that Denmark possessed a modern European literature written by Holberg
himself.

By profession Holberg was an historian, and he was the
author of a great many books on European history, on the
history of Denmark and Norway, on ecclesiastical history,
the history of the Jews, and books on Natural Law, and on
the philosophy of Law. His main work as an historian is
his *History of the Danish Kingdom* ("Danmarks Riges Historie"), in three volumes (1732—35), which won him a
place in the line of great Danish historians which began
with Saxo and included Anders Sørensen Vedel and Arild
Huitfeldt. His interest was mainly in modern times;   to
him antiquity and the Middle Ages represented ignorance
and barbarism. He was little impressed with warriors and
conquerors, but admired practical reformers and productive

creators. "A useful citizen" was the epitaph he wished for himself.

Holberg remained a bachelor till his death. Through the money he earned by his writing, and on account of his parsimonious way of life, he became a wealthy man, and because he left his fortune for the re-establishment of the College at Sorø, he was made a Baron. He died in 1754.

Just as Holberg represented the critical and rationalistic tendencies of his time. HANS ADOLF BRORSON (1694—1764) was an exponent of the emotional tendencies of the same period. Brorson, who was originally a parson in North Slesvig and eventually became Bishop of Ribe, came early under the influence of German Pietism, which he interpreted in his hymns and sacred poetry. He produced only two collections of lyrical poetry, one called *The Rare Ornament of Faith* ("Troens rare Klenodie", 1739), the other *The Swan's Song* ("Svanesangen", published posthumously). Both consist mainly of hymns, of which several are translations from the German.

Brorson's hymns are inspired by a deep religious mysticism, combined with a longing for the liberation of the soul from the imprisonment of temporal life. It is the suffering Christ rather than the victorious Christ who appears in Brorson's hymns, and one of his favourite sources of inspiration is the Song of Solomon; so, for instance, he describes with fine and delicate art the relationship between the Soul and Christ in the simile of a bride's longing for her bridegroom — a theme usually so tastelessly and nauseatingly treated by the German Pietists. The two first stanzas of his hymn *Until the Day Breaks* ("Her vil ties"), with its dialogue between the bridegroom (first stanza) and the bride (second stanza), may serve as an example:

> Now no murmur, bide but firmer,
> bide but firmer, O faint of soul!

4*

Slowly our summer we shall outrun her,
we shall outrun her and reach our goal.
Now no murmur, bide but firmer,
bide but firmer, O faint of soul.

Times that chasten seldom hasten,
seldom hasten, 'tis not their way.
As the days lengthen, winter will strengthen,
winter will strengthen and bring dismay.
Times that chasten seldom hasten,
seldom hasten, 'tis not their way.

Her vil ties, her vil bies,
her vil bies, o svage Sind!
Vist skal vi hente, kun ved at vente,
kun ved at vente, vor Sommer ind.
Her vil ties, her vil bies,
her vil bies, o svage Sind!

Trange Tider langsomt skrider,
langsomt skrider, det har den Art.
Dagene længes, Vinteren strænges,
Vinteren strænges, og det er svart.
Trange Tider langsomt skrider,
langsomt skrider, det har den Art.

Compared with Kingo's vigorous verse, Brorson's may
sound weak and effeminate, but if one listens carefully to
the singing of the Dying Swan, one can hear the purest
and loveliest of music, carrying a message, of agony relieved
by an unconquerable faith in God.

AMBROSIUS STUB (1705–58) is another fine lyric poet
contemporary with Holberg and Brorson, unrecognized in
his own lifetime, and therefore a tragic character, whose
fate was to become jester to the wealthy squires of Denmark. His poems — or those which have survived —

are mainly religious and moralizing *Arias* or occasional pieces, witty improvised epigrams, or drinking songs. In many ways his poetry is suggestive of Robert Herrick. Behind the 18th century artificiality of metaphors and similes and other stylistic finery, there is a genuine love of Nature in Stub's poems, a sense of personal experience, and a vivacious, graceful tone, which has kept the best of his poems alive through the centuries. Here is an example of his light and charming impromptus, an epigram written on the occasion of the wedding of a certain Miss Lamare after she had left the *Duekloster* (i. e. Dove Convent) at Odense:

> Now fill them with wine full,
> those cups you have there,
> and let us be mindful
> of little Lamare.
> Sweet dove from the convent,
> fly mated, afar!
> Miss soon becomes Mrs.,
> and Mrs. Mamma!

> *Ved Vinen den klare*
> *Erindres vi nu,*
> *At Frøken Lamare*
> *Bør kommes i Hu;*
> *Du Klosterets Due,*
> *Flyv parret herfra,*
> *Af Frøken blir Frue*
> *Af Frue Mama!*

Between 1740 and 1770 nothing much of great importance happened in Danish literature, and this period can boast of no first-rate creative writer. A multitude of less eminent writers: philosophers, historians, critics, editors, etc., followed in Holberg's footsteps, discussing contemporary subjects and adapting European Rationalism to Danish conditions. This was to a great extent a period of journalism rather than of literature, a period of didactic verse rather than of lyrical poetry. JENS SCHIELDERUP SNEEDORFF (1724–64) was the editor of *The Patriotic Spectator* ("Den patriotiske Tilskuer"), and C. B. TULLIN (1728–65), a disciple of Young and Pope, the author of various boring didactic poems (e. g. *On the Excellence of the Creation with Regard to the Order and the Connection of Created Things*).

Towards the end of the 18th century, however, a significant revival of Danish literature took place. JOHAN HERMAN WESSEL (1742–85), a poet of Norwegian extraction, was a Bohemian and an idler, whose name is immortal in Danish literature as one of its greatest humorists. His dramatic work, *Love without Stockings* ("Kærlighed uden Strømper", 1772), the only long work he ever had the energy to write, is undoubtedly one of the most comic tragedies in literature, but one must read it in the original Danish, for it hardly lends itself to translation. Like Holberg's *Peder Paars* it is written in alexandrines, and as in *Peder Paars* the irony depends upon the putting of ordinary characters into a heroic setting; but Wessel's tragedy is far more elegant and light in its form than Holberg's satire, and it is written in graceful alexandrines, which Holberg's certainly were not. *Love without Stockings* must be seen against the background of the dramatic fashion of Wessel's time, when Holberg's comedies had been superseded by Danish imitations of Italian operas and French tragedies. These were heroic plays about the conflict between Love and Virtue, culminating in a series of suicides. It was against the unnaturalness of these dramas, and especially of the tragedies written by his compatriots NIELS KROG BREDAL and JOHAN NORDAHL BRUN, that Wessel directed his ridicule, when he wrote the tragedy in which with great artistic skill he out-Heroded Herod. *Love without Stockings* contains a hero and a heroine, with a confidant and a confidante, plus a rival and his confidant, and there is the usual conflict between Love and Virtue. But the hero is neither a prince nor a nobleman, only an ordinary tailor, and the heroine is a servant girl. The conflict arises over the hero's lack of a pair of long stockings, essential to his wedding, which he is forced to steal from his rival. This is the conflict between Love and Virtue which brings about the tragic end: in the final scene each of the characters commits suicide one by one, until the stage looks like a battlefield, littered with corpses. In an epilogue (added by Wessel later) Mercury descends from the sky and brings them all to life again, and the play ends in a wild extravaganza with the refrain: "The crazier, the better."

Wessel wrote *Love without Stockings* for fun, simply because it amused him, but it was such a success that it put an end to imitations of French and Italian classicism in Danish drama.

Of Wessel's light humorous poems and versified narratives, many have been loved and admired by generation after generation. His verse story, *The Blacksmith and the Baker* ("Smeden og Bageren"), is a good example of these sauntering verses, in which Wessel, with a great many amusing digressions, tells an anecdote. The moral in *The Blacksmith and the Baker* — for these stories usually have a humorous moral — is that if, for some reason you cannot hang the man who committed the crime, you can always hang someone else. Wessel's small impromptus are quick-witted and nimble; he was a master of brief humorous verse. His little poem in *Aftenposten* may serve as an example:

> Dare I compose *The Post* a stanza
> on how to deal with influenza?
> Crush cloves at morning in a cup,
> mix them in mead, and drink it up.

If long before the evening greet us
your cough don't get its full quietus,
then you may strike a vengeful note:
"Go, cut, Sir Leech, your lying throat!"

Tør jeg besvære Aftenposten
Med ringe Raad imod Kiighosten:
Stød Nelliker en Morgen smaae,
Kom dem i Miød, og drik dem saa.
Hvis du er ikke inden Aften
Som den, der aldrig havde havt'en;
Saa kan du sige allenfals:
Hr. Medicus! Løgn i jer Hals!

Spiritually, Wessel was a descendant of Holberg — an 18th century rationalist of the English and French school. Together with other Norwegian men of letters who lived in Copenhagen he spent his evenings in the "Norske Selskab" — a Norwegian club where, among other things, a feeling of Norwegian patriotism found its first poetic forms; but, like Wessel, its members mostly cultivated French elegance and *esprit*.

At the same time, in other fields, a revival of emotional poetry was taking place. This was greatly influenced by contemporary German literature (especially Goethe, Schiller and Klopstock) and by English literature (especially Shakespeare, Milton, Ossian, Percy's *Reliques,* Young's *Night Thoughts,* and Gray's *Elegy).* The feeling and content of the poem were considered by this school as more important than correctness of style and metre.

JOHANNES EWALD (1743—81) — by many regarded as Denmark's greatest lyrical poet — is the exponent of Danish Pre-Romanticism. From his passionate, sensitive and chaotic mind came rich, inspired poetry, sometimes simple and subdued, but with deep feeling — as in the poem in which he mourned the death of Christian VI, *Hold Taare, op at trille* — sometimes solemn and majestic — as in *King Christian;* sometimes passionately religious — as in his *Ode to the Soul* ("Ode til Sjælen"); sometimes in agony and distress — as in *The Penitent* ("Pønitenten"); and sometimes grateful and happy — as in *The Blessings of Rungsted* ("Rungsteds Lyksaligheder"), and *To My Moltke* ("Til min Moltke").

In real life Ewald was a tragic, unhappy character, bitterly disappointed in love, a hopeless drunkard, physically broken down. But in his frail body was a restless and indomitable spirit, a lover of mankind and a worshipper of God. He filled the outdated form of the ode with new and fascinating contents — his poetry was passionate — full of the enraptured, harmonious expressions of the genuine poet. In a strange way Ewald was both a forerunner of 19th century Danish Romanticism and at the same time bound by 18th century literary traditions. For him, Art was a craft to be learned by a study of the classic models; and he sticks so closely to the literary forms in vogue in his own century that one can only appreciate him fully if one has a knowledge of these. And yet he was the first poet who delved into Scandinavian antiquity and discovered the poetic wealth in the myths, in Saxo Grammaticus, in the sagas, and in the medieval ballads. It was his study of Shakespeare, Milton, Rousseau and Ossian which led him to use incidents in the history of his own country as plots for his dramas; especially *Rolf Krage* (1770), the first important Danish tragedy, and *The Death of Balder* ("Balders Død", 1773), the first example of tragedy in blank verse. But Ewald found heroism also in everyday life, and his poetic drama, *The Fishermen* ("Fiskerne", 1780), was the first serious Danish drama in which ordinary people were treated heroically. A new patriotic sentiment, hitherto unknown to Danish poetry, appears in this play; but on the whole its greatness lies more in its lyrical passages than in

its dramatic quality. In this play Ewald pays homage to
the sea surrounding Denmark in a poem which later became
the Danish National Anthem. Here are its first and last
stanzas in English: —

> King Christian stood mid fume and smoke
>   by towering mast.
> So fiercely fell each hammer-stroke
> that Gothic brain and helmet broke,
> and down went every foe in smoke
>   with poop and mast.
> Now fly, they cry, fly, all who can —
> or yield to Denmark's Christian
>   at last.
>
> Path of the Dane to fame and power,
>   dark-rolling wave!
> Thy friend receive this fateful hour
> who dauntless still though dangers lower,
> will spurn like thee the tempest's power,
>   dark-rolling wave!
> Through hazards bold and battle's din
> lead me in triumph till I win
>   my grave.

> *Kong Christian stod ved højen Mast,*
> *I Røg og Damp.*
> *Hans Værge hamrede saa fast,*
> *At Gothens Hjelm og Hjerne brast.*
> *Da sank hvert fjendtligt Spejl og Mast*
> *I Røg og Damp.*
> *Fly, skreg de, fly, hvad flygte kan!*
> *Hvo staar for Danmarks Christian*
> *I Kamp?*

Du Danskes Vej til Ros og Magt,
Sortladne Hav!
Modtag din Ven, som uforsagt,
Tør møde Faren med Foragt,
Saa stolt, som du, med Stormens Magt,
Sortladne Hav!
Og rask igennem Larm og Spil
Og Kamp og Sejer før mig til
Min Grav.

Although mainly a lyrical poet Ewald wrote one prose work which has become a classic, his autobiography, entitled *Life and Opinions* ("Levned og Meninger") in imitation of Laurence Sterne, who influenced its style considerably. It was meant as a confession intended only for the eyes of his mother and his pastor; but the pleasure of writing carried him away, and the result is an intoxicating mixture, in which humour and gentle irony mingle with expressions of the profoundest grief. The importance of the book lies in its revelation of the poet's mind — Denmark's most sensitive poet, with the possible exception of Hans Andersen.

Both Wessel and Ewald died at an early age, before the century was out, and the end of the 18th century is marked by much poetic dilettantism. Politically it was an age of social reforms, and political and social matters were much to the fore; but it is astonishing to see how little influence the French Revolution and its ideas had on contemporary Danish literature. P. A. HEIBERG (1758—1841) and MALTHE CONRAD BRUUN (1775—1826) were the only exponents of a militant Radicalism, and neither of them is a very great poet. P. A. Heiberg was, however, a great and outstanding personality, and it is his tragic life — he was expelled from Denmark for his Radical opinions and lived for forty years in France as a political refugee — which has made his name

so well known. His critical and satirical prose is often
good journalism, and his best poems are full of searing
irony, but are now remembered mainly for their sarcastic
slogans, some of which have become proverbial.

In spite of Ewald, rationalistic tendencies predominated
at the end of the 18th century, and this period produced
innumerable pamphlets, most of which were forgotten as
quickly as they were written. It was also the age of social
clubs, and drinking songs, written for the members of
these clubs, abound. KNUD LYHNE RAHBEK (1760—1830),
a poet and critic whose versatility was greater than his gifts,
was the author of many such songs. After Ewald and Wessel the general level of dramatic art dropped considerably.
General taste favoured the optimistic and idyllic, and apart
from the charming comedy, *The Gold Box* ("Gulddaasen",
1793), by CHRISTIAN OLUFSEN (1764—1827) hardly any of
the plays of this period have survived.

The last great writer of the 18th century was JENS BAG-
GESEN (1764—1826), who began his literary career by imitating the satires of Holberg and Wessel but gradually developed a style of his own. He was a man of quickly changing
mood, and his poetry varies according. He wrote, now in
Danish, now in German, now sentimentally, now elegantly
and facetiously. His turbulent, impetuous spirit never left
him in peace. In 1789 he travelled through Germany and
Switzerland to Paris, and on his return wrote a book on
his journey, *The Labyrinth* ("Labyrinthen", 1792—93), a
charming arabesque, impressionistic in style, full of Baggesen's ebullient temperament. In many ways it resembles
Ewald's memoirs, and was also strongly influenced by
Sterne.

At the beginning of the 19th century Baggesen decided
to leave his native land and settle abroad, and with strange
prophetic instinct dedicated his lyre to young Adam
Oehlenschläger. But a few years later he returned, and

found a completely changed Denmark. Literary Romanticism had now won the day, and Baggesen for a short time became a convert to the new creed, but abandoned it again; and in consequence several years of his life were spent in a futile feud with Oehlenschläger, whom he criticised (not without some justice) for not understanding the limitations of his own poetic genius. During these years Baggesen developed a brilliant technique in rhymed polemical verse, but it only showed to what extent he himself belonged to the 18th century. Of his many poems only a handful have survived — not one of them a masterpiece. His worst faults as a poet are his versatility and lack of stability, and his main poetic merits are his grace and charm. None of his best poems has been translated into English, but I will quote the first two stanzas and the last one of the sentimental and nostalgic poem, *My Childhood* ("Da jeg var lille"), one of his most popular:

> There was a time when I was very little,
> when my whole frame was but a cubit tall;
> the tears, as I recall it, trickle sweetly,
> and therefore 'tis a time I oft recall.
>
> I frolicked in my mother's fond embraces
> and rode astride a loving father's knee;
> dejection, spite, anxiety and brooding —
> like love and money, these were Greek to me.
>
> — — —
>
> They fled, they fled, those happy days of childhood,
> and all the quiet joys which they begat;
> and now I've nothing but remembrance left me —
> God grant I never, never part from that!
>
> *Der var en Tid, da jeg var meget lille,*
> *Min hele Krop var knap en Alen lang;*

Sødt, naar jeg denne tænker, Taarer trille,
Og derfor tænker jeg den mangen Gang.

Jeg spøged i min ømme Moders Arme
Og sad til Hest paa bedste Faders Knæ,
Og kendte Frygt og Grublen, Sorg og Harme
Saa lidt som Penge, Græsk og Galathe.

— — —

De svandt, de svandt, de blide Barndoms Dage!
Min Rolighed, min Fryd med dem svandt hen —
Jeg kun Erindringen har nu tilbage;
Gud! lad mig aldrig, aldrig tabe den!

CHAPTER IV

SWEDISH LITERATURE IN THE 18TH CENTURY

Sweden's career as a great power did not come to an abrupt termination with the end of the 17th century, for the first years of the 18th century witnessed some of Charles XII's boldest triumphs as a strategist on the Continent. Not until 1718, after his defeat and death, did the fantastic and insecurely balanced fabric of his empire collapse, and Sweden revert to the status of a minor power. By that time her people had already felt the pinch of poverty, whilst the material resources of the country, so carefully accumulated by Charles XI through fiscal reforms and the sequestration of noble property, had all been squandered on the costly foreign campaigns. Faced with disastrous news from abroad and the necessity to eat bread made out of bark at home, the nation lost its ebullience but not its courage. The literature of the period reflects this soberer attitude.

The excessive indulgence in pompous words and forms, which had marred the work of some of Stiernhielm's successors in the last decades of the 17th century, was a quite natural reaction to the discovery of the linguistic possibilities of Swedish: the elaborate apostrophes of the odes of G. DAHLSTIERNA (1661—1709), and the grotesque witticisms of I. HOLMSTRÖM (1660—1708) corresponded to earlier Baroque tendencies in French and German letters, and had been stimulated by the "marinism" of Italy. The Swedes did not indulge for long in the worst extravagances of this fashion; the corrective influence of French classical standards gradually asserted itself, partly thanks to the precept and example of S. TRIEWALD (1688–1743) and to the teachings of the purist P. LAGERLÖF (1648–1699). Nor should the changing texture of society be underestimated as a factor in the literary development at the turn of the century; the political and economic conditions resulting in and from the increased autocracy of government, the bureaucratization of the nobles, and the rise of the middle-classes, affected literature. Thus the light-hearted occasional verses of JOHAN RUNIUS (1679–1713) were written to please his bourgeois friends, and skilfully record their amusements, whilst the formless exercises of the poetess SOPHIE BRENNER (1659–1730) in French, German, and Swedish verse, reveal those rather trite didactic tendencies which were to become so indissolubly associated with the Western bourgeoisie during the coming century. The charming lyrics and hymns of the Finn JACOB FRESE (1691–1729) have a more intimate, melancholy note than Spegel's or Swedberg's religious verses, foreshadowing some of that pietistic sentimentality which, a little later, was to infuse itself so markedly into the currents of the 18th century. Frese expressed some of the resigned fortitude of the generation which experienced the fall of Charles XII.

Yet literature did not change character overnight when the national hero fell at Fredrikshald. The year 1732 — that is, a date well on into the so-called "Frihetstiden" — is commonly taken to mark the beginning of the new era in Swedish letters: the appearance that year of the first number of *The Swedish Argus* ("Den Swänske Argus") formally ushers in the Age of Enlightenment and "den yngre Nysvenskan"; and with *The Swedish Argus* OLOF VON DALIN (1708–1763) made his bow to the public — anonymously — for the articles in this periodical, modelled chiefly on the *Spectator,* were nearly all from his pen. This was something of a *tour de force* for a young man of 24. Dalin was one of the first, and outstanding, products of the University of Lund in Southern Sweden, founded in 1668 to facilitate the Swedification of the southern provinces reconquered from Denmark. With a combination of classical and modern learning acquired from his master at Lund, A. Rydelius, and with worldly knowledge gained as a tutor in a highly cultured aristocratic family and as a civil servant in Stockholm, Dalin, through *Argus*, immediately became a popular writer, and then shed his anonymity. Success, in fact, accompanied Dalin all through his life as writer and courtier. In a sense it is the r e a s o n for his importance, for it was as popularizer of other thinkers' ideas, as educator of the growing reading public, that he earned his niche in the gallery of Swedish littérateurs. From the start he seems to have had a remarkable facility for absorbing ideas, and for clothing them in expressive, ingenious language. Herein lay the strength of *Argus*. These second-hand ideas — the ideals of reason, common-sense, and moderation — were applied to the abuses and faults of contemporary Sweden, particularly of the capital, which increasingly set the fashion of the day. Dalin conceals his didacticism under wit and satire, and the most amusing sections of the *Argus* series are various dialogues, reproduced in the ordinary language of the day, between masters and servants, between fashionable coxcombs, and so on. His prose, considered as a flexible instrument, shows the most marked advance on anything preceding it in Sweden: it is in fact modern prose. What Dalin accomplished for Swedish prose, not least with the allegorical *Tale of the Horse* ("Sagan om Hästen") of 1740, was really his greatest single achievement in literature.

Argus also constituted the first genuine venture in literary journalism in Sweden, with the possible exception of *Den sedolärande Mercurius*, for the 17th century *Post-*

Tijdenden had no literary pretensions. Even though *Argus* enjoyed only a rather brief career, it pointed the way to others. It was typical of this age that so much serious discussion was ventilated in the press, and that so much literary work was published there; in earlier centuries the Church would have acted as literary midwife for this kind of thing. Thus, as the 18th century advances, the tone of Swedish literature becomes secular, even profane; the constricting bonds of orthodoxy are slackened among the upper classes, and the political intrigues of "Frihetstiden" (1719–1772) undermine the authority both of Crown and Church. The new and bolder Continental ideas were adopted more readily because of this general decline in authority, and in their turn, of course, affected politics. Nevertheless both Crown (under Gustav III) and Church offered stout resistance. French culture was perhaps the dominant influence on Sweden during this period (from 1745 on), and French philosophy, tragedies, lampoons, were all the rage; but English influence came a good second, even though at times it only reached this Northern outpost of civilisation via the French capital. In literature English models were perhaps more influential towards the end of the 18th century; it was rather in respect of political ideas that, under the uneasy and on the whole abortive party system of "Hats" and "Caps" — the system which prevailed during "Frihetstiden" — men looked to England, as the home of constitutional freedom. They also looked towards England as the home of the natural sciences; and, after all, the new, increasingly materialistic, views of the Age of Enlightenment were founded on the new discoveries, while science as such was venerated more and more.

Dalin had studied both French and English authors, but in much of his output after *Argus* one feels that the French influence predominates, not always happily. In the classical verse tragedy *Brynhilda* and the epic *Swedish Freedom* ("Svenska Friheten") Dalin attempted to rival Voltaire, but his efforts, though respectable, can hardly be called inspired. Again like the versatile Voltaire, he wrote a history (of Sweden) and a number of odes, and got himself involved in a political *contretemps:* but here he was more fortunate than Voltaire, in that, though his offences were more serious, his punishment was pretty light. Within a few years he was back at Court, more cherished than ever, the favourite of the brillant Queen Lovisa Ulrika and of Carl Gustav Tessin, courtier, architect, writer, and patron of the arts. Yet in Dalin a certain simplicity seems to have survived, which allowed him to write, by the side of his "slick", amusing, occasional poetry, folksongs and ballads, not just designed as burlesques (though some were so intended), but also with the object of expressing simple, human sentiments. It is for these songs that he has been remembered as a poet. Moreover, with all his new-fangled and foreign airs and graces, Dalin remained in several respects a believer in the orthodoxy and nationalism (as in respect of Charles XII) of his predecessors, and the agile courtier could not quite accept the bouncing optimism of 18th century Enlightenment.

The sciences, as has been indicated, occupied the central position in the affections of the educated sections of society in this age, utility being the criterion according to which activities were judged. It was in this field, especially, that CARL VON LINNÉ (1707—1778), one of the very few internationally famous Swedes of his day, was so conspicuous. This is not the place to discuss his achievements as a botanist, but the lustre he shed throughout Europe on Swedish scholarship, together with his personality, had, without doubt, a stimulating effect on culture in general in his native land. As Rector, too, of Uppsala University, Linné had a practical opportunity of leading the study of

5*

the natural sciences according to new principles. Though the bulk of his writings were composed, for obvious reasons, in Latin, he reveals in his works in the Swedish language (e. g., descriptions of his journeys to Öland, Lapland, etc.) all that keen eye for detail and that vivid feeling for the beauties of nature and that gratitude for the mercy of God in revealing them to man, that made Linné both a great scientist and a real poet — in prose. His appreciation of nature helped to open the eyes of some of the younger generation of writers to the particular, as opposed to the general, in nature — such men as G. P. CREUTZ (1731— 1785), G. F. GYLLENBORG (1731—1808), and above all CARL MICHAEL BELLMAN (1740—1795). As Swedish prose stylist, however, Linné was not lauded by his contemporaries, but much more by the 19th century: and yet the fresh realism of J. WALLENBERG'S autobiographical travelogue *My Son on the Galleon* ("Min Son på Galejan"), which aimed, in part, at parodying Linné, had been learnt from the master among others.

The other great international figure who made Sweden known abroad during these years, was EMMANUEL SWEDENBORG (1688—1772), son of Bishop Swedberg of Skara. His was a character much less appealing than that of the charming and impulsive Linné, but, like Linné, he combined profound and original scientific thought with deep religious faith. As a scientist he was more versatile than Linné, and his religion was not the, mainly orthodox, Lutheranism to which the latter conformed. In fact, Swedenborg evolved a faith of his own, after a prolonged spiritual crisis in the 1740's, and his many religious writings in Latin record the details of his mystic visions of Heaven and Hell. The various rewards and punishments are elaborated with scientific precision and a curiously practical approach.

Swedenborg, indeed, was destined to exert an influence along two different lines, on actual religion, and on literature. His disciples in England founded a Church in his name in that country, after his death, and whilst many of his Swedish contemporaries ridiculed his ideas, the visionary appeal of his faith, picked up at secondhand and ignorantly distorted, combined with the growing contempt for orthodox religion among the educated to encourage the genesis of secret circles, some large, some small, dabbling in bogus mysticism and the occult sciences. For the loss of faith in the state religion, in the latter half of the century, under the pressure of rationalistic materialism, had provoked the customary reaction of superstition, as, for example, in the Roman Empire during the 1st century A.D., throughout all Western Europe and not least in Sweden. Hence the popularity of so-called Swedenborgian ideas, which Swedenborg himself would probably have been the first to reject. Such superstitious ideas, which affected even Gustav III, were violently attacked by the really enlightened rationalists, such as J. H. KELLGREN (1751—1795), to whom I must later return.

In literature, Swedenborg's visions were destined to kindle the imagination of Goethe and Balzac, to mention no others, while in Sweden they aroused the admiration of several writers, for example, of C. J. L. Almquist and of Strindberg in his later period. Swedenborg's more immediate effect, through the emphasis he laid on the individual and the imagination, was in arousing echoes among some of the Pre-Romantics.

The craze for societies manifested itself more innocently, during this age, in the foundation of academies and learned communities. The society known as *Tankebyggarna*, founded in 1753 by a dilettante gentleman, has, unlike many similar bodies, gone down to posterity on account of three of its members, FRU NORDENFLYCHT (1718—1763), Creutz, and Gyllenborg: the latter two were still the merest apprentices in literature when they joined the society. Fru Nor-

denflycht, on the other hand, had already published a number of verses, making her début with *The Mourning Turtle-
dove* ("Den sörjande turturduvan") in 1743. A member
of the bourgeoisie, she had married a naval chaplain, and
his sudden and premature death had released in her the
springs of poetry. Such personal and emotional reactions
were to characterize Fru Nordenflycht throughout her life.
Whilst Dalin was intellectually flexible enough to get the
feel of various literary fashions, and so technically skilful
that he could reproduce them in his own work, he practically never expresses any *personal* emotion in his verses, and
never reveals any spiritual conflicts. Fru Nordenflycht,
representing the second generation of the Swedish Age of
Enlightenment, is aware, in quite another way, of the pull
of contradictory ideals and feelings, and pours out her emotions in verse and letters. Being a woman, and a highly passionate woman at that, she is more subject to influences than
her contemporaries Creutz and Gyllenborg, but not sharp
enough to weigh up properly the issues raised. By her
quality of enthusiasm she dominated *Tankebyggarna*, whilst
Creutz and Gyllenborg, with a much profounder knowledge
of French and other cultures, introduced her to recent
foreign thought. These three shaped the literary output
of the society, published in 1753—1756 and in revised form
in 1759—1762, under the title *Literary Works* ("Vitterhets-
arbeten"). Dalin's generation had been intent rather on
the artistic forms connected with the new influences, and
Dalin himself particularly on the classical ideals, as embodied
in Racine and Boileau, of the French 17th century. The
philosophical problems raised, for instance, by Voltaire,
Montesquieu, and Bayle, had, perhaps, not yet crystallized
in their consciousness: these problems obviously grew
more, rather than less, complicated, as the century pro-
gressed. It was Fru Nordenflycht who, first among Swedish
writers to do so, showed, in her literary output, traces of

Rousseau's influence.   Personal as ever, she had absorbed
Rousseau's doctrines through the last love of her life,
Fischerström, and like Rousseau's heroines she openly gives
vent to her passionate feelings for the younger man, in
poems which rank high among the lyrics of the century and
outweigh the mediocrity of her more ambitious literary
work, and in letters, which are actually written in French:
"Ma cabane," she characteristically says, "est devenue un
ciel pour moi par votre tendresse."
Fru Nordenflycht showed no particular interest in the
finer points of style.   Form, however, was the main concern of the two younger members of the group, both aristo-
crats, both courtiers, both highly cultured.   It was, incidentally, characteristic of the improved social status of Swedish
authors that the finer flowers of the aristocracy should
mingle on an equal footing with the brighter luminaries
of the bourgeoisie in such bodies as Vitterhetsakademien
and later in Gustav III's Swedish Academy.
Creutz and Gyllenborg, at first glance, present a decep-
tive similarity — a "Rosencrantz and Guildenstern" effect.
On closer analysis this impression is dispelled.   Of the two
Creutz was much the better poet, carrying his learning with
exquisite grace, and embodying it in flowing and varied
metres.   The slightness of his output, which consists of a
small number of lyrics and an idyll in five cantos, *Atis and
Camilla* (1761), made his reputation as "a poet's poet",
before he, practically speaking, abandoned writing and
turned his talents to diplomacy: he became a succesful
ambassador to France.   *Atis and Camilla*, based on the
conventional French interpretation of classical mythology, is
a rococo pastoral resolved by divine intervention, which yet
contains glimpses of real nature, of course carefully selected
for their beauty.   Here we find a reflection of Rousseau's
doctrine of the evils of civilisation and his search for
unspoilt nature.   By conviction, however, Creutz was an

Epicurean, singing like Herrick of the roses that must be quickly gathered.

Gyllenborg, herein unlike his friend, was a Stoic, both his reading and his temperament having encouraged in him that brand of pessimistic resignation which became fashionable later in Revolutionary France. Echoes of classical and other erudition, together with the doctrines of Rousseau, are perceptible in his two best poems, *The Contemner of the World* ("Världsföraktaren", 1762) and *The Misery of Man* ("Människans Elände"). In *The Winter Song* ("Vinterkvädet", 1759), a poem in a genre exploited by Creutz, with many loans from Thomson's *Seasons*, he sang of the joys of winter. Its principal interest for literature is that here the old legend of "göticism", was revived and given a more up-to-date garb à la Montesquieu; and thus Gyllenborg provides a link, in this and other works, with the coming Romantic theories on this subject. I shall have to return to these theories in a subsequent chapter. The rhetorical verses of Gyllenborg from his later life need not delay us here.

In the period between Fru Nordenflycht's death (in 1763) and the first flowering of the Gustavian Age (about 1777), one writer alone stands out, namely BELLMAN. He is indeed above time and space. He is the only Swedish poet — with the possible exception of Fröding — to attain to universal stature. If Bellman had been a French or an English poet, he would by now have been a world classic, read by millions, and vulgarised by the wireless. For Bellman himself set his lyrics to music, they were intended to be sung, therein being t r u e lyrics, and as Kellgren pointed out as early as 1790 in his famous preface to the first edition of *The Epistles of Fredman* ("Fredmans Epistlar"), music and verse are here so skilfully interwoven that they are inseparable. That Bellman had often openly taken contemporary airs, French song hits, or old folk-tunes, and adapted them to his purpose, rather than compose new ones, does not detract from his originality and skill. Through this happy marriage of words and music Bellman's songs have made themselves immensely loved in the Scandinavian countries, and are still sung and imitated. Bellman's contemporaries saw in him at first only a gay trifler, a mocker at pomp and ceremony, a boon companion who could be counted on to amuse any party — in fact a popular man. He came actually from a good and serious bourgeois home, was well educated, and his first literary efforts were religious poems. Faced by the secular tendencies in 18th century literature, one is tempted to forget how much religious writing the century produced — not least under the deepening influence of pietistic movements and as a result of the continual recruitment of bourgeois poets. But this writing seldom rose to the heights of literature.

Soon, however, Bellman found his real *métier*. By way of Bible parodies and satires on the secret societies of the time, as in *The Order of Bacchus* ("Bacchi Orden"), he passed on to true lyrics. *The Epistles of Fredman*, already mentioned, and *The Songs of Fredman* ("Fredmans Sånger") contain the quintessential Bellman. Published respectively in 1790 and 1791, these collections, or rather the bulk of them, had been composed much earlier (1768–1774). At the time of their publication the poet was already, in a worldly sense, a broken man, consumptive, debt-ridden, and not untouched by the cumulative effects of years of heavy drinking. Yet his spirit, with its attractive element of childlike lightheartedness, had not deserted him.

Bellman's temperament, artistic in the deepest sense of the word, shines through these seemingly improvised, but, in reality, carefully constructed lyrics. *Joie de vivre* had inspired them, but the fatalistic consciousness of the ephemeral nature of existence underlies the greatest of them. The shadows indicated in the picture serve to emphasise the brilliance of the colours and the sharpness of the outlines, just as the drum in the accompaniment gives depth to the harmonies of violin and flute. Conversely, Bellman gives relief to his descriptions of the low life of Stockholm by unexpected references to classical mythology, appealing to the imagination of the hearer and at the same time amusing him by the startling juxtaposition. Thus Ulla Winblad, a drab of the town, is compared to Venus Anadyomene. These are in a sense rococo effects, the graceful and sensuous arabesques of a Boucher translated into words — but with a difference. It is Bellman's combination of the realistic and the stylized, his amused interest in human nature around him and his keen but humorous observation of the light gestures and quick words that reveal it, which, joined with his technical mastery of language and metre, make him an immortal poet. The Stockholm that he described, the sordid but picturesque "City between the Bridges" from the dissipated and bankrupt decline of "Frihetstiden", is peopled by a curious crew of drunkards, rascals, and prostitutes, led by Fredman, a ruined watchmaker. Bellman often sets these characters against the background of Stockholm's suburbs, the smiling banks of Lake Mälaren with its little islands, which they frequent on holidays, and so, in these songs, he took possession in the name of poetry, for the first time, of both Stockholm and the Swedish countryside. Bellman's impressions of nature, stylized though they are, have a vitality lacking in Creutz' landscapes. Bellman was not interested in literary fashions as such, though he had learned both from the poets of "Stormaktstiden" and from Creutz, nor, it appears, in the ideologies that absorbed so many of his contemporaries. For his seeming disregard of classical standards the Gustavian poets despised him, until Kellgren, revising his earlier judgment, defended him *coram publico*. Yet it is not least on account of this indifference to passing fashions that Bellman's work has survived untouched by time.

Gustav III's political coup in 1772 had a unifying and reviving effect upon the nation as a whole. After the corruption and intrigues of the '60's, the air was — temporarily — cleared. For literature and the arts the personality of the new and autocratic king was of particular importance, in that Gustav III, imitating the Bourbon princes, loved to see himself as their patron. Especially did the king concern himself with the theatre and the opera, and it was as a result of royal patronage that Sweden now developed a proper theatrical tradition, towards the end of the '70's. That is, it developed standards of acting and production. Gustav III's court theatre at Drottningholm is still one of Europe's show pieces.

However, native dramatists of real talent still failed to come forward. We have seen that Dalin had tried his hand at tragedy, and comedy too, and OLOF CELSIUS had produced, just before Dalin, a tragedy *Ingeborg* (1737), whilst the politician CARL GYLLENBORG (not to be confused with the poet) had succeeded, in the same year, in turning out quite a lively comedy, *The Swedish Coxcomb* ("Svenska sprätthöken"). Yet none of these works, nor their sparse successors during the ensuing decades, can be classed as living drama. But now many of the leading poets, Kellgren, LEOPOLD, Gyllenborg, OXENSTIERNA, even Bellman, more or less reluctantly, were compelled by the king to write plays, who himself wrote or sketched the outlines of dramas and operas. Thus, for example, Kellgren was entrusted with the task of writing the libretto for the opera *Gustav Vasa*. National feeling and pseudo-classical technique was the recipe followed in so many of these works, but true vitality was lacking. Nor were any first-class comedies produced under Gustav's aegis, though some were at any rate charming and amusing.

In the genre of the novel, the century had even less to
offer, in spite of the development of prose as a medium.
Urban Hiärne's *Stratonice* (about 1650) is classed as a novel
by some critics, but is in fact hardly more than a pastoral
tale. During the 18th century the demand for fiction
was satisfied by translations of foreign novels, and by Swedish versions of the Icelandic sagas, which became very
popular. Their influence is discernible in the first genuine
Swedish novel, MÖRK's and TÖRNGREN's *Adalrik and Giöthilda*
(1742—1744). Mörk's second novel, *Thecla,* has slightly
higher literary pretensions. Lack of interest in psychology,
and lack of understanding of it, no doubt account for the
failure of the Swedish novel to develop during this century:
the anonymous work entitled *A Swedish Nobleman's Adventures in Foreign Parts* ("En svensk adelsmans äfventyr i
utrikes orter", 1759—1780) indicates the kind of thing that
took the place of the novel proper. Genuine memoirs,
later on, more introspective diaries, as the taste for confession developed, also became increasingly fashionable. Not
a little of the charm and wit of Gustav III's court and
courtiers has survived to our times thanks to the works of
A. L. HAMILTON, G. J. ADLERBETH, and G. J. EHRENSVÄRD,
to mention no others.

Yet in spite of frigid dramas and naive novels, the Gustavian era was a brilliant one — in poetry and polemics.
And however cramping, in some respects, Gustav's influence
was — for, among other things, freedom of political speech
was severely curtailed — the king did provide, through his
court, a centre and a standard, and often, too, financial
encouragement for struggling writers. Literature enjoyed
a social prestige it had never before possessed in Swedish
history, and never has possessed again.

The generation of J. H. Kellgren, J. G. Oxenstierna
(1750—1818), C. G. af Leopold (1756—1829), FRU LENN-
GREN (1754—1817), to mention some of its leading figures,

took over the aesthetic principles of *Tankebyggarna*. Their own verses revealed classical perfection expressed with much greater suppleness of form and word (whilst they embodied more complex influences), apart from the more pompous odes of Leopold. Leopold's first essay in this genre (1778), in fact, brought him into conflict with Kellgren, who, shortly before, had started his work as critic on *Stockholms-posten*, a new literary organ which he dominated. Kellgren, as well as being the greatest poet of this generation, became too its arbiter of taste. THOMAS THORILD (1759–1808) and his pupil BENGT LIDNER (1757–1793), who represented the revolutionary element in this generation, were both subjected to his penetrating wit, and when Kellgren was too ill to continue the feud, Leopold took over the task from him. Thorild's writings are evidence of a renewed influence from Germany, in their author's emotionalism and "Sturm-und-Drang" attitude to life and literature. Lidner's works, of which his odes, such as *The Death of Countess Spastara* ("Grevinnan Spastaras död"), rank highest, reveal both this influence, and that of Milton and Young. They were immensely popular. Thorild and Lidner were akin to Rousseau in their sentimentality and their worship of the individual, and in this respect both deserve the epithet Pre-Romantic. So that the feud between Kellgren and Thorild really, in some ways, anticipates the Swedish battle between Classic and Romantic, fought in the next century. Curiously enough, however, Thorild and Kellgren share certain ideas, and Kellgren, too, was affected by certain aspects of Rousseau, by Danish Pre-Romanticism, by the English poets, by Ossian, and later on even by Thorild himself.

But whilst Thorild, in his *Dithyramb* of 1786, offered a worthy poetic illustration of his principles, much of his poetry seems turgid, and a good deal of his prose is too uneven, too abrupt in style to appeal to the reader (for example, his *Criticism of Critics* ("Kritik över Kritiker"), etc.). Kellgren, on the other hand, was a master of both media, and the principles for which he fought so wittily, lucidity, elegance, common-sense, were brilliantly exemplified in his own poetry, in *My Laughing-Stocks* ("Mina Löjen", of 1778), *Our Illusions* ("Våra Villor"), of 1780, and in the two classic attacks *à la* Voltaire on the obscurantism and superstition of the time, *Being Mad Doesn't Make one a Genius* ("Man äger ej snille för det man är galen"), and *The Enemies of Light* ("Ljusets fiender"), respectively dated 1787 and 1792. Kellgren's increasing Radicalism (at first, like Thorild, he welcomed the French Revolution) had already brought him into collision with the authorities, and after 1789 he opposed the king. The Reuterholm regency that took over after Gustav's assassination in 1792 considered him a dangerous opponent.

It was typical of Kellgren that he continued to develop both intellectually and emotionally right up to his premature death. Unlike Leopold, who took his stand on the most conservative of platforms, expressing his views and sentiments in technically accomplished verses, Kellgren combined intellectual passion with a dynamic temperament. Quite early in his career he had composed masterly love poetry, of a sensuous subtlety, that was new in Swedish literature. In *The New Creation* ("Den nya Skapelsen") of 1789, under the impact of a new and altogether deeper feeling, and under the influence of Milton and others, he expressed loftier but no less passionate experiences. In this work his epicurean-ethical philosophy was married to his eroticism:

> Thou, who of beauty and of graces
> A pure and heavenly prototype art ...

> *Du, som av skönhet och behagen*
> *en ren och himmelsk urbild ger!*

Kellgren's death from consumption put an end to the creation of such masterpieces.

Oxenstierna occupies a strange position. In his outward aspects a perfect Gustavian courtier and wit, he turned out epigrams and occasional verse to please his royal master, and did so with a skill and a command of classical technique that he had learned from Creutz. Yet by inclination he was a budding Romantic, and his contemplative, emotional approach to nature, as it is reflected in *The Harvests* ("Skördarna"), indicates, more openly than does any other Swedish work of the period, the influence of Rousseau's teachings, and also the example of Saint-Lambert. The poem, like much of Oxenstierna's best work, was actually written before 1774, but not published until 1796, and then in revised form and by that time Oxenstierna could no longer rank as a precursor of Romanticism. Hee, too, took up the Gothic themes which were to appeal so strongly to the Swedish Romantic movement.

Like Kellgren, Fru Lenngren was connected with *Stockholmsposten*, of which her husband was an editor, but her collaboration on the paper was carried on under a veil of secrecy. Fru Lenngren did not like bluestockings of Fru Nordenflycht's type! She had made her literary début as a young woman in the 1770's, with verse satires, then returned to authorship in the '90's when Kellgren's illness adversely affected the journal, and during the years 1795—1800 she produced many of her best poems. Her genres were the realistic satire and the ballad or idyll, the latter frequently with a sting in it, and her shafts are aimed at the extravagances and futilities of the aristocracy. So, in *The Portraits* ("Porträtterna"), the arrogant stupidity of the countess is ridiculed in a miniature masterpiece. In her appreciation of bourgeois values, of reason and moderation at their most prosaic, Fru Lenngren represents the encroaching power of the middle-classes, and, in spite of the amusing malice of her pen and her vigorous humour, she is not entirely free from their sentimentality. Like the Gustavian Classicists, she handled her technique skilfully and unobtrusively, and it is not surprising that she won the admiration of the Academician Rosenstein, of Gyllenborg, and of Leopold.

At first influenced by Fru Lenngren, but later on also affecting her in turn, was F. M. FRANZÉN (1772—1847), a poet of philosophical odes, but also of sentimental idylls. His idealism, the emphasis he lays on the religious element, and also his use of imagery, all provide links with the Romantics, but in his later works he reverted to classical usages partly under the pressure exerted by the Swedish Academy. Thus, as the 18th century runs out, the old tenets are re-stated, more loudly than before, under the coercion of Leopold. Already, however, BENJAMIN HÖIJER (1767—1812) was lecturing at Uppsala on the German philosophy that was to usher in the next era in literature.

CHAPTER V

DANISH LITERATURE 1800—1870

The Romantic Movement came to Denmark from Germany. It was inspired, partly by the German Jena-Romanticists, partly by the classicism of Goethe and Schiller. Schelling's philosophy was interpreted in Denmark by the philosopher HENRIK STEFFENS, but Oehlenschläger, Ingemann, Grundtvig and Hauch, gave it a form peculiar to Denmark, and a shape very different from the original. It is only in the poetry of SCHACK VON STAFFELDT (1769—1826), in the youthful attempts of Ingemann, and in some of Oehlenschläger's very early poems that there is any close relationship to the morbidity and crazy mysticism of German Romanticism.

At the beginning of the 19th century the literary stage of Denmark was, so to speak, ready for a change. After Baggesen had left Denmark, the lack of any outstanding author was remarkable. Ewald's Pre-Romantic poetry had, however, paved the way for a revival of feeling, and had suggested a new conception of the function of the poet and of poetry. Instead of regarding the poet as nothing but a craftsman skilled in his particular trade, he was now looked upon as divinely inspired with power to see things hidden from other mortals and the ability to express himself in the language of the Gods. The 18th century worship of reason seemed to these new writers to have taken Denmark nowhere — only into a blind alley of stilted descriptions

of nature, form without content, a literature, boringly
moral, more concerned with making its readers into good
citizens than into happy men and women.
ADAM OEHLENSCHLÄGER (1779–1850) inaugurated the
new movement and became its leader. It was Steffens who
converted him, but Steffens was right when he said: "I gave
to him only himself." The first immediate result of a long
talk with Steffens, was that Oehlenschläger went home and
wrote his poem *The Gold Horns* ("Guldhornene", 1802).
It was written in an ecstasy of inspiration, and told what,
for Oehlenschläger, was the poetic truth about the theft
of the famous gold horns: they had been given to the
Danes by the old Scandinavian Gods, a portent which had
not been appreciated or understood, and so the Gods had
taken them back. Oehlenschläger tried to reproduce the
metres of Danish and Norse heroic poetry: —

> They pry in pages
> Of ancient sages,
> They search in the glooms
> Of mounded tombs
> On swords and shields
> In ruined fields,
> On Runic stones
> Among crumbled bones.

> *De higer og søger*
> *i gamle Bøger,*
> *i oplukte Høie*
> *med speidende Øie,*
> *paa Sværd og Skiolde*
> *i muldne Volde,*
> *paa Runestene*
> *blandt smuldnede Bene.*

A forgotten Denmark was rediscovered — a Denmark of antiquity and of the Middle Ages. Scandinavian mythology was revived to such an extent that in some of their early poems both Oehlenschläger and Grundtvig discard "pale Christ" in favour of the old pagan gods. In the same way, Love and Nature were rediscovered. The whole of Danish Romanticism is embodied in Oehlenschläger's dramatic poem *Midsummer Night's Play* ("St. Hans Aftenspil", 1802), which contains, at the same time, a witty satire against 18th century Rationalism and literature.

The youthful inspiration, and the ecstasy with which Oehlenschläger set out, lasted for five years. In three groups of poems and dramas Oehlenschläger gives evidence of poetic genius which has no parallel in Danish literature. The range of subjects covered is enormous. There are many beautiful poems, such as *Hakon Jarl's Death* ("Hakon Jarls Død"), and a wealth of ballads with medieval and modern themes; dramatic works — in addition to *Midsummer Night's Play* the poetic drama *Aladdin,* whose main character is a born genius, carefree and innocent: what others strive to obtain through intellectual reflection is given to him as a free gift; *Hakon Jarl* — the first and best of Oehlenschläger's Northern tragedies; *Balder the Good* ("Baldur hin Gode") — a mythological tragedy in Greek style. There are great poetic cycles, such as *The Langeland Journey* ("Langelandsrejsen") and the philosophical *Life of Jesus Christ Symbolized in Nature* ("Jesu Kristi gjentagne Liv i den aarlige Natur"); there are long epic poems, such as *Thor's Journey to Jotunheim* ("Thors Rejse til Jotunheim") and *Vaulundur's Saga,* a prose version of an old Edda poem. The richness of subject matter is extraordinary and the technical skill in handling a variety of metres impressive. During these years Oehlenschläger's creative powers appeared to be without limit; he was absolute monarch of

6*

the kingdom of Danish poetry. He came, he saw, he conquered.
Oehlenschläger never surpassed, however, the richness
and quality of these early years. He continued writing, but
only very rarely reached such heights as he had done in
his youth. The youthful rebel became a sedate, respectable citizen, a professor of literature who considered himself above criticism. Had he been British he would have
made the ideal Poet Laureate (he *was* actually laureated
by Tegnér, at Lund in Sweden, in 1829). In one work
only, the cycle of dramatic poems entitled *Helge* (1814),
did he reach the standard of his early work, and personally
I regard parts of this cycle as the best poems Oehlenschläger ever wrote. His later Northern tragedies, *Axel og Val-
borg, Stærkodder, Hagbard og Signe, Væringerne i Mikla-
gaard,* and *Palnatoke,* have all considerable poetic quality,
and they are interesting, because they represent the creation
of Danish historical tragedy, but they are not good theatre,
and their simplicity and naivety have made it difficult for
later generations, with a taste for the more complicated,
fully to appreciate them.
    N. F. S. GRUNDTVIG (1783–1872) is a gigantic figure, not
only in Danish literature, but also as an educationalist, an
historian, a philological scholar, a religious reformer, and
a politician. By his admirers — and they are numerous
even today — he was and is looked on as a prophet. If one
is to have a full understanding of 19th and 20th century
Denmark, one must understand Grundtvig and his ideas.
The Danish Folk High Schools were directly inspired by
him, and the whole pattern of Danish democracy is closely
linked with Grundtvig's ideas on "folkelighed".
    Grundtvig was one of the most prolific Danish writers of
the 19th century, but of his collected works only a fraction
can be termed *belles lettres*. And yet this group includes
a vast number of poems, several of them personal, reflecting

his own spiritual development, such as *The Garden of Udby* ("Udby Have"), *The Hill at Egelykke* ("Strandbakken ved Egelykke"), *To My Mother* ("Til min Moder") and the strangely prophetic *New Year's Morning* ("Nyaarsmorgen"): a number of dramatic and narrative poems, such as *Roskilde Rhymes* ("Roskilde-Rim"), *Chronicle Rhymes* ("Krønike-Rim") and *Paaskeliljen;* and many biblical and historical poems — for Grundtvig retold most of the Bible stories, and many historical events, in verse. Among his poems are some beautiful memorial stanzas, such as his inscription in memory of the men of the "Prince Christian" who fell in the battle of Zealand's Odde in 1808: —

The good ships closed in the evening gloom,
and deep was the glow they gave;
they played right over the open tomb
and crimsoned the surging wave.

Here was I set as a bauta-stone,
for clans in the North carved clear:
Danes were the men who, bone on bone,
moulder beneath me here;
Danes in their stock, their tongue, their zeal,
even their names shall live as leal
sons of our sires of old.

De Snækker mødtes i Kvæld paa Hav,
og Luften begyndte at gløde,
de leged alt over den aabne Grav,
og Bølgerne gjordes saa røde.

Her er jeg sat til en Bavtasten,
at vidne for Slægter i Norden:
Danske de vare, hvis møre Ben
under mig smuldre i Jorden,

danske af Tunge, af Æt og af Id,
thi skal de nævnes i løbende Tid
Fædrenes værdige Sønner.

Grundtvig has written a vast number of songs, "for school
and home", songs in praise of his native land, and songs
in which his ideas of spiritual freedom are embodied. But
most of his best poetry is in the hymns he wrote, nearly
1,500. Several, however, are translations and adaptations
of old Danish, German and Anglo-Saxon hymns, and of
Latin sacred poetry. Grundtvig was certainly one of the
most prolific hymnists in the world, and for Danes every
event in the Christian year is closely connected with one
or other of Grundtvig's hymns. The main reason why so
few of them have been translated is probably Grundtvig's
free use of Danish idiom. His unorthodox Christianity is
closely linked with his love of the Danish countryside and
Danish history, as can be clearly seen in his masterly version
of a medieval hymn, *Day Song* ("Dagvisen").

Grundtvig shared the Romantic enthusiasm for the anti-
quities of Scandinavia, and he interpreted the Scandinavian
myths as poetic visions; he retranslated both Saxo Grammaticus and Snorri, and translated *Beowulf* into Danish,
before it had even appeared in English. His *Handbook of
World History* ("Haandbog i Verdenshistorie"), in three
volumes, is, like his other historical works, a strange mixture of scholarship, prophetic vision and insanity.

In religious and spiritual matters Grundtvig's influence
was far greater than Kierkegaard's. In his student days he
was, as he said of himself, "spiritually dead". Following
a romantic worship of pagan gods, he became a zealous
Christian, for a time even extremely orthodox. But, as he
grew older, he became increasingly more liberal, fought
bitterly against the dogmatic professors of theology, and
demanded complete freedom in all spiritual matters.

Compared with Grundtvig, B. S. INGEMANN (1789—1862) seems small and insignificant. Of his prose works, only his historical novels deserve mention. They were written, and it was at Grundtvig's suggestion, between 1824 and 1836. In four of these novels: *Valdemar Sejr, The Childhood of Erik Menved* ("Erik Menveds Barndom"), *King Erik and the Outlaws* ("Kong Erik og de Fredløse"), and *Prince Otto of Denmark* ("Prins Otto af Danmark") — and in two long epic poems, Ingemann made an important contribution to the popularization of the idea of Danish medieval history as the "golden age" of Denmark. The aim of these novels was to inspire contemporary thought with the Romantic ideas of chivalry and national pride. Walter Scott had done the same thing in English literature with his Waverley novels, and the naive simplicity as well as the poetic quality of Ingemann's romances made them as popular to generations of Danes as the Waverley novels were in England and Scotland. In spite of their historical inaccuracies, they did much to strengthen national pride in Denmark.

Ingemann's poetic cycle about *Holger Danske,* the legendary national hero, was conceived in the same spirit.

As a poet, however, Ingemann's only claim to greatness are his *Morning and Evening Songs,* which are among the purest lyric poetry of the 19th century. They are religious poems — but not hymns — written by an unsophisticated, childlike mind, depicting, with exquisite beauty, a world of innocence and pious goodness, but not banal, because they are sincere and free of any form of pretence. Nature is seen through the eyes of a child: the glorious sunset on a summer's evening is the sun's going to rest in a beautiful castle built by God himself: —

> A thousand turrets flash their gold,
> amber the gateway's lustre;

and there, in ocean mirrored bold,
tall radiant columns cluster.
God's sun goes into its golden keep,
mantled in purple glorious.
Where rose-clouds over the castle sweep
waves light's own banner, victorious.

Fra tusind Taarne funkler Guld;
Porten skinner som Ravet;
Med Straalestøtter underfuld
sig Borgen spejler i Havet.
Guds Sol gaar i sit Guldslot ind,
skinner i Purpurklæder.
I Rosensky paa Borgens Tind
staar Lysets Banner med Hæder.

CARSTEN HAUCH (1790—1872) was a dramatist, a novelist,
and a lyrical poet. Goethe and Shakespeare, and his admiration of Oehlenschläger, made him a convert to the Danish
Romantic movement. His personal integrity and his admir-
able honesty penetrate both his creative work and his
memoirs.

Hauch's dramas are often sinister, tragic, and philosophic.
Some of them, such as *Bajazet, Tiberius, Gregor VII, Svend*
Grathe and *Marsk Stig,* are complex psychological dramas,
often with a personal background, but in a historical setting. *The Sisters of Kinnekullen* ("Søstrene paa Kinnekullen") is his most successful and one of the pillars of
Danish Romantic drama, in which the vanity of striving
after material gain is demonstrated by the use of a mixture
of the natural and supernatural.

As a novelist, Hauch, like Ingemann, was inspired by
Sir Walter Scott. His historical novels also reflect Hauch's
philosophy of resignation, and contempt for superficial
values. The scene is often laid outside Denmark, e. g. in
Vilhelm Zabern (Norway), *The Alchymist* ("Guldmageren")

(Germany), *A Polish Family* ("En polsk Familie") (Poland) and *Robert Fulton* (America). It was as a lyric poet, however, that Hauch was at his greatest. He never became popular, unlike Oehlenschläger whom he admired greatly, and by whom he was certainly influenced, especially in his ballads. He had not the same easy approach to poetry as Oehlenschläger, and his introspection and philosophic attitude demanded much of his readers. The effort is worth making, however, for Hauch's descriptions of nature, his poetic confessions, the penetration of his memorial poetry — especially his poems about *H. C. Ørsted* and *Christiane Oehlenschläger* — are the expressions of a manly and heroic mind which despised the easy way, never sought fame or popularity, and believed only in an ultimate righteousness. From the world of sorrow and cares and vanity he turned his eyes to the stars, finding comfort and consolation in the serene stillness and sense of eternity reflected in the Milky Way: —

> For grief is but the wrong side
> of the flaming robe of bliss;
> the eternal light is shadowed
> in the dim springs of the abyss.

> *Thi Smerten er kun Vrangen*
> *Af Salighedens Dragt,*
> *I Dybets dunkle Kilder*
> *Speiler sig Lysets Pragt.*

*

During the first quarter of the 19th century the early Romantic movement was unchallenged. Then appeared two men who brought a new element of reason and realism into Danish literature. Their names are Poul Møller and Steen Steensen Blicher.

Poul Møller (1794–1838) was the author of the first

novel in Danish literature dealing with contemporary events. *The Adventures of a Danish Undergraduate* ("En dansk Students Eventyr") was written in 1824, but published posthumously and incomplete, for several pages of the manuscript were missing. Although originally planned as an historical novel on the pattern of Walter Scott, it was eventually completely changed, and described student life, as Poul Møller knew it. It is a charming book, light and gay and full of humour. Psychologically, it is interesting, because the author has split his own personality into those of the two main characters, Curly Frits, a charming and irresponsible youth who falls constantly in love — and his cousin, the Magister, whose learning has cut him off from life and killed his spontaneity and power of action: a scholar lost in reflection, comic and pathetic at the same time. The dry and sober Bertel is another important character, witty, obstinate, anti-romantic. This novel heralded a new realistic approach, and thus occupies an important place in the history of Danish literature.

Poul Møller was also the author of several charming light poems, some of the best of which were written during a journey to China, when he felt a nostalgic longing for Denmark and tried to recapture the atmosphere of daily life in Copenhagen. Some of his poems are in the form of small dramatic scenes, others in the form of fables, sometimes reflecting personal disappointment or disillusionment. Of high artistic merit also are his *Leaves from Death's Diary* ("Blade af Dødens Dagbog"). He wrote brilliant aphorisms and philosophical essays, which demonstrate his satirical powers and his rejection of the purely abstract and metaphysical: — "All poetry that does not come from life is a lie."

STEEN STEENSEN BLICHER (1782—1848) was a Jutlander by birth and upbringing and spent his life as a poor parson there. Ossian's melancholy poetry, which he read as an

undergraduate in Copenhagen, filled him with nostalgia
for the Jutland moors: —

My home is in the russet heather land,
my laughing childhood lit the moorland gloom;
my tender footsteps trod the yellow sand,
dark mounds companioned all my boyhood's bloom.

For me the flowerless fields are just as fair,
my heath of brown as beautiful as Eden;
there let my bones one day find quiet, where
my fathers' graves are lying, heather-laden.

Min Fødestavn er Lyngens brune Land,
min Barndoms Sol har smilt paa mørken Hede,
min spæde Fod har traadt den gule Sand,
bag sorte Høje bor min Ungdoms Glæde.

Skøn er for mig den blomsterløse Vang,
min brune Hede er en Edens Have —
der hvile ogsaa mine Ben engang
blandt mine Fædres lyngbegroede Grave.

Blicher translated Ossian into Danish, and Ossian's influence on him is obvious in his early poetry, but he gradually developed his own style, gentle and subdued, equally
fascinating in its expressions of sad resignation and in its
warm humour.   In *Birds of Passage* ("Trækfuglene", 1838)
he interprets human nature, as in the sad self-portrait of a
caged bird longing for freedom, in the opening *Prelude*
("Præludium").   His best poems are in Jutland dialect;   in
these, great events are treated in the vernacular, with
characteristic irony and understatement.

In 1824 — the same year in which Poul Møller wrote
The Adventures of a Danish Undergraduate — Blicher
wrote the first of many stories (*noveller*), entitled *The
Journal of a Parish Clerk* ("En Landsbydegns Dagbog"), a

masterpiece of 19th century Danish prose. Although the
subject was taken from Danish history (the story is based
on the life of Marie Grubbe) it was far removed from the
idyllic embellishments of history then in vogue, and it is
a work of art, perfect in its style, and convincing in its
psychology. In Blicher's stories, as in his poetry, the note
he strikes varies from sorrow and resignation to humour
and irony, and one can best understand his stories if one
knows his own unhappy background: the poor, lonely
country parson, unhappily married, constantly in debt —
finding comfort only in his solitary wanderings on the Jutland moors, in his talks with peasant and gypsies — and in
his drinking. All the best of Blicher's stories, *The Robbers'
Den* ("Røverstuen"), *The Parson at Vejlbye* ("Præsten i
Vejlbye"), *The Hosier and his Daughter* ("Hosekræmme-
ren"), *Three Holiday Eves* ("De tre Helligaftner"), *Alas,
How Changed!* ("Ak, hvor forandret") and his brilliant
dialect story *Æ Bindstouw*, are stories about Jutland, based
on an intimate knowledge of the conditions he describes.
There are often traces of the 18th century narrative style,
and the general feeling is anti-romantic. Blicher preaches
a gospel of disillusion and disappointment, for life does not
keep its promises: the Romanticism of the fairy-tale is not
true to life.

Passing from Blicher to JOHAN LUDVIG HEIBERG (1791–
1860) is like passing from the wilds of Jutland to a *salon*
in a cultured Copenhagen home. J. L. Heiberg was the
son of two Danish writers; his father was P. A. Heiberg
(see pp. 59–60), and his mother was THOMASINE GYLLEM-
BOURG (1773–1856), whose *Everyday Stories* ("Hverdags-
historier") were much admired in her own time, but are
hardly read today.

At his zenith, Heiberg was the dictator of literary taste
in Copenhagen. He was a man of great influence, and
his wife, JOHANNE LOUISE HEIBERG, the leading lady of the

Royal Theatre, of which Heiberg himself was a director.
He was a gifted critic, especially in dramatic matters, but
he was an intellectual snob, with a contempt for the common herd, and more concerned with form than content.
As a dramatist Heiberg attempted to revivify Danish
drama by importing French *vaudeville*. His light comedies, in which the dialogue is frequently interrupted by
song, were received with acclamation, following the pon-
derous tragedies of Oehlenschläger and Hauch. These comedies have no serious content — but the wrappings are
exquisite. *April Fools* ("Aprilsnarrene"), *The Inseparable*
("De uadskillelige"), *No* ("Nej"), *The Critic and the Ani-
mal* ("Rescensenten og Dyret") are very light indeed, and
Heiberg defended them in a serious essay, in which he
contended that they would pave the way for the revival of
Danish comedy.

In some of his romantic plays, such as *Elverhøj* and *Syv-
soverdag*, there is an interplay between the worlds of
fantasy and reality: those of "poetic reality" and of
pedestrian reality. *Elverhøj*, especially, with its patriotic
fervour, has become a *pièce de résistance* and is constantly
performed.

Heiberg's finest dramatic achievement is the apocalyptic
comedy, *A Soul after Death* ("En Sjæl efter Døden", 1841).
In spite of its many contemporary allusions and its Hegelian
philosophy it may still be read with great pleasure and
much amusement. It is a verse-drama, the satire of which
is directed against the "average" citizen, whose soulless
existence Heiberg despised. The Soul — for we meet him
when his body is already dead — wanders full of self-
confidence in all his ignorance towards the gates of Heaven,
where Saint Peter rejects him, after an interrogation exposing his ignorance of the essence of Christianity. He then
goes to Elysium, where he reveals to Aristophanes, who
examines him, a shocking ignorance of the spirit of the

Classics. Finally, he is admitted to Hell by that hospitable and gentlemanly doorkeeper, Mephistopheles, and the subtle irony of the play is that here the Soul feels himself to be at home and perfectly happy. Hell is nothing but a replica of the soulless and superficial life he led in Copenhagen.

After Heiberg's death, Madame Heiberg published her memoirs, entitled *A Life — Re-lived in Memory* ("Et Liv gjenoplevet i Erindringen") — one of the finest books of reminiscences in Danish literature.

HENRIK HERTZ (1797—1870) was a close friend of Heiberg's and of his family. To him, also, perfection of form was more important than content. It was Baggesen's style he was imitating when he published — anonymously — *Letters of a Ghost* ("Gjenganger-Breve", 1830), in which, maliciously and wittily, he took a number of contemporary poets to task for their sins against artistic form.

Hertz contributed several light comedies in a bourgeois setting to the Danish stage, and some romantic plays. *Svend Dyring's House* ("Svend Dyrings Hus") is a refined pastiche, based on medieval ballads, *King René's Daughter* ("Kong Renés Datter") a very fine play about a blind girl who recovers her sight through the power of love and poetry.

Hertz's poems are often nothing more than clever imitation of style, especially that of Bellman (see pp. 72—75) and of the ballad, but they are always harmonious, often humorous, and sometimes have an undertone of melancholy and resignation.

*

A gradual change had taken place in the trend of Danish literature. The realistic tendencies of Poul Møller and Blicher, and the "poetic Realism" of Heiberg and Hertz, had led it along new paths, less simple and more thoughtful than before. In the 1830's a revival of Danish poetry took place, led by four men, three of whom were concerned only with love and nature, treated in a purely aesthetic manner.

CHRISTIAN WINTHER (1796—1876) was a Zealander, and it was the praises of the Zeland scene he sang. His worship of woman finds expressions in many ways: in his naive *Woodcuts* ("Træsnit"), in his many versified tales, in the collection of poems written to his future wife, published under the title *To Someone* ("Til Een"), but by his enemies maliciously nicknamed *To Everyone*. In his best poems, such as *A Summer Night* ("En Sommernat"), and *Fly, Bird, Fly* ("Flyv, Fugl, flyv"), fine descriptive writing conveys an idea of abstract love: —

Fly, bird, fly, over Furresøen's surges,
follow two lovers awhile.
Fashion your song from their music that merges
laughter and sorrow and guile.
Singer I am, and my song must recapture
all of Love's secret deceit;
sing of the torment, interpret the rapture,
conquest and bitter defeat.

Flyv, Fugl, flyv over Furresøens Bølge,
Stræk dine Vinger nu vel!
Ser du to elskende, dem skal du følge,
Dybt skal du speide deres Sjæl.
Er jeg en Sanger, saa bør jeg jo vide
Kærligheds smigrende Lyst,
Alt, hvad et Hjerte kan rumme og lide,
Burde jo tolke min Røst.

Winther's greatest work is the long verse novel *The Flight of the Stag* ("Hjortens Flugt", 1855). This is a long epic poem, the scene of which is laid in Zealand in the Middle Ages, and Folmer the Singer, a wandering minstrel, is easily recognized as Winther himself. The constantly changing

scene and the many different characters make it possible
for Winther to treat his two favourite subjects in a variety
of ways.

Winther was influenced by both Byron and Heine; his
instrument has fewer strings, but many of his love poems
are comparable to Heine's best.

LUDVIG BØDTCHER (1793–1874) is another purely lyric
poet, who spent a great part of his life in Italy. He wrote
only a handful of poems, of which several were inspired by
the Italian scene. He was an onlooker in life, a fine and
gentle aesthete, whose poems are delicate, sensitive, and
artistically sober; always melodious, flowing, and full of
rare and fascinating beauty. Here is the first stanza of
his poem *In the Spring* ("I Foraaret"):

Now lulled are the pregnant winds of spring
buds open, and flowers their perfume fling,
and waters that languished in winter's chain
break glittering loose again.
From sheltered shade
in darkening glade
my ears may capture
a nightingale's rapture;
and deeply my heart those tones inspire
with sighs, and longing, and sweet desire.

Nu sænker sig Vaarens svangrende Luft,
Og Knopperne briste, og Blomsten faaer Duft,
Og Bølgen, som længe smægted i Tvang,
Gaaer atter sin blinkende Gang; —
I dunkle Lund,
I dæmrende Stund,
Bag Løv, som skjærmer,
En Nattergal sværmer, —
Og Tonerne synke dybt i mit Bryst
Som Suk, som Savn, som smeltende Lyst!

EMIL AARESTRUP (1800—56) was not a poet by profession; he was a country doctor, happily married, and with a host of children; even the arrangement of these tickled his musical ear, for he wrote to a Copenhagen friend: "My proud boast of having twelve children, six of the masculine and six of the feminine sex, has thus not been unjustified, and while avoiding a dull symmetry, harmony has been achieved by the following variation: a boy, a girl, a girl, a girl; a boy, a girl, a girl; a boy, a girl; a boy, a boy, *a boy!* Your ear for music and sense of form and colour will find the arrangement in accordance with the rules for grouping, colouring, and thoroughbass. That is the overture to the true drama of the Aarestrupian family."

Like Bødtcher, Aarestrup was an aesthete, but more refined, more Gallic in his taste; he was an Epicurean, a lover and a connoisseur of beauty, which to him first and foremost meant the beauty of the female body. Winther is a great love poet, but Aarestrup is the erotic poet *par excellence* in Danish literature. His *Ritournelles* are pearls of elegance and sarcasm. He can portray a woman in three lines: —

She's just fifteen, so lanky-limbed and pliant.
How airy is her stride, how pert her pacing!
And when she puts her tongue out, how defiant!

En Femtenaars, en lang og smidig Unge!
Hvor luftig hendes Gang, hvor knibsk Fodskiftet!
Og i sin Trodsighed hun rækker Tunge.

There is often a certain cynicism in his last line: —

Deep longing turned your eyes to tear-brimmed pools.
You wrung your hands, I wailed a wild farewell . . .
But heaven laughed, and the wood whispered: "Fools!"

Dit Øje smægtede i store Taarer,
du vred din Haand, jeg jamrede: "Farvel!"
Men Himlen lo, og Skoven hvisked: "Daarer!"

He is a master of the concentrated short story: —

Four days' bombardment — notes without cessation;
the fifth, an evening truce, negotiation;
and on the sixth night — well? — capitulation.

I fire Døgn med Breve bombardertes;
den femte Aftenstund parlamentertes;
den sjette Nat — hvad saa? — kapitulertes.

Aarestrup's *Erotic Scenes* ("Erotiske Situationer") is a
collection of finely chiselled poems of passionate, sensual
love. His sense of rhyme and metre is perfect, and in spite
of the limitation of the subject, he never becomes monotonous.

In the 1830's Byronism swept Europe, including Denmark, where young FREDERIK PALUDAN-MÜLLER (1809—76)
became its chief protagonist. His superficial, easy-flowing,
and elegant verse novel, *The Dancing Girl* ("Danserinden",
1833), was written on the model of *Don Juan* and *Childe
Harold,* and so were several others of his early poems. But
after a personal crisis, Paludan-Müller turned his back on
the idol of his youth and retired from the turmoil and
vanity of life, eventually becoming a complete hermit, an
uncompromising moralist, whose philosophy was that of
renunciation, and who condemned what to him were the
weaknesses of the Danish character: lack of discipline and
obedience, lack of will power, and superficiality of mind.
His poem *The Day of Judgment* ("Basunen") should be
read against this background: —

Kneel, kneel, O earth; your glory cast aside,
and, humbly clad, take off your mask of pride.
In heaven's clouds the angel host appears,
        and Judgment nears.

Down, down in dust, what scorns the dust to scan —
ye stones of nature and great walls of man;
each turret crowned, and tower whose height appalled,
        to ruin called.

Knæl, knæl, o Jord! og, iført Sæk og Aske,
Afkast din Herligheds og Stoltheds Maske!
I Himlens Skyer er Engleskaren kommen,
        Den følger Dommen.

Ned, ned i Støv, hvad knejser og hvad trodser:
Naturens Sten- og Kunstens Mur-Kolosser!
Hvert kronet Spir, og alle høje Taarne,
        Til Fald udkaarne.

Paludan-Müller's greatest contribution to Danish literature is his verse novel *Adam Homo*, an epic in twelve
cantos, written 1841—48. In this, we follow a man from
the cradle to the grave, see him becoming more and more
shallow, throwing away the faith of his childhood, the love
of a pure and innocent woman, his honesty and his ideals,
until, having discarded every fundamental value, he has
reached the highest social level. By contrast, Alma, the
woman who loves him, develops spiritually while sinking
socially. After death, when Adam's soul is weighed, Alma
saves him from damnation by putting the weight of her
love on the scales and accompanies him to Purgatory in
order to save his soul. The *Alma Sonnets*, which are part
of *Adam Homo*, make up the only sonnet cycle of any
importance in Danish literature.

7*

Among Paludan-Müller's other poems there are several with subjects taken from Greek mythology, e. g. *Venus, The Wedding of the Dryad* ("Dryadens Bryllup"), *Amor and Psyche, Tithon* and *Adonis*. In these poems Paludan-Müller condemned the world and the flesh, and his contempt for worldly splendour is further expressed in the poems *Benedict of Nursia* ("Benedict fra Nursia") and *Kalanus*. A constantly recurring theme in Paludan-Müller's poetry is Death, for death in blind obedience to God meant for him the liberation of the soul from the vanity and sin of the world. In his three great biblical poems, *Cain* ("Kain"), *The Death of Abel* ("Abels Død") and *Ahasuerus*, the idea of death predominates.

Paludan-Müller was a severe and castigating moralist, a poet who had come to scorn the purely aesthetic point of view to which he himself had subscribed when young. His poetry was the poetry of ideas, but it has often great beauty of form.

*

Left, right! Left, right! ... Down the country-road came a soldier marching. Left, right! Left, right! ... He had his knapsack on his back and a sword at his side, for he had been at the war, and now he was on his way home. But then he met an old witch on the road. Oh! she was ugly — her lower lip hung right down on her chest. "Good evening, soldier," she said, "what a nice sword you've got, and what a big knapsack! You're a proper soldier! Now I'll show you how to get as much money as you want!" "Thank you very much, old dame!" said the soldier. The soldier was HANS CHRISTIAN ANDERSEN (1805—75), who marched like a new Aladdin right into the Fairy Kingdom of literature, and became Emperor of the most beautiful world of all, the world of children's imagination. *The Tinderbox* ("Fyrtøjet") was the first of Andersen's fairy-tales, published in 1835 in an insignificant little book together with three other stories: *The Princess and the Pea* ("Prinsessen paa Ærten"), *Little Claus and Big Claus* ("Lille Claus og Store Claus") and *Little Ida's Flowers* ("Den lille Idas Blomster"). Thirty years of agonized suffering and struggle for recognition lay behind; but the poor shoemaker's son from Odense had decided already as a child that he would become famous. His background was that of grinding poverty, the lowest of the low, with a history of immorality, insanity and criminal tendencies among his ancestors. He was, as he said himself in 1833, "a swamp plant", and in a way his whole life was a struggle to rid himself of his background. Before he wrote his first fairy-tales he had tried to win fame as a singer, a dancer, an actor, a playwright, a poet, and a novelist. The success of his first novel, *The Improvisatore* ("Improvisatoren", 1835), encouraged him to try his hand at writing fairy-tales. He did not realise then that he was destined to raise the literature of children's stories to heights which it had never reached before, and to make it equally fascinating to children and grown-ups alike. (Unfortunately, the grown-ups have, in some countries, committed the same mistake which they have made with Defoe's *Robinson Crusoe,* and Swift's *Gulliver's Travels* — that of pushing Andersen's fairy-tales and stories into the nursery and locking the door on them.) In 1835, fame was approaching for Andersen: world fame of a kind unknown to any previous Danish writer — but happiness seemed further away than ever. Andersen was like the fir-tree in his own story, never able to enjoy the moment, but always looking forward to something still better in the future.

Before Andersen died he had written 164 stories and fairy-tales; some are based on Danish folk-tales, some on Danish history; the plots of others are from foreign sources; but most of them are his own invention, often springing

from some personal event, great or small, happy or unhappy. "The fairy-tales lay in my thoughts like seeds; all
that was necessary was a breeze, a ray of sunshine, or a drop
of bitter wormwood — and they burst into flower." No
more subjective writer has ever lived. Everyone knows
that *The Ugly Duckling* ("Den grimme Ælling") is Andersen's version of his own life story. But he has told it over
and over again, sometimes in hopeful, sometimes in hopeless mood, and sometimes with fine irony at his own
expense. Andersen himself, his friends and his enemies,
appear in the fairy-tales and stories in a thousand different
forms.

In the fairy-tales one sees Andersen's childlike belief in
the ultimate victory of the good and innocent over the evil
and calculating. Here is Andersen's belief in God and in
the immortality of the soul. But his philosophy is much
more varied than that. *The Bell* ("Klokken") is a fine
allegorical sermon on the triumph of virtue and innocence.
The Shadow ("Skyggen") is a bitter and cynical tale of how
a parasitical and empty imitator stole fame, and finally the
very existence, from the good and learned man, and married
the beautiful princess. Andersen's philosophy is not in
either: it is in both. H. C. Ørsted, the famous Danish
physicist, was one of the first to appreciate Andersen's true
worth, and it was Ørsted who pointed out that, "Andersen
is greatest in his humour". This is quite true, but it is a
fact which has not been fully appreciated outside Denmark,
possibly because of the poor quality of most of the translations. What Andersen wrote was true poetry — tragic,
comic, simple, or humorous — and his tales are of such
universal appeal that even today many of them have equal
fascination for an Odense child, an English child or a
Hindu child, and very few of them date.

Andersen's contribution to lyric poetry consists of a few
short sensitive love poems, some nature poems, a number

of patriotic and children's songs, and some versified tales. His best novels are *The Improvisatore*, with its fine descriptions of Italian scenery, and *Only a Fiddler* ("Kun en Spillemand") and *O. T.*, with their realistic descriptions of Danish life. All his novels are poorly disguised autobiographies; they are always about a genius and his struggle for fame. He did write his autobiography — but without telling the whole truth — under the title *The Story of My Life* ("Mit Livs Eventyr", 1855); a more candid description, however, of his childhood and youth is to be found in the reminiscences he wrote for a girl with whom he was in love, and which were published in Danish under the title *Levnedsbogen;* but it is his letters, of which 16 volumes have been so far published, which throw the most light on his strange and fascinating personality.

*

It is remarkable how little Danish literature was influenced by the political turmoil outside Denmark during the first forty years of the 19th century. Absolutism was taken for granted, even by Grundtvig, and the European revolutions produced only one literary reaction, Poul Møller's poem *The Artist among the Rebels* ("Kunstneren mellem Oprørerne", 1837), in which he takes sides *against* the rebels.

In 1840, however, a young Jewish writer, Meïr Aaron Goldschmidt (1819–87), founded a weekly paper in Copenhagen, *The Corsair* ("Corsaren"), of which for six years he was editor. It was an extraordinarily witty and well written paper, expressing the most unorthodox views: a Radical, even revolutionary, paper, definitely anti-royalist in outlook. The whole of Copenhagen was shocked — and bought the paper secretly. Official censorship had no difficulty in finding pretexts for having number after number banned; but Goldschmidt developed a brilliant ambiguity in his articles, unparalleled until the first years of the German Occupation a hundred years later. After a feud with Kierkegaard, who had invited *The Corsair* to attack him, Goldschmidt gave up the paper and went abroad for some years; and that was the end of him as a revolutionary spirit. His literary importance, however, was not at an end.

In 1845 Goldschmidt published his first novel, *A Jew* ("En Jøde"), which was a bitter attack on the ostracism of the Jews among the Danes, and during the next few years he wrote a number of stories from his intimate knowledge of Jewish traditions, Jewish life, and Jewish psychology. *Maser, Levi and Ibald, Mendel Herz,* and that little masterpiece of pathos, *Avromche Nightingale* ("Avromche Nattergal"), are all psychologically convincing, and written by a man who understood the Jews, because he was one of them.

In his other novels and stories Goldschmidt gives intimate descriptions of Danish provincial life, e. g. *Reminiscences from My Uncle's House* ("Fortællinger fra min Onkels Hus") or makes long expositions of his ideas on retributive justice, e. g. *Homeless ("Hjemløs")* and *The Heir* ("Arvingen"). From the artistic point of view, his short stories and his thrilling novel *The Raven* ("Ravnen") are the best, and in his *Memoirs* ("Livserindringer og Resultater") he attempts to interpret his own life in the light of his ideas about Nemesis.

*

As is proper for the man who preached a gospel of extreme individualism, Søren Kierkegaard (1813–55) holds an entirely isolated position in Danish literature, unattached to any group or school of writers, and with hardly any followers. The English-speaking world has only just discovered him, and since the war his philosophy has been the subject of many books and essays in England and America. Seen from without, Kierkegaard's life appears uneventful, but what a drama if you see it from within, through Kierkegaard's own eyes. As a child he was under the domination of his father, a father who could never forget that as a poor shepherd's boy he had once cursed God — and it seems that Kierkegaard also knew, or believed, that, before they were married, his father had raped his mother. Throughout his childhood Kierkegaard was isolated from other children, in a morbid atmosphere of religious gloom, in which performing actions in imagination was considered more important than performing them in reality. Against his father's wish he studied philosophy and aesthetics at Copenhagen, but after his father's death he submitted, and took a degree in theology. As an undergraduate he had a reputation for brilliance, irony and sarcasm. In 1840, Kierkegaard became engaged to Regine Olsen, but they were never married, because although they loved one another he felt it his duty to break off the engagement — after vainly attempting to make her do so in order that no one might think that she had been jilted. But in the small and very provincial town of Copenhagen the whole story was generally discussed and Kierkegaard condemned.

A few years after this, Kierkegaard began his career as a writer, and between 1843 and 1846 he published a number of philosophical works under various *noms de plume*. The most important are *Either/Or* ("Enten-Eller", 1843) and *Stages on Life's Way* ("Stadier paa Livets Vej", 1845). The former, which contains, among other things, a collection of brilliant aphorisms, entitled *Diapsalmata*, and the "novel" entitled *The Diary of a Seducer* ("Forførerens Dagbog"), is his interpretation of two different conceptions of life: the aesthetic and the ethic. Kierkegaard has identified himself with the characters in *Either/Or*, e. g. Don Juan, the perfect example of one aspect of the aesthete: the Seducer, for whom woman, an innocent woman in particular, is an object of enjoyment; and the *paterfamilias,* devoted to duty, and described as an example of one aspect of the ethic, for whom woman is more beautiful as a wife than as a virgin, but most beautiful as a mother. The final stage, the religious stage, in which suffering and isolation are the key words, is just suggested at the end of *Either/Or,* and fully analysed in *Stages on Life's Way;* in the fragment entitled *Guilty — Not Guilty* ("Skyldig — Ikke skyldig"), Kierkegaard tells again the story of his own engagement. Three other books, all analyses of religious psychology, were published under various pseudonyms: *Fear and Trembling* ("Frygt og Bæven") — described as a dialectical lyric; *Repetition* ("Gjentagelsen"), an essay in experimental psychology; and *The Concept of Dread* ("Begrebet Angst"). At the same time he published under his own name the first of his *Edifying Discourses* ("Opbyggelige Taler").

It was obvious that Denmark had produced not only a great thinker, but also a great writer. *Either/Or* and *Stages on Life's Way,* in particular, are important landmarks in Danish literature.

In 1846, Kierkegaard published *Concluding Unscientific Postscript* ("Afsluttende uvidenskabelig Efterskrift"), in which he acknowledged all his books previously published under pseudonyms. At this point, he had intended to stop writing and settle down as a country parson. But in the same year the feud with *The Corsair* started, and Kierkegaard suffered unspeakably from being ridiculed in sarcastic articles and malicious cartoons. He felt and understood the feelings of a martyr suffering for his faith, and this led him to a deeper realisation of the essence of Christianity. Following this he wrote several books in which he attacked the theologians for turning Christianity into

a philosophy, and of which *The Sickness Unto Death* ("Sygdommen til Døden", 1849) and *Training in Christianity* ("Indøvelse i Christendom", 1850) are two. For Kierkegaard Christianity was a paradox which must be personally experienced by the individual, in isolation, or — in his own idiom — to be a Christian was to be "alone in a small boat in 70,000 fathoms of water".
The theologians made no reply to Kierkegaard's attack. Then, in 1854, Bishop Mynster, the Primate of Denmark, died, and Bishop Martensen, his successor, who conducted the funeral service, called Mynster "a witness of truth, a link in the holy chain from the Apostles to our days". That was too much for Kierkegaard, who protested violently, and the last year of his life was spent in a violent and passionate attack on "official Christianity", which he considered the most abominable hypocrisy. In articles and essays and in the nine numbers of a magazine, *The Moment* ("Øieblikket"), which he himself edited, he attacked, with scorn, bitterness and irony, all clergymen ("those perjurers and actors") and all professors of theology ("It is one thing to suffer, another thing to become professor of someone else's suffering"). The effort killed him, but he died without receiving the sacrament, rather than take it from the hand of a clergyman.

*

The 1850's and 1860's produced hardly any new Danish writers of importance. The poetry of CARL PLOUG (1813–94) has little inspiration, and the undergraduate poems and Grundtvigian songs of JENS CHRISTIAN HOSTRUP (1818–92) are without much originality. Hostrup's light comedies also are entertaining rather than literary. CHRISTIAN RICHARDT (1831–92) and VILHELM KAALUND (1818–85) did little more than rehash the better known Romantic themes. The novels of VILHELM BERGSØE, CARIT ETLAR and H. F. EWALD are entertaining and often exciting, but can hardly be called innovations. The only important contribution to the development of the Danish novel is HANS EGEDE SCHACK's *The Fantasts* ("Phantasterne", 1857), a psychological novel on the danger of excessive day-dreaming. Apart from this the stage was still occupied only by writers who had made their *début* before 1850. They were growing old; it was the end of an act.

CHAPTER VI

SWEDISH LITERATURE 1800—1870

From the capricious and intolerant personality of Gustav IV Adolf literature was hardly likely to derive any particular stimulus; and it is not surprising that the first decade of the 19th century offers for the most part pompous odes, drinking songs that were pale — or noisy — imitations of Bellman's, written by VALERIUS and WALLIN, and crude ballads in the style of the German "Schauerromantik." By an apparent paradox, it was the loss of Finland in 1808 and the deposition of the king in the following year which revived the national spirit, and initiated a new epoch of experiment and inspiration in Swedish literature. Nationalism, driven inwards, sought consolation in dreams of past glory and hopes of a brighter future.

But of course other, deeper reasons, apart from the impact of national disaster[1], help to explain the triumph of Romanticism. Of these, the most important was the influence of German idealistic philosophy on the generation of the '90's, who, partly through periodicals, partly through the spoken word of University teachers, were brought into contact with the teachings of Kant, Schelling, and Fichte. HÖIJER was the outstanding exponent of the new philosophy:

---

[1] It is probably impossible for anyone who is not a Swede to appreciate fully the political and emotional significance for the Swedes of the fate of Finland. It is a factor which continually recurs in the history of Sweden after 1808, and still does so at the present day.

he had the gift of kindling enthusiasm, among his young hearers at Uppsala, not only for philosophy, but also for the literature of Germany, the writings of Goethe and Schiller, and the first products of the German Romantic Movement. We have already seen, too, how various trends and signs towards the end of the preceding century had heralded the approach of Romanticism.

Significant of the change in attitude was the shifting of the literary centre of gravity from the capital to the University towns, especially Uppsala, though later on, with the coming of Liberalism, Stockholm was to recapture her leading position, and though, too, various Romantic *frondeurs* such as HAMMARSKÖLD carried on their campaigns from the capital. Romantic literature, in fact, became esoteric rather than social and worldly. Isolated from the bustle of practical affairs, it tended to become too rarefied and remote, too academic and philosophical. That is why so much of what the Romantics (Nyromantiker) produced never became popular, and why it is now so difficult for the modern reader to disentangle its intrinsic beauty from the wrappings of philosophical obscurity.

*

Of the so-called "fosforister" — they received their name from the periodical *Phosphorus,* published by the literary society *Aurora,* with which many of this group were at one time associated — PER DANIEL AMADEUS ATTERBOM (1790—1855) was undeniably the most eminent. He was generally reckoned as their leader, by virtue of his poetic achievements and the range of his ideas, but he had no marked polemical gifts — and complicated polemics wasted a good deal of the time and energy of the Romantic generation during the decade 1810—1820. I shall not spend time on discussing these quarrels here. Indeed, Atterbom was a dreamy, diffident, introspective youth, a clergyman's son

of precocious talent, who required the continual encouragement, at Uppsala, of tougher friends and fellow-authors such
as V. PALMBLAD (1788–1852). The latter combined classical erudition with practical sense and a gift for fighting
in the literary field. It was thanks to Palmblad's publishing activities that the ephemeral literary periodicals, in
which the Romantics printed their writings, were in fact
able to appear. His ready pen often supplied them with
provocative contributions, aimed at the classical tenets of
the Old School, the Academy, of which Valerius and
especially WALLMARK were the chief champions.

The "fosforister" and their allies wished poetry to express ideal values, to interpret the individual's emotions
and moods, to evoke the infinite: in order to achieve or
attempt all these things they desired much greater freedom
of form and diction than was customary at that time. Palmblad's own serious, though rather tedious, efforts in literature were "long short stories", that is, "noveller", such as
Amala (1817), and, later on, novels, for instance *The Falkenswärd Family* ("Familjen Falkenswärd", 1844–1845).
By that time the Romantic Movement had long since lost
its ardour and the freshness of its inspiration.

Atterbom first showed his poetic abilities in the Prologue
to *Phosphorus* (1810), in which he attempted to express
both philosophical and aesthetic ideas and called for the
revival of "true" poetry. The thoughts put forward are
obscure — indeed there was an element of d e l i b e r a t e
mystification, here as in many Romantic works — yet his
handling of metre, in this case i. a. *ottave rime,* and his diction, showed that he was already a genuine poet. He went
on to the cycle called *The Flowers* ("Blommorna", 1812–
1837), in which, much more simply than in his other works,
he interprets Schelling's nature-philosophy through the
symbols which he saw around him, in the gardens and
forests of the countryside. Atterbom had a very keen sense

of the beauties of the physical world, a sense which ERIK
STAGNELIUS (1793—1823) shared with him.

However, Atterbom's outstanding work was not in these,
but in the two poetic dramas, *The Blue Bird* ("Fågel Blå"),
never completed, and the five "adventures" or cantos of
The Isle of Bliss ("Lycksalighetens Ö", 1824—1827). By the
time he was writing this latter work Atterbom had travelled
abroad, had met and subsequently married his wife, to
whom he remained extraordinarily devoted until her death,
and had come to terms with life. He had courageously
decided that aestheticism was not the solution to life, that
only through unselfishness and suffering can man attain
to truth and happiness, and that these can never be reached
in this world. These ideas are expressed in the play by
means of complicated symbolism and imagery, in the story
of Astolf, the young king of the land of the Hyperboreans
(Sweden), and of Felicia, his bride, queen of the Isle of
Bliss, which latter the two inhabit in love and harmony, until Fate, or, rather, Nyx, goddess of Night, intervenes. Astolf
dies, and Felicia, at the end, expresses those sentiments of
resigned renunciation which are really the poet's own. It
is interesting to see how, profoundly influenced though he
was by Schelling's terminology, Atterbom, in this work,
also reveals that he has returned to his childhood beliefs.

A revival of religious faith marked many of the Swedish writers of this age (as happened, too, in France and
Germany) — a reaction against the apparent cynical world-
liness of the later 18th century. Thus J. O. WALLIN (1779—
1839), a bishop and member of the Academy, turned, partly
under the influence of Romanticism, to writing hymns,
which became famous for their sincerity and beauty. An
Uppsala friend of Atterbom, S. HEDBORN, did some of his
best work in hymn form: his other achievements were in
the folksong, the genre of poetry so much loved by the
German Romantics, Tieck, Eichendorff, and others. Apart

from Hedborn and Geijer, very few of the Swedish Romantic writers were really successful in this genre. Like Tieck, Atterbom had based his verse-dramas on folk-tales, but nothing could be less "folklig" than the ethereal fancies of *The Isle of Bliss,* nor could anything be less dramatic. Atterbom's work became, and has remained, a "läsdrama", a drama for reading not acting, which reflects the complex influences of German philosophy and German Romanticism, of Goethe's and Schiller's "new humanism", of S h a k e - s p e a r e and Ossian, and which embodies, too, the author's conception of "göticism". In spite of its predominantly esoteric character and its obscurities, it possesses great beauty, beauty of rhythm and melody, of colour and phrase. The nightingales sing in the groves of the island, and Felicia and Astolf exchange vows of love in verses of great charm.

In its musical harmony and its idealism, its yearning for eternal truth and beauty, this work represents *par excellence* Romantic ambitions (and not those of Sweden alone): that is why so much space has been devoted to it here. Even its faults are typical of the generation to which it belongs. The ambitions were shared by several other writers, such as, for example, P. ELGSTRÖM (1781—1810), G. INGELGREN (1782—1813), and the much greater poet E. STAGNELIUS. Stagnelius, son of a bishop, belonged to no group: ugly and uncouth, he lived a friendless life in Stockholm, after having studied at Lund as well as Uppsala, and died young, probably as a result of excesses. His works, most of which were not published till after his death, include epics and plays, as well as lyric poems. Stagnelius' was a much more complicated, passionate nature than Atterbom's. He was torn between an idealism of an even more complex, mystical sort, based among other things on Neo-Platonism, Schelling, and Chateaubriand, and an extremely sensual eroticism; and these conflicting impulses are symbolized in his poems, as in the collection *Lilies of Sharon* ("Liljor i Saron") and others. Stagnelius could convey intensity of emotion and involved philosophical thought with a lucidity and mastery of language that Atterbom lacked. He had learned much from the ancient Classics, which he had mastered at an early age; indeed in *Sigurd Ring* and *Visbur* he tried to write Greek tragedies on Nordic themes, but the results, though technically accomplished, were lifeless. The greatest of his works, and the last — *The Bacchae* ("Bacchanterna") — treats of the fate of Orpheus, and shows what masterpieces Stagnelius might have gone on to write, as poet though not as dramatist, if he had lived. Even with what he did achieve he became, stylistically at least, far more influential in Swedish literature than Atterbom.

No more vivid contrast to Stagnelius could possibly be imagined than ERIK GUSTAV GEIJER (1783—1847). Geijer, rather older than Stagnelius and Atterbom, came to Uppsala with the intention of subsequently pursuing the practical business career of his ancestors, who were iron-founders in Värmland: only gradually did he come to realise that — like Atterbom — he wished to devote his life to academic work. Before he settled down in Uppsala, where he eventually became professor of history, he travelled in England (in 1809) as tutor to a wealthy young Swede. His impressions of England, recorded in letter form, and published, together with reminiscences of his childhood, in the charming little volume *Memories* ("Min-nen", 1834), give a lively picture of the sordidness and wealth of England during the early stages of the Industrial Revolution, and also of the fresh intelligence of the writer himself. Geijer appears to be interested in everything, the roads, the inns, the food, the theatre, and so on, and in the political constitution of Britain, and this lively interest in phenomena was to characterise him throughout his life. Realistic and versatile, where Stagnelius was introspective and one-sided, Geijer, through his dynamic, attractive personality, dominated the circle of "fosforister" in Uppsala, and indeed a much wider sphere as well. To Atterbom he was for years a faithful friend and counsellor, and exerted a very important influence on him, until political differences separated them in 1838; for Atterbom, by then professor of aesthetics, remained an out-and-out Conservative to the end of his life, whereas Geijer went over to Liberalism, by a courageous apostasy, costly to his own interests, which shook the intellectual circles of Sweden and heartened the Liberal set around the paper *Aftonbladet*, headed by its editor L. HIERTA.

Geijer's writings are largely historical and philosophical, consisting of works such as *The Annals of the Swedish Kingdom* ("Svea Rikets Hävder", 1825), that reflect the different stages of his ideological development and are important because of their influence on Swedish thought. He had been much affected by Kant, Schelling, and Fichte, and later in life he read Hegel and the post-Hegelian German materialist thinkers: to the end, however, he himself remained a Christian idealist. Unfortunately, whilst a lively and popular lecturer, he reveals himself, in his weighty written works, as an indifferent prose stylist; and he is chiefly remembered, in literature, for his *Poems* ("Dikter"), which make up only a slender volume. The bulk of these were composed in 1811—1814, and in the late '30's, epochs that coincided with periods of especial emotional stress for the writer. For though Geijer did his best to present a serene countenance to the world, his optimism, his belief that "sorrow is sin", was not maintained without periods of deep personal conflict. He set many of his poems, including hymns, to music, which was really his favourite artistic medium: here, too, he shows his remarkable versatility.

It was above all Geijer's first period of poetical activity that made him famous and influential, and incidentally turned the so-called *Götiska Förbundet* in Stockholm into a literary society, though only for a time. This body had begun in 1811 as one of the orders then so popular, with very strongly nationalist ideals. Geijer took the lead in producing a periodical, *Iduna*, the first number of which largely consisted of his own poems, *The Last Skald* ("Den siste skalden"), *The Viking* ("Vikingen"), *The Yeoman Farmer* ("Odalbonden"), and others. In his belief in the courage and simplicity of the heroic past, in his desire to use Nordic subjects as literary themes, Geijer was an adherent of "göticism", but he avoided the exaggerations of a LING, the first and inept reviver in this generation of these ideas. Geijer and Ling were in fact both pupils of the Danish poet Oehlenschläger (see pp. 82–84). It is significant that with the coming of Romanticism Danish influence, as well as German, was to reassert itself in Swedish letters: Geijer is an excellent example of the effect of both Danish and German influence, and it is important to notice that he also admired Shakespeare.

Geijer's success did much to stimulate the influence of "göticism", not least on ESAIAS TEGNÉR (1782–1846), to whom I must return. Geijer contributed to other organs of the Romantic Movement, without ever being a genuine "fosforist". His poems are remarkable for their concrete simplicity and apparent artlessness, so evocative, for all their naivety, of mood and feeling in nature and man, as for instance in *The Little Charcoal-Burner* ("Den lille kolargossen"):

It is so dark far, far away in the forest.

Det är så mörkt långt, långt bort i skogen.

In this and other poems Geijer approaches the lyrical qualities of Goethe, whom he so much admired.

*

The prince of poetry in the Sweden of Carl Johan Berna-
dotte was, however, without doubt, Esaias Tegnér. Geijer,
in many ways critical of him, has described a meeting with
him, in youth, in passages which can still conjure up the
wayward brilliance of the young poet:
"One knew the course of his thoughts as little as the sun-
beams' passage through the leaves. ... Everything he said,
glittered."[1]
Longing for light and clarity were indeed vital elements in
Tegnér's poetry.

Tegnér became the great classic writer of that epoch,
"classic" in the sense that he was much read and admired
by many sections of the nation. Inheriting the tradition
of Kellgren and Oxenstierna, and also of the rhetorical
Leopold, he developed and modernised them under the
influence of Oehlenschläger, Geijer, Goethe, and Schiller.
It was Tegnér whose epigrams in verse and bons mots were
repeated with appreciation. Wit was a quality not usual
among the Swedish Romantics, though not altogether lacking in Hammarsköld, C. Livijn, and J. C. Askelöf: Tegnér's, however, really sparkled. He certainly learnt a good
deal from the "Nyromantiker", and drew on many of their
sources, such as Kant and Schelling, but the obscurities and
the "jingle-jangle", as he called it, of "fosforism" irritated
him. Of Atterbom's Isle of Bliss he maliciously said that
it made him dizzy, it was like going up in a balloon, and
Hammarsköld (Hammer-shield) he christened, by an unkind
pun, "Hammarspik" (Hammer-nail). Tegnér, then, whilst
contributing for some time to Iduna, never took his stand
with the Romantics, nor did he, finally, throw in his
lot with the Old School. In the magnificent speech he
made in Lund, on the occasion of the tercentenary of the
Reformation (1817), he attacked the aridity and material-

[1] "Man visste lika litet gången av hans tankar som solstrålens väg genom
löfven ... allt, hvad han sade, blänkte."

ism of the Age of Enlightenment, as well as the obscurantism of the New School.

He had already (i. e. before 1817) demonstrated his own
powers in lovely odes and lyrics such as *Svea* (1811) and
Song to the Sun ("Sång till solen", 1813) and in delightful
occasional verse which recalls Bellman's charm: he had
also showed that patriotism, politics, and philosophy could
inspire him, as well as erotic passion.   Tegnér was ready
to welcome Norway as a brother-country, as in *Nore* (1814),
he admired Napoleon for his opposition to Russia — *The
Hero* ("Hjälten", 1813) — and sang in praise of liberty and
noble deeds.   He was an ardent patriot, a growing Conservative, yet his nationalism — and, as is well known, during
this period of European history nationalism was everywhere
developing fast — did not hinder him from following
international affairs with the greatest interest from the
little backwater of Lund.   Here he became ensconced as
professor of Greek in 1812, and was ordained a clergyman
for the practical reason that a living would help to support
his increasing family.   The charming *Morning Psalm of
the Poet* ("Skaldens morgonpsalm") is a prayer for poetical
inspiration and for the physical means whereby that inspiration can be translated into verse.   That Tegnér should
petition for poetry, not for virtue, was typical of his attitude.
Increasingly, as he matured, his work was to set forth
his lofty conception of poetry as revelation of divine truth
and thus as another aspect of religion.   But that at the same
time he should consider the practical question of finance
is evidence of his complexity.   He was, for instance, an
excellent administrator, and appreciated the pleasures of
the senses, but also had in him a strong element of melancholy, which from time to time upset his mental balance.
His fits of pessimism and introspective bitterness increased
as he grew older, curtailing his literary activity, until at
last — for a while — his mind completely gave way.   Before

this he had long since left Lund, to become Bishop of Växjö. Tegnér's longing for clarity and light was thus partly motivated by an intense desire to overcome the darker side of his own nature: his fascinating and excellently written letters provide plentiful evidence of his mental states.

The zenith of Tegnér's poetic career was reached in the years 1820—1825, during which he composed, for example, *The Children of the Lord's Supper* ("Nattvardsbarnen"), *Axel*, a Byronic romance that has dated, the magnificent *Epilogue to the Degree-giving at Lund* 1820 ("Epilog vid Magisterpromotionen i Lund 1820"), and *Frithiofs Saga* (1820—1825). The third decade of the 19th century, indeed, forms a kind of brief Golden Age in Swedish literature: the Old School and the New come to terms; and Atterbom, Tegnér, Stagnelius, E. SJÖBERG, known by his pseudonym VITALIS, another shortlived recluse, and other, minor, writers produced some of their best work.

In *Frithiofs Saga* Tegnér attempted an epic poem on an old Icelandic theme (see p. 15) in 24 cantos, varying in length and metre. It deals with the love of the Viking hero Frithiof for Ingeborg, the daughter of King Bele, a love which she returns, though she is forced by her brothers Helge and Halfdan to marry her older and more powerful suitor King Ring, while Frithiof is away on the seas. On his return Frithiof, enraged by the loss of his love, desecrates Balder's temple, and is then sent away into exile. Later he returns in disguise to the court of King Ring, where he overcomes the temptation to kill his rival. But he has been recognised: Ring kills himself in the old Nordic fashion, to make way for the younger man, and the people are ready to elect Frithiof king and protector of Ingeborg's young son. He, however, will not accept either throne or wife until Balder, the power of good, has forgiven him;

and it is on this note of atonement and reconciliation that the poem ends, in Balder's rebuilt temple.

Thus Tegnér followed the main lines of the old story, whilst giving it a modern interpretation by the emphasis laid on psychological values and by his elaboration of the sentimental passages between Ingeborg and Frithiof. Too modern those passages may seem to a reader of to-day: but Tegnér was not deterred by such considerations, and his Swedish and German and even English contemporaries — for the work was translated forthwith — received the poem with enthusiasm. He had wanted to sing of the heroic Swedish past: the fact that he actually chose a Norwegian subject provoked no criticism. His achievement is that, in spite of faults, the poem still remains a living work, fresh and vigorous, and this is due, in great part, to his use of metres. Like Oehlenschläger in his *Helge,* Tegnér[1], with great virtuosity, varied his rhythm according to the mood of the story, now rapid, now contemplative, now emotional. He recaptured, too, the grandeur of the Homeric hexameter, and the concrete yet imaginative diction of the Greek epic poet, with whom he had been familiar since childhood. So, for example, in *Frithiof's Inheritance:*

Now on grave-heights lay King Bele and Torsten the
⠀⠀⠀⠀⠀⠀⠀⠀⠀⠀⠀⠀⠀⠀⠀⠀⠀⠀⠀⠀⠀⠀⠀⠀⠀ancient,
Even as themselves had decreed; for on either side of the
⠀⠀⠀⠀⠀⠀⠀⠀⠀⠀⠀⠀⠀⠀⠀⠀⠀⠀⠀⠀⠀⠀⠀⠀⠀⠀⠀inlet
Mound faced mound o'er the waves — twin breasts through
⠀⠀⠀⠀⠀⠀⠀⠀⠀⠀⠀⠀⠀⠀⠀⠀⠀⠀⠀⠀⠀Death separated.
So by the Folk-Ting's voice gained equal shares in the
⠀⠀⠀⠀⠀⠀⠀⠀⠀⠀⠀⠀⠀⠀⠀⠀⠀⠀⠀⠀⠀⠀⠀kingship
Helge and Halvdan both; but Frithiof, brotherless orphan,
Shared with none, but in peace established his dwelling in
⠀⠀⠀⠀⠀⠀⠀⠀⠀⠀⠀⠀⠀⠀⠀⠀⠀⠀⠀⠀⠀⠀Framness.

[1] Tegnér freely admitted his debt to this author and work. (See p. 84).

Vore nu satte i hög kung Bele och Thorsten den gamle
där de själve befallt; på var sin sida om fjärden
högarna lyfte sin rund, två bröst dem döden har åtskilt.
Helge och Halfdan, på folkets beslut, nu togo i samarv
riket efter sin far, men Frithiof som endaste sonen,
delte med ingen och fäste i lugn sin boning på Framnäs.

The other factor which gives vitality and lasting force
to the poem was Tegnér's own emotional stress during
its composition. The desire to achieve an harmonious
solution to his own intellectual problems, and the impact
of two emotional relationships, are both reflected in the
verse.

One might say of many Swedish writers that, if they had
been born into a greater and richer country, they would,
thanks to tradition and opportunity, have become much
greater figures. Of none, with the exception of Strindberg,
is this truer than of Tegnér. Restricted as he was, first by
a professorial chair, then by a bishopric in a small provincial
town, he felt, and resented, the confined spheres in which
he had to live, and the lack of free intellectual intercourse
in the Sweden of his day. By a grim irony, his only two
journeys to the Continent proper took him, one to a spa,
the other to a lunatic asylum.

*

Thus far, in this generation, poetry has occupied us almost exclusively, but the best work of C. J. L. ALMQUIST
(1793–1866) was practically all written in prose: the exception is provided by the remarkable lyrics *Songes,* and
by one or two of his more successful verse dramas. This
does not mean that Almquist had no poetical ambitions,
for, like Tegnér, he had a lofty conception of the nature
of poetry; and he infused into that conception the religious
mysticism which he had absorbed in childhood from
the Moravian Brethren, and at Uppsala from his read-

ing of Swedenborg, combined with the exaltation which he had learned from the German Romantics. Checked by an uncle's intervention from publishing his first ambitious literary work, *Amorina,* in 1823, he took refuge in the countryside, and put into practice his Rousseauistic beliefs in life on the land, going so far as to take a country girl as his wife. Both the marriage and the farming turned out to be failures, and Almquist returned to Stockholm after a year, there to earn his living by teaching. Later he became a clergyman, later still a journalist, and finally, driven by fear of arrest for an alleged (but never proved) attempt to murder a money-lender, he fled the country in 1851. The remainder of this somewhat sensational life was spent in America, where he made a bigamous marriage. Then, on his way back to Sweden, Almquist died in Germany in 1866.

During the years 1823—1851 Almquist developed an enormous, uneven productivity, on which it is impossible to comment adequately here. It was unfortunate that the misadventure with *Amorina* kept him so long from publishing at all, so that not until 1832 did the first series of works covered by the title *The Book of the Wild Rose* ("Törnrosens bok", 1832—1851) begin to appear: these volumes included historical novels, such as *The Hermitage* ("Hermitaget"), "noveller", such as *Araminta May,* plays such as *Signora Luna,* satires, romances, and epic poems, such as *Arthur's Chase* ("Arturs Jagt"). The second series (1839—1850), "imperialoktavupplagan", as it was called, contained many works written before 1830, for example, the excellent satire on bureaucracy, *Ormus and Ariman,* which indicates how early Almquist had developed his critical, almost anarchical, views on society. By delaying publication of these things, Almquist received neither the healthy stimulus nor the criticism which he needed. His Romanticism, in some aspects more extreme than that of the "fosforister", and often more varied and effective, as in the historical novel about Gustav III's Court, *The Queen's Jewel* ("Drottningens Juvelsmycke"), represents one side of a dual nature: the reverse, a realism which observed nature, men, and society with a sharp eye, and expressed these observations in clear, flexible prose, is already evident in his earliest writings. This realistic tendency grows stronger towards the end of the '30's, after a silence of three years, though the Romantic elements persist to the end. In the meantime, Almquist had been affected by the Socialist doctrines of Fourier and other French contemporaries, and his own critical attitude towards Government and Church, together with his awareness of social problems, drove him into the Liberal ranks. The Liberals, while increasingly powerful, remained socially *déclassés*: Almquist was to outstrip them all in provocative opinion.

Almquist's most lasting work was done in the genre of the "novell", which he virtually created, so far as Swedish literature was concerned. Here his interest in psychology and in background are happily combined, as in *The Palace* ("Palatset", 1838), and more especially in the stories about peasant life, *The Chapel* ("Kapellet"), and *Skällnora Mill* ("Skällnora kvarn") of the same year, in which he pays tribute to honest poverty. That he had far out-distanced contemporary ideas was proved by *That's all right* ("Det går an"), which outraged opinion by its suggestion that a free relationship between the young woman (Sara) and a man (Sergeant Albert), outside marriage, could be moral and happy. With this story and others Almquist showed how literature could be used as an effective means of debating intellectual and social problems, something which was not to occur again in Sweden until the period of Strindberg and others in the '80's ("Åttiotalet").

A curious ambivalence marks the intriguing personality and works of Almquist. No doubt this is responsible for the extraordinary differences of opinion concerning him, which have continued to exist. His potboilers and "folk-skrifter" were devoured by the middle-classes of his day, the growing reading public that wanted more fiction and ensured the popularity of novels such as those by AUGUST BLANCHE (1811—1868). At the same time the Finnish-Swedish poet J. L. RUNEBERG (1804—1877) selected Almquist for particular praise, in 1839, whilst otherwise condemning the whole tendency of contemporary Swedish literature. There is unfortunately no space in this book to discuss Finnish-Swedish literature, but of Runeberg it must at least be said that his lyrics, such as the collection of 1833 and his epic poems, especially *The Legends of Ensign Stål* ("Fänrik Ståls sägner"), published in 1848 and 1860, were destined to exercise a powerful influence on Swedish literature proper, and to set up new standards of "poetic Realism."

*

This influence, however, was some time in taking effect; and meanwhile, in the '40's and '50's, the currents of Romanticism petered out into insignificant trickles, with the so-called "epigonen" literature, pale imitations of the previous generation, with some feeble additions of supposed realism. Such was the work of the aesthete B. E. MALM-STRÖM (1816—1865), in spite of his admiration for Runeberg, and such, too, was that of his senior NICANDER (1799—1839). Even more sentimental were the ballads of C. W. BÖTTIGER, full of tears and roses. These poets were much admired, and possessed considerable technical skill, but their interest for us is solely in the evidence they provide of contemporary taste. The steadily increasing prosperity of Sweden during the uneventful years after 1830 rather encouraged a general apathy in respect of the arts. The bombastic enthusiasm of the students at Lund and Uppsala for the "Scandinavianism" of the 1840's would

appear *prima facie* to contradict this, yet their enthusiasm
was mere wind, and their attitude unrealistic to a degree;
and unfortunately the whole of this political movement in
Sweden came to little. Young student poets such as
C. V. A. STRANDBERG (pseudonym TALIS QUALIS, 1818–
1877) produced a few good rhetorical odes under its
stimulus, but much of this kind of verse degenerated into
"punsch-vältalighet"– "punch-eloquence" – produced by
superannuated students such as J. NYBOM. A more satis-
factory kind of student poetry was written by G. WENNER-
BERG (1817–1901), whose *Youths* ("Gluntarne"), set to
music, told of the pleasures of student life, and can still
evoke a nostalgic longing for the Uppsala of the 1840's.
Yet these idylls, too, were essentially "epigonen" literature,
in spite of their apparent freshness.

*

Meanwhile the art of the novel had made some progress.
We have seen already how little had been achieved in this
genre during the 18th century: but FREDERIK CEDER-
BORGH'S *Uno von Thrasenberg* (1809–1810) gave promise
at last of a Realistic school of novel-writing in Sweden. This
work is the story of a young nobleman's experiences in
Stockholm, on his arrival from his country home, and
gave its author opportunities for satirizing the bureaucracy
of the capital and the dissipated life of the aristocracy.
Yet the Romantics, with the exception of Almquist, did
little with the novel; Almquist's tales were, in a sense,
too personal and wayward to help build up a native
tradition, though, certainly, they influenced subsequent
literature; and, curiously enough, it was a trio of women
who succeeded, however crudely and imperfectly, in
developing the Swedish novel during the first half of
the 19th century. Of the three, FREDRIKA BREMER (1801
–1865) is the most famous, as a result of her work for

female emancipation, through which she became internationally known. *The Neighbours* ("Grannarna", 1837), a picture of upper middle-class life, is the best thing she did, thanks to the character of "ma chère mère", the General's widow, a creature of flesh and blood, who shows up the many anaemic, romanticized people, in Fredrika Bremer's other stories. For, in order to appeal to contemporary taste, the authoress introduced melodramatic intrigues, the return of the prodigal son in disguise, *et hoc genus omne*, and made her views on feminine education and, later, Liberal reform more acceptable by sentimental interludes. Such romanesque incidents and characters occur frequently, too, in the works of her fellow-writers, SOPHIE VON KNORRING (1797—1848), and EMILIE FLYGARE-CARLÉN (1807—1892). The former was by birth an aristocrat, and her novels, such as *The Cousins* ("Cousinerna"), deal chiefly with her own class. Her general theme is the triumph of duty over inclination. *The Crofter* ("Torparen") was written in answer to Almquist's *That's all right,* and, as the title indicates, Fru Knorring here concerned herself for once with the poorer classes. This is undoubtedly her best work. Emilie Flygare-Carlén, familiar from childhood with the west coast of Sweden, set many of her novels in this background, and described the life of fishermen and excise officers and merchants. Her best-known book, *The Rose of Thistle Island* ("Rosen på Tistelön", 1847) is still readable. Though a poor stylist, she had a better gift for telling a story and a much more accurate knowledge of the seamy side of life than her more genteel sister-novelists. Like them, she debated, however wordily, problems in her stories, the best of which were written before 1860.

*

Runeberg was the ideal and model for the "Pseudonym Poets" ("Signaturerna"), the Uppsala literary society which,

in 1863, tried to initiate a revival in Swedish letters. E.
BÄCKSTRÖM (1841–1886), lyricist and playwright, C. D. AF
WIRSÉN (1842–1912), later a conservative and negative
critic of the literature of the '80's and '90's, made with
others, their début under its aegis. But the revival merely
produced imitative poetry in slightly different forms, and
only Count C. SNOILSKY (1841–1903), who originally belonged to this group, had genuine talent. Snoilsky, inspired
by the cause of freedom, and by his travels in the South,
sang of the beauty of Italy in his *Poems* ("Dikter"), published in 1869. Later on he attempted to express the conflicts and problems of revolutionary and industrialized
Europe, but these poems belong to the later decades of the
century.

One writer, *par excellence,* represents the transition from
the idealism of the "Nyromantik" to the Naturalism of the
'80's. VIKTOR RYDBERG (1828–1895) was a Radical, largely
self-educated, journalist, who ended up as professor at the
newly founded University (Högskola) of Stockholm, and as
the Grand Old Man of the Swedish Academy. Novelist,
poet, philosopher, he owes his place in the history of Swedish literature before 1870 principally to his ideological
novel *The last Athenian* ("Den siste athenaren", 1859)
and his philosophical treatise *The Bible's Doctrine concerning Christ* ("Bibelns lära om Kristus", 1862). In both these
works he attacks the narrow orthodoxy of the Church,
implicitly or explicitly. Rydberg was a fighter for broader
perspectives and loftier ideals, in fact for a better world,
but to a certain degree his work, in spite of its idealism,
helped to prepare the triumph of a materialistic conception
of life. Rydberg was to view with horror the rule of Frode
the ruthless king of the industrial slaves, whom he depicted
in *The New Grotte Song* ("Den nya Grottesången").

CHAPTER VII

NORWEGIAN LITERATURE 1814–1870

In 1814 occurred that event which was to overshadow all others in the history of Norway; the removal of the Danish yoke and the establishment of the free Constitution of Eidsvoll. Union with Sweden followed which lasted until 1905 but for nearly all practical purposes Norway had again become an independent state and this newly-won freedom gave an impetus to the national life which can hardly be over-estimated; not least did it stimulate the cultural life of the country.

Since the 16th century Danish literature had held sway in Norway practically unchallenged, and such Norwegians as wrote were completely dominated by Danish literary fashions and traditions and, of course, Danish was the language they used. Some of these writers achieved considerable fame in the Danish literary world, notably Ludvig Holberg (see pp. 46–51) and Johan Herman Wessel (see pp. 54–56); also worthy of mention is PETTER DASS (1647–1707), a clergyman of Scottish extraction, whose *Trumpet of the North* ("Nordlands Trompet") describes the province of Nordland in fresh and vigorous verse. Towards the end of the 18th century Norwegian writers in Copenhagen founded their own literary society, *Det norske Selskab* (The Norwegian Society), but there is little which distinguishes them in style or language as purely Norwegian writers; in subject matter, however, much of what was written by Norwegians in the years before 1814 is marked by a somewhat excessive and bombastic patriotism.

HENRIK WERGELAND (1808–1845) is the first writer of the new Norway of whom we need take note. His life and work are symbolic of the national renascence. By temperament he was a Romantic but possessed a goodly leaven of 18th century Rationalism, qualities which are reflected in his enormous output, running into more than 20 large volumes in the collected edition of his works. The major part of this has but a literary-historic interest for the present-day reader, and ranges from articles for the enlightenment of the common man to large-scale works in verse. It comprises also works of history, tragedies, farces and polemical articles galore, much of it marked by an intense patriotism: it was, in fact, Wergeland who was largely responsible for getting his compatriots to celebrate 17th May as Norway's National Day. It is, however, in his shorter poems that Wergeland's genius achieves its highest expression. Some of these are marked by a wonderful feeling for nature as, for example, in the opening lines of the poem, *A Good Year for Norway* ("Godt Aar for Norge"); here the poet feels the rain falling softly on him, so softly that he asks if the angels have not first caught it up in their wings, so that the flowers will not be alarmed or the grass startled in its gentle quivering, or the bee, sleeping in the lily, awakened. Or again in the poem called *Myself* ("Mig selv") which was written as a reply to an attack on him in the newspaper, *Morgenbladet,* where, amongst other things, he was accused of being out of humour:

I in bad spirits, did you say? I, who need only a glimpse
        of the sun
To break out into loud laughter from a joy I cannot
        explain?

When I smell a green leaf, dazed I forget poverty,
    riches, friends and foes.

My cat rubbing against my cheek smoothens all heart-
    sores.
Into my dog's eye I lower my sorrows as in a deep well.

My ivy has grown. Out of my window it has borne on
    its broad leaves
All the memories I do not care to keep.

The first spring rain will fall on the leaves and wipe out
    some faithless names.
They will fall down with the drops and poison the
    burrows of the earth-worm.

I who read rapture in each petal of the hundred-leaved
    rose, that gift of spring —
Me should a wretched rag cause to quench one second
    with vexation?

That would be like killing sky-blue and rose-coloured
    butterflies.
Such crime, verily, my heart recoils from.

Jeg i slet Lune, Morgenblad? Jeg, som kun behøver et Glimt
af Solen
for at briste i høi Latter af en Glæde, jeg ikke kan forklare
mig?

Naar jeg lugter til et grønt Blad, glemmer jeg bedøvet
Fattigdom, Rigdom, Fiender og Venner.

Min Kats Strygen mod min Kind udglatter alle Hjertesaar.
I min Hunds Øie sænker jeg mine Sorger som i en dyb
Brønd.

Min Vedbend er vokset. Didudaf mit Vindu har den baaret
paa sine brede Blade
alle de Erindringer, jeg ikke bryder mig om at gjemme.

Den første Foraarsregn vil falde paa Bladene og udviske
nogle troløse Navne.
De ville falde ned med Draaberne og forgifte Regnormens
Huler.

Jeg, som læser Henrykkelser paa hvert af Centifoliens, den
Vaargaves, hundrede Blade —
mig skulde en slet Avis bringe til at dvæle en Sekund med
Ærgrelse?

Det vilde være som at dræbe himmelblaa og rosenrøde
Sommerfugle.
Den Synd gyser mit Hjerte for i sit Inderste.

Of his longer poems, *Jan van Huysum's Flower-piece*
("Jan van Huysum's Blomsterstykke", 1840), inspired by
one of the Dutch master's paintings, and *The English Pilot*
("Den engelske Lods", 1844) are richest in imagination and
poetic power. In the former Wergeland identifies the
flowers of van Huysum's painting with human figures
whose fates they share. The *English Pilot* is a narrative
poem of a rather melodramatic nature about an English
nobleman who seduces the wife of Jonny the pilot, but
contains, also, some descriptive passages of remarkable
beauty; most famous is the poem called *The Appearance
of England*, depicting the appearance of the cliffs of Dover:

> That which glitters in the west,
> Twixt the waves and cloud-banks over,
> That is England, sun-caressed:
> See the cliffs of Dover!

9*

> *Det som skinner*
> *vester hist*
> *mellem Sky og Havsensvover,*
> *Det er England,*
> *solbelyst,*
> *Klipperne ved Dover.*

and the poem goes on to glorify England as the home of free institutions. Love of freedom and detestation of tyranny and oppression inspired Wergeland to write his dramatic poems, *Cæsaris* (1833) and *The Spaniard* ("Spaniolen", 1833), dedicated respectively to fighters for freedom in Poland and Spain, and his championship of the Jews, who at that time were barred from entering Norway, received poetic expression in two of his finest works *The Jew,* ("Jøden", 1842) and *The Jewess* ("Jødinden", 1844). Many of Wergeland's most sensitive and best-loved poems were written practically on his death-bed. *To my Wallflower* ("Til min Gyldenlak") is one of the most celebrated and gives poignant expression to Wergeland's love of flowers which remained with him to the last.

> Wallflower mine, ere thy bright hues fade,
> I shall be that whereof all is made;
> Ere thou hast shattered thy crown of gold,
>   I shall be mould.

> When "Open the window!" I cry, from my bed,
> My last look lights on thy golden head;
> My soul will kiss it as over thee
>   It flieth free.

> Twice do I kiss thy lips so sweet,
> Thine is the first, as it is meet;
> The second, dearest, my will bestows
>   On my fair rose.

In bloom no more I shall it see;
So give it my greeting, when that shall be,
And say I wished on my grave should all
    Its petals fall.

Yes, say I wish that upon my breast
The rose thou gavest my kiss shall rest;
And, Wallflower, be in Death's dark porch
    Its bridal torch!

Gyldenlak, før du din Glans har tabt,
da er jeg det hvoraf alt er skabt;
ja før du mister din Krones Guld,
    da er jeg Muld.

Idet jeg raaber: med Vinduet op!
mit sidste Blik faar din Gyldentop.
Min Sjæl dig kysser, idet forbi
    den flyver fri.

Togange jeg kysser din søde Mund.
Dit er det første med Rettens Grund.
Det andet give du, kjære husk,
    min Rosenbusk!

Udsprungen faar jeg den ei at se;
thi bring min Hilsen, naar det vil ske;
og sig, jeg ønsker, at paa min Grav
    den blomstrer af.

Ja sig, jeg ønsker, at paa mit Bryst
den Rose laa, du fra mig har kyst;
og, Gyldenlak, vær i Dødens Hus
    dens Brudeblus!

Wergeland's largest work is the great, rambling, faulty
masterpiece called *Creation, Man and Messiah* ("Skabelsen,

Mennesket og Messias"). It appeared in 1830 and, in spite of its many defects, is a remarkable work and contains some of Wergeland's most felicitous poetic flights. It sets out to explain in the spirit of 18th century optimism the creation and the spiritual mysteries of life. Few readers, Norwegian or otherwise, would nowadays have the stamina required to plough through its great length: it can best be approached through a revised and shortened version called *Man* ("Mennesket"), which appeared in 1845. Wergeland's often extravagant literary style, his noisy personality, and not impeccable personal life, did not make for his acceptance in the orthodox literary and academic circles of Christiania. The reverse was, in fact, the case. He was detested by many and particularly opposed to him was the circle gathered round the poet JOHAN SEBASTIAN WELHAVEN (1807—1873). Welhaven was of a more conservative and orthodox nature than Wergeland and this, together with his upbringing and environment, made him well-suited to represent the continuance of the Danish literary tradition in Norway. His well-turned, if not particularly original, poetry is not wholly deserving of neglect, and whilst few read Welhaven at the present day and remember him mainly on account of his polemical exchanges with Wergeland and as the object of the unrequited passion of Wergeland's sister, Camilla, the reader would find enlightenment concerning his poetic principles in the poem, *The Spirit of the Poem* ("Digtets Aand"). Here he lays down that the function of poetry is to express the otherwise inexpressible, but adds, that this can only be achieved if the poet confines himself within the boundaries imposed by reason and language. This should be borne in mind before proceeding to other of his poems. Some of them are purely polemical, especially *The Dawn of Norway* ("Norges Dæmring"), where, by calling attention to the provincialism and lack of standards prevailing in Norway at the time, he satirizes what he imagined was the narrow nationalism of Wergeland and his supporters. Other of his poems, like *The Republicans* ("Republikanerne"), are reminiscent of travels abroad, but barbed at the same time: here his target is windy enthusiasm of outsiders for oppressed minorities. In his so-called *Poems from Antiquity*, he uses themes from classical antiquity and the Bible, lightly to clothe much that is polemical. Later he used material from the popular ballads and folklore of Norway in his *National Romances*, which are expressive of a rather pale, drawing-room National Romanticism. Some of his finest poems are to be found in his last collections published in 1848 and 1860, many of them marked by quiet resignation and deep religious feeling. One of the most beautiful is the poem called, *The Departed* ("Den Salige"), from the collection of 1848.

The "high" Romantic movement in the German sense hardly manifested itself in Norway at all. Instead, National Romanticism, always latent in the Norwegian, achieved in the period 1840–1860 complete preponderance in the nation's artistic life. In painting, J. C. Dahl, Adolf Tidemand and Hans Gude depicted, in these terms, the majesty of Norwegian nature and the life of the peasant; in music, Edvard Grieg skilfully adapted folk-melodies and motives to the requirements of classical form; in literature, its manifestations were manysided. Most important was, perhaps, the awakened interest in the old ballads and folk-tales from the Middle Ages, which, as has been already mentioned, had been preserved by oral tradition out in the country districts. This interest inspired the collecting zeal of two Norwegians whose names were destined to become household words, Jørgen Moe (1813–1882) and Peter Christen Asbjørnsen (1812–1885). Moe was the son of a farmer from Ringerike in Eastern Norway and while still a student became interested in the popular tales and ballads of his part of the country. He became early acquainted with Asbjørnsen who, also from childhood, had conceived a great affection for the pithiness of the folk-tales he had learnt from his father, an Oslo master-glazier. Together, Asbjørnsen and Moe collected and published a large number of folk-tales, both *folkeeventyr* and *folkesagn*, thus rescuing in the nick of time a national treasure which oral tradition could hardly have preserved much longer. The special difficulty which confronted Asbjørnsen and Moe when they came to give written form to these tales was the actual language to be used. To present them in the current *riksmål*, which was practically indistinguishable from Danish, would have entailed the loss of their essential character. On the other hand, to render them in dialect form would have made them largely incomprehensible to the majority of educated Norwegians who, after all, comprised the reading public. They therefore compromised very successfully. The outer clothing and orthography were Danish, but in choice of vocabulary and particularly of syntax they adhered very closely to the spoken Norwegian of the places where the folk-tales were collected.

The language question brings us to another very important aspect of the National Romantic movement. Patriotic Norwegians after 1814 soon began to feel that some attempt should be made to give written form to the rural dialects which, in effect, constituted the speech of the major part of the population. It was thought particularly harmful that country children, in order to become literate, should have to do so via the medium of Danish, practically a foreign language to them. Fortunately a philologist of considerable dimensions was to emerge to give shape to these aspirations. This was IVAR AASEN (1813–1896). Aasen was a poor peasant lad, born in the region of Sunnmøre. In spite of great handicaps he managed to educate himself sufficiently to obtain a post as a rural school-master. He became early interested in the relationship of his own native dialect to the Old Norse language and embodied his researches in a grammar of the *Sunnmørsk* dialect. This piece of work aroused the interest of "Videnskabernes Selskab" (Society for the Advancement of Knowledge) in Trondheim which granted him a sum of money to investigate other country dialects. In 1848 he published his *A Grammar of the Norwegian Language* ("Det norske Folkesprogs Grammatik") and in 1850 *Dictionary of the Norwegian Language* ("Ordbog over det norske Folkesprog"), works which were to be the foundations on which all future language-research in Norway was to be built. Aasen was, however, not content to be only a philologist: he created a standard Norwegian, called *Landsmål* (The country language), out of the different dialects and wrote much poetry in it. None of this has any great literary value, but is interesting as expressive of peasant outlook and mentality, and some poems have achieved great popularity, particularly *The Old Mountains* ("Dei gamle Fjelli") and *The Norwegian* ("Nordmannen"); they are part of his cycle of poems called *The Wood Anemone* ("Symra", 1863) which represents, perhaps, his best work as a poet. Also amongst his popular works is a play, *The Heir* ("Ervingen", 1855), not a very serious piece of work but one which is still sometimes performed.

More considerable as a literary artist in the field of *Nynorsk* (New Norwegian, as *Landsmål* has since become called), was AASMUND OLAFSEN VINJE (1818–1870). Like Aasen, he was of peasant origin and was born in Telemark in South-western Norway in the poorest circumstances. He was a man with exceptional intellectual gifts and an unquenchable thirst for knowledge. As a young man he became an itinerant rural schoolmaster, and by combining this underpaid occupation with a variety of others, including making wooden shoes and distilling spirits, he managed to acquire the means to enter a teachers' training college.

But he did not stop there;   at the age of 32 he entered
the University at Christiania and eventually took a degree
in law.   For some years he was a journalist and in 1858,
having decided that he would write Danish no more,
founded his own newspaper called *The Dalesman* ("Dølen"),
which was written mainly by himself and in his own form
of New Norwegian.   Vinje was a first-class journalist and
many of his articles can still be read with pleasure.   He was
no fanatical National Romantic: he knew too well the real
state of affairs in the country districts to be that, and he
was by temperament a rationalist;   much, in fact, of what
he wrote can be considered as a counter-blast to the prevailing notions regarding the excellence of the peasantry.   In
the summer of 1860 Vinje took a trip to Trondheim to be
present at the crowning of Karl XV in the cathedral there, a
journey which was productive of *Travel Memories* ("Ferda-
minni"), perhaps the most delightful thing he wrote.
Within the framework of the journey he reflects on persons,
things and life with a wisdom tinged by the mild melancholy
so characteristic of much of what he wrote.   His most
ambitious work is the long poem *Big Boy* ("Store Gut",
1866), dealing with peasant life at the end of the 18th century.   More approachable are his many short lyric poems
often expressive of a deep feeling for nature and a longing
for scenes of childhood.   Of special interest to English-
speaking readers is his *Britain and the British,* which was
published, in English, in Edinburgh.   It contains the, often
unflattering, impressions of a stay in England and Scotland
in 1863 which Vinje made in order to study the British jury
system.
   The Realism to be noted in Vinje, whilst not, strictly
speaking, in pact with what was to follow, was indicative
of the approach of a new literary epoch that was largely to
supersede National Romanticism.   In the van of the new
movement was CAMILLA COLLETT (1813—1895), already

mentioned as the sister of Henrik Wergeland. She appears to have been an unusually gifted woman, a born rebel, particularly against the prevailing social conventions as they applied to her own sex. Her unrequited love for the poet Welhaven added, no doubt, an edge to her other dissatisfactions and after her marriage to an understanding University professor, P. J. Collett, she took, largely on his advice, to authorship. The emancipation of women (of the upper and middle-classes) from the tyranny of social convention is her theme; the political aspect of women's position in society interested her less. Best known of her books and polemical writings is the novel *The Sheriff's Daughters* ("Amtmandens Døtre"), which appeared in 1855. It is a work which few can read with patience nowadays but it, nevertheless, constitutes a mile-stone in the history of Norwegian literature for, whilst other Norwegian writers, including the young Henrik Ibsen and Bjørnstjerne Bjørnson were still under the spell of the National Romantic movement, Camilla Collett had anticipated the advice of Georg Brandes, (see pp. 145–49), and was debating problems with a vengeance. Briefly, *The Sheriff's Daughters* deals with the problem of the woman of the middle-classes for whom marriage, and usually a marriage where the dictates of the heart receive little consideration, is the only possible career. The book is written with the passion of crusading zeal which convinces in spite of the antiquated style of the book and general lack of artistry.

Whilst Fru Collett had been engaged on such matters, the man who was to become Norway's most famous literary figure, HENRIK IBSEN (1828–1906), was occupied in Bergen at the theatre, recently established there, combining the functions of dramatic coach and house poet, a position he took over in 1851, after six years as a pharmacist's assistant in the small sea-port town of Grimstad in Southern Norway. Already in his Grimstad days he had written his first drama,

Cataline, but no success attended it and only the generosity of a friend got it published. With his one-act play *The Warrior's Barrow* ("Kjæmpehøjen", 1850), he achieved some small success, but this, and two or three efforts from about the same time, can be disregarded, as is usually the case in the collected editions of his works. *Lady Inger of Østraad* ("Fru Inger til Østraad", 1854), published 1857, and *The Feast at Solhaug* ("Gildet paa Solhaug", 1855), published 1856, are worthy of more serious attention. Both are set in the Norway of the early 16th century and they can, as far as choice of subject goes, be reckoned as part of the National Romantic movement. They are competent pieces of work, containing the germs of much that was to be developed in Ibsen's later work, but, as is to be expected, showing traces of powerful outside influences, notably from Denmark and France. The sagas and early Norwegian history were to provide material for two further plays, *The Vikings in Helgeland* ("Hærmændene paa Helgeland", 1858) and *The Pretenders* ("Kongsemnerne", 1863). In the first Ibsen attempts to reproduce the pithy and archaic style of the sagas, not, it must be admitted, with any signal success; the play, in fact, strikes one today as stiff and unnatural and the characterization crude. On a much higher plane is *The Pretenders.* Here the psychological penetration is masterly and in the characters of Haakon, the king born to success, and his rival, Duke Skule, the man of ability paralyzed by doubt, we find reflected something of Ibsen's own beliefs and doubts at the time concerning his abilities as a writer. Another aspect of this had already been touched on in *Love's Comedy* ("Kjærlighedens Komedie", 1862) and in the poem *On the Moors* ("Paa Vidderne", 1860), where the problems of the ethical and aesthetic in life, particularly as they apply to the creative artist, and the creative artist's place in society, are implicit. *Love's Comedy* is also a satire on courtship, betrothal and marriage, and in some ways a ripost to Camilla Collett's *Sheriff's Daughters*. Ibsen appears to cast a vote in favour of the marriage of convenience or, at least, to show that when women have a free choice in the matter of their partner in marriage, they play safe and carefully avoid the snares of romantic marriage.

In 1857 Ibsen left Bergen for Christiania to take over the direction of the Norwegian Theatre there. The next seven years were to be the most miserable in his life but in 1864, having been awarded a small travelling scholarship which had been supplemented by private benefaction, he journeyed to Rome and there began the long period of some 30 years' voluntary exile from his native land, an exile only to be broken by short and infrequent return visits. It was in Italy that *Brand* (1866) was written, the work which was to lay the foundations of Ibsen's literary fame. It concerns the clergyman Brand, a man of unrelenting principles, who demands from himself, his flock and the world at large, "all or nothing". Compromise in any shape or form is anathema to him and rather than deviate a hair's breadth from his principles he denies the last solace of the Church to his dying and unrepentant mother and sacrifices successively the lives of his child and wife and finally himself. That such a figure should have been conceived under Italian skies seems perhaps incongruous, but so it was. *Brand* was followed in 1867 by *Per Gynt* of which Ibsen has said, that it "wrote itself" after *Brand*. Whilst *Brand* owes much to the writings of Søren Kierkegaard (see pp. 104–7) and has its setting in the harsh, rain-drenched fjord country of Sunnmøre, *Per Gynt* belongs to the brighter aspect of Gudbrandsdalen and is based, to some extent, on a *folkesagn* from those parts. Per is a country-lad who, in complete contrast to the uncompromising Brand, solves all the problems of life by the simple process of avoiding them — by "going round" — and by practising the most blatant self-deception. There can be no doubt that *Brand* and *Per Gynt* contain many things Ibsen thought necessary to bring home to his fellow-countrymen. It seems that he detected a certain spinelessness in them, a lamentable willingness to easy compromise. Brand, Ibsen said, was "himself in his best moments". All the same, the play shows quite clearly what consequences the complete rejection of the spirit of compromise entails. Ibsen's compatriots applauded the piece, but whether it was in a spirit of self-satisfaction, or because they felt invigorated after a merited moral castigation, it is difficult to say. Both conceptions, in any case, received a corrective in Per Gynt, whom most Norwegians since have tended to regard as typifying the national character, but, as has often been pointed out, Per Gynts are not a product peculiar to Norway — the universality of the type has long been recognized. It should be noted that both Brand and Per Gynt undergo, at the last, some measure of conversion culminating, in the case of Brand, in the acknowledgement (I think the last words of the play should be interpreted thus) that God is a god of love and, in the case of Per, in his abjectness on discovering that he, like the onion, was devoid of any core or real self at all. Both these plays represent the poet Ibsen at his greatest, the lighter touch in *Per Gynt* perfectly matching the grave beauty of *Brand*. *Per Gynt* was Ibsen's last play in verse, and, henceforth (with the solitary exception of *Emperor and Galilean*) he was to deal with contemporary personages and problems.

Ibsen's slightly younger contemporary, BJØRNSTJERNE BJØRNSON (1832—1910), occupies a special place in the affections of his countrymen. In his day he was celebrated as an orator of dimensions, as a man of affairs and as champion of all sorts of causes. He was, in fact, by temperament the complete reverse of the reserved, formal and doubting Ibsen. Always full of confidence and irrepressible, Bjørnson

soon received recognition as a writer. In 1857 appeared
the first of his stories of peasant life, *Synnøve Solbakken*,
closely followed by *Arne* and *A Happy Boy* ("En glad Gut")
and later by others. These stories have for many years
been amongst the best-loved works of Norwegian literature,
but Bjørnson's contemporaries thought them "raw", containing, as they do, an element of Realism which shocked a
generation imbued with a pious reverence for the purity
and simplicity of rural life as they found it exemplified,
very much to their taste, in the paintings of Adolf Tidemand. The fact is that the new Realism was slowly but
surely making its way into Norwegian literature and, as far
as rural life was concerned, the revelations of the sociologist,
Eilert Sundt, regarding the state of affairs in the country
districts, disclosing that drunkeness, immorality and squalor
were prevalent, played their part in giving currency to
saner views on the peasantry and dispelling many of the
illusions of old-fashioned National Romanticism. Later
generations have complained that Bjørnson's stories of
peasant life depict the rural dweller in "søndagsklær" (in
his Sunday-best) and give a far too idyllic picture of the
rural scene. Let it be said here that the present-day reader
will probably feel that they are somewhat sentimental. All
the same they provide delightful reading, and contain
qualities of style and a compactness and freshness often
lacking in his later and more ambitious works. Bjørnson
was also a man of the theatre. In 1857 he was appointed
chief of the theatre in Bergen and in the same year his play,
Between the Battles ("Mellem Slagene") was performed at
the Christiania Theatre. Further plays based on episodes
from Norwegian history followed, notably, *Sigurd Slembe*
(1862). This play has much in common in subject with
Ibsen's *The Pretenders*. Sigurd Slembe is a pretender
to the Norwegian throne, with a better right than Duke
Skule had in Ibsen's play but, like Skule, he fails to make

good his claim. Bjørnson emphasizes the indisciplined in Sigurd's character and shows how he is motivated by ambition rather than a belief in his destiny as a king. He is a man whose great abilities mark him out as a leader, yet whose defects of character make disaster certain for him. Bjørnson was never tired of pointing out the evil consequences of faulty self-discipline and lack of forbearance in the face of provocation; in his Peasant Stories the lesson is often repeated. In *Sigurd Slembe* Bjørnson succeeded better than in any other of his historical plays in creating an authentic historical atmosphere with real figures and, at the same time, provided himself with a vehicle for the handling of ideas. In *Mary Queen of Scots* ("Maria Stuart i Skotland", 1864) he succeeds less well — it is a colourful play, but the character of Mary was too foreign to Bjørnson to be understood by him.

CHAPTER VIII

DANISH LITERATURE 1870–1950

(a) 1870–1900.

The loss of Slesvig in 1864 following the Danish-Prussian War meant that Denmark's happy illusions were completely shattered. She woke up from her romantic dreams to bitter reality. But the time was ripe for reorientation in many fields. An important social and political development was taking place, also in Denmark. The Danes were beginning to realise that their literature was stagnant and entirely out of touch with the new scientific, philosophical and political ideas outside, such as Darwinism, Utilitarianism, Positivism, and Socialism. Young writers were still using the Romantic style; but this had now lost its charm and its appeal. There was a latent tension: something new had to come.

It came. *Det moderne gennembrud* is the Danish term used to describe the new movement in which a modern (i. e. Naturalistic or Realistic) literature 'broke through' — a movement of which Georg Brandes was the spiritual leader.

GEORG BRANDES (1842–1927) was not a creative writer, and yet his influence on Scandinavian literature after 1870 was greater than that of any other single person. He came from a family of Danish Jews, and early devoted his life to literary studies. His reading of Kierkegaard temporarily shattered his agnosticism, and his acquaintance with the works of Taine and Sainte-Beuve taught him the method of criticism depending on psychological analysis, and gave him a profound understanding of the great perspectives in literature. John Stuart Mill, whom he met personally, and whose two books *The Subjection of Women* and *Utilitarianism* he translated into Danish, influenced his social views. He felt it his mission to awaken the Danes and bring Denmark out of her backwater and isolation. Henrik Ibsen, whom he met in Germany, confirmed him in this conviction and said to him: "Now you must go home and tease the Danes; and I will taunt the Norwegians," and in a letter, Ibsen charged Brandes to become the leader of the "revolution of the spirit" for which he himself was fighting.

The great battle started on November 3, 1871. That was the day on which Georg Brandes gave the first, in the University of Copenhagen, of a series of public lectures which inaugurated a new epoch in Danish literature. From the introductory lecture it was clear that a revolution had begun. The lecturer — who was already well known for several scholarly works — did not attempt to conceal that his new *rôle* was that of agitator. His object was to wake up the Danes, "who are usually forty years behind Europe," and who were still sticking to the Romantic traditions of the beginning of the century, that is to a reaction against Radical ideas which had, in fact, never reached Denmark at all. He stated as his main principle his belief in "the right of independent research and the ultimate victory of independent thought." He attacked the abstract idealism of Danish 19th century literature, and demanded from the modern that it concern itself with life and reality, not with dreams and fantasy, and that it work in the service of Progress, not in the service of Reaction. It was he who said: "That a literature lives today, shows itself by its setting us problems to debate."

Brandes's lectures continued for many years and were

published 1871–87 in six volumes under the title *Main Currents in Nineteenth Century Literature* ("Hovedstrømninger i det nittende Aarhundredes Literatur"). They are like a drama in six acts. The first three volumes describe Reaction increasing in Europe, but the fourth volume, entitled *Naturalism in England* ("Naturalismen i England") is the turning point. Byron is seen as a hero with whom, together with Keats, Shelley and Thomas Moore, begins a new period of progressive literature. In the two last volumes, Victor Hugo, George Sand and Heinrich Heine play the part of hero, and show the final defeat of Reaction in France and Germany.

Brandes's first lectures caused an enormous stir in Denmark. Radical Copenhagen intelligentsia were immediately attracted, Conservative opinion shocked and scandalized by this 'atheist Jew', who mocked the literary traditions of Denmark and wanted to turn everything upside down. Brandes paid the penalty, for he was not awarded the chair of aesthetics which fell vacant in 1872 – a clear injustice, as a result of which he went to Germany, where he remained for a number of years; while there, he wrote the first books on which his European fame is based.

Apart from the *Main Currents,* Brandes, during the 'seventies and 'eighties, wrote a number of scholarly studies, most of them tinged with rebellious Radicalism and European in outlook. His books on *Søren Kierkegaard, Ferdinand Lasalle,* and *Disraeli* (English title *Lord Beaconsfield*) were all written during the 'seventies. In the following decade he wrote *The Men of the 'Modern Breaking-Through'* ("Det moderne Gennembruds Mænd"), a book in which the general surveyed his Scandinavian troops and brothers-in-arms; and *Ludvig Holberg,* a brilliant introduction to the work of Holberg, in which there is implied a comparison between Holberg's and his own 'European mission'. Among other books, *Danish Poets* ("Danske Digtere"), containing a remarkable analysis of Bødtcher, Hauch, Paludan-Müller and Winther, shows his ability to appreciate writers whose views differed widely from his own. During the 'eighties, Brandes began to lose faith in democracy and developed, under the influence of Nietzsche whom he made known to Denmark, a philosophy of "aristocratic Radicalism". In his book entitled *Great Men, the Main Source of Culture* ("Det store Menneske, Kulturens Kilde", 1890) he expresses his belief in Nietzsche's 'hero worship'. The many biographies of great men — *Shakespeare, Goethe, Voltaire, Cæsar* and *Michelangelo* — written during the next thirty years, reflect this attitude, and indeed his own *Autobiography* ("Levned", 1905–08) might be mentioned in this connexion. His famous book on *Shakespeare* is a good example of these 'hero books', for although he did an immense amount of research on the subject, it is his use of psychological interpretation which makes the book interesting. He attempts to solve the Shakespearean riddles and elucidate the so-called "dark period" in Shakespeare's life by a process of personal identification with Shakespeare. The result is an inspired and fascinating book, in which, however, Shakespeare appears as the romantic figure Brandes would like him to be. It is not quite without justice that Brandes commented bitterly as an old man that he was "an old romanticist who had spent his life attacking Romanticism."

In a number of books and articles Brandes discussed contemporary problems in European politics. His *Impressions of Poland* ("Indtryk fra Polen", 1888), his *Impressions of Russia* ("Indtryk fra Rusland", 1888), and his two books on the First World War and its consequences should be mentioned, along with a number of articles in which he protested against the injustices suffered by national and racial minorities in Europe. He was the only Dane of his generation to whom all Europe listened. His hatred of violence and tyranny was great, and he never lacked courage in expressing it.

As a young man Brandes was denounced as "a prophet of ungodliness, suicide and free love", and in his old age the attack was resumed, on his writing some anti-theological books, among which *Jesus, a Myth* ("Sagnet om Jesus") is best known. The worship of Greek culture, to which he remained faithful throughout his life, is beautifully expressed in one of his last books, *Hellas, Travels in Greece* ("Hellas", 1925).

A Naturalistic and Realistic literature would have arisen in Denmark if Georg Brandes had never existed, but its special form, not only in Denmark, but also in Sweden and Norway, was to a great extent due to his inspiration and guidance. He was passionate, and his passion was infectious. His own generation, and the next, were both faced with the problem of accepting or rejecting his ideas. Even today discussion about him has not ceased.

One of the first Danish writers to be influenced by Brandes was J. P. JACOBSEN (1847–85), who published his first work the year after Brandes had demanded a new literature, based on a realisation of contemporary problems. Jacobsen responded with *Mogens* (1872), the story of a young man who lives in a world of dreams, from which a tragic meeting with reality awakens him to bitter disillusionment. He seeks escape in dissipation, until a woman's love restores his belief in human happiness, this time in a real, not a dream, world.

The story of Mogens reflected to a great extent Jacobsen's own development. He had also been a romantic dreamer, as his early (then unpublished) poems and lyrical monologues bear witness. But the sensitive dreamer was at the same time a sober natural scientist, a botanist, who had distinguished himself with a thesis on fresh-water algae, had read Darwin, and had translated both *The Origin of*

Species and *The Descent of Man* into Danish. He went through a religious crisis, from which he emerged a declared atheist, but his mind was split between scientific observation and romantic dreaming, which prevented him from finding his true literary form. With *Mogens* he had made his choice, for the philosophy underlying it is closely related to that which Brandes preaches in *Main Currents*.

The style in which *Mogens* is written is a classic example of Naturalism, with its detailed, almost scientific, description of Nature, and of man as part of Nature, guided by his instincts and desires. The botanist is recognizable, especially in the introduction, in which every tree, every plant, and indeed every natural event, is described in the minutest detail: an embroidery of words; a musical and harmonious style, with a frequent use of inversion and alliteration. In France, Zola had defined a work of art as "a corner of Nature, seen through a temperament." *Mogens* was Jacobsen's corner of Nature, photographically accurate, but seen through his eminently artistic temperament. A Danish Naturalistic literature had been inaugurated.

Two novels, a volume of stories, and a small number of poems — that is J. P. Jacobsen's entire contribution to Danish literature. He died young — he suffered from consumption and knew that he had only a short time to live — but he was also a very slow worker: every sentence he wrote was filed and polished, and he was always at great pains to find exactly the qualifying adjective or adverb covering the precise shade of meaning he had in mind. As a result, his style is often precious and overloaded, and leaves nothing to the reader's imagination; but in spite of this, he was a sensitive artist, and his books have survived.

J. P. Jacobsen's first novel, *Marie Grubbe,* appeared in 1876. It is a psychological study of a 17th century lady, whose strange fate had also inspired both Blicher and Andersen to write about her. Before writing the book, Jacobsen made extensive studies of 17th century language, social manners, fashions, architecture, furniture, and so on, so that every detail would be absolutely accurate from an historical point of view. But more important than historical accuracy was the solving of a psychological riddle; like Flaubert and Zola he looked on human beings as human animals; it is by her instincts and secret desires that Marie Grubbe is forced into self-degradation.

Jacobsen's other novel, *Niels Lyhne* (1880), which depicts contemporary life, is the story of a man's evolution, and here again he is concerned with the problem of dream *versus* reality — his own problem, which he never solved, except in his books. It is a novel which sets problems to debate; especially those of atheism, of free love, and of marriage. But first and foremost it is concerned with the difficulties of being a consistent atheist. There is no abstract idealism in this book; its disillusioned philosophy is based on the idea that life is a difficult and complicated process, which must be "taken as it is" and allowed to "follow its own laws", and that we must learn to face death, "the difficult death", which is the gateway to nothing at all.

Death plays an important part in all Jacobsen's works. In the story *Fru Fønss,* that of a woman's choice between her children and the man she loves, Fru Fønss's farewell letter to her children shows Jacobsen's awareness of his own approaching death.

It is as a writer of stories that Jacobsen ranks highest. *A Shot in the Fog* ("Et Skud i Taagen"), *Two Worlds* ("To Verdener"), and *The Plague in Bergamo* ("Pesten i Bergamo") especially, are beautiful word pictures; they have all the charm of the sketches of a great artist and leave far more to the imagination than do the novels.

His few poems, especially his *Arabesques,* have a rare and indefinable beauty; there were, after all, emotions and sentiments which the Naturalistic prose writer could express only in poetry.

HOLGER DRACHMANN (1846–1908) made his literary début in 1872 with a volume of poems. He was then a staunch supporter of Brandes: unorthodox, rebellious, infected with revolutionary ideas and with a contempt for the stuffy atmosphere of Denmark as compared with the fresh air of Europe. In 1871 he had spent some time in London, where he met Socialist dock-workers from the East End, and French *communards* who had fled to England following the defeat of the Paris Commune. These meetings inspired his poem *English Socialists* ("Engelske Socialister"), and similar revolutionary notes are struck in *King Mob* and other of his early poems.

Gradually, however, Drachmann gave up his revolutionary *rôle* and took up an attitude of anti-orthodox individualism, a Bohemian disguised as a happy-go-lucky and carefree *landsknecht*, with anti-bourgeois tendencies and democratic sympathies for ordinary people, especially fishermen and sailors.

It was only after the dissolution of his first marriage that he gave up posing, and produced some genuine poetry, full of introspection and bitter self-accusation. He gave up acting and developed a form of expression which was completely his own. The poem *Sakuntala*, written in Munich after he had seen a performance of the Indian play of that name, reflected his anguish. Here is the first stanza: —

> I could not slumber for longing;
> there brushed my brow
> sweet blossomy air,
> streaming in here at my window
> like a river of perfume rare;
> I listened as lofty palm-trees
> softly soughed

their plaintive song
that whispered me, where I waited long:
Sakuntala, Sakuntala.

Jeg kunde for Længsel ej sove,
en Blomstervind
slog mig imod,
strømmed herind ad mit Vindu
som en vellugtaandende Flod;
jeg hørte de høje Palmer
suse svagt
med sød Musik;
det hvisked, ihvor jeg stod og gik:
Sakuntala, Sakuntala.

In the 'eighties, Drachmann turned violently against Brandes and his Radical views, and became a poet of romantic and patriotic sentiment. Following his second marriage, the revolutionary turned Conservative, and wrote poems in praise of peaceful married life. His poem *East of the Sun and West of the Moon* ("Østen for Sol og vesten for Maane", 1880) and his play entitled *Once Upon a Time* — ("Der var engang —", 1885) were both in the Romantic tradition which he had previously scorned. Drachmann had abandoned the Naturalistic world of grey everyday problems in favour of the shining fairy-tale world of imaginative poetry. That did not last long either. Drachmann fell in love with a young actress in a Copenhagen music-hall, his second marriage was dissolved, and "Edith" — as he called the girl — became the inspiration not only of some of his finest love poems, but also of his only important novel, *Signed Away* ("Forskrevet", 1890). In this work, the two main characters reflect the two sides of Drachmann's personality: the aesthete, and the rebellious Bohemian. Among his later works his *Melodramas* deserve special mention, and especially the verse drama in which he retells the Edda legend of *Wayland the Smith* ("Vølund Smed", 1894). Drachmann holds a very high place in Danish literature as a lyric poet, passionate, impulsive, and capricious. As a brother-in-arms he was unreliable, for his very temperament was lyrical and impressionable, with quickly changing moods, greatly influenced by the women in his life. He saw his own changeable nature in the sea, and this was a favourite subject to which he returned time after time. His poetic faults are easy to see, his wordiness, his egotism, his poses, but in his best poems he can be compared to Swinburne. In his mastery of verse and phrase, and his imagery, he ranks with Ewald as a superb lyric poet; but he is also indebted to Oehlenschläger, Winther and Aarestrup; to Heine and Byron; his translation of *Don Juan* is probably the best in any language.

The novels and peasant stories of SOPHUS SCHANDORPH (1836—1901) are prose Realism of little artistic value. VILHELM TOPSØE (1840—81), who was politically an opponent of Georg Brandes, is a more refined Realist, a fine psychologist depicting contemporary life with subtle irony. EDVARD BRANDES (1847—1931) — a brother of Georg — treats contemporary problems in his not very inspired plays.

*

The moral in Andersen's story *The Ugly Duckling* was expressed in these words: "It doesn't matter about being born in a duckyard, as long as you are hatched from a swan's egg". This represented Andersen's — and the, then generally, accepted — Romantic conception of the genius, as in Oehlenschläger's *Aladdin:* the genius predestined to greatness. A great new author, a man who was to become Denmark's greatest novelist, turned the moral of Andersen's tale upside down in a story entitled *Eagle's Flight* ("Ørneflugt"), which ended with these words: "For after all, it is no use having been hatched from an eagle's egg, if you've been brought up in the duckyard."

This new writer was HENRIK PONTOPPIDAN (1857–1943), who stands head and shoulders above all other novelists of this period. His first works were some stories, published in the 'eighties under the titles *Pictures of Village Life* ("Landsbybilleder") and *From the Cottages* ("Fra Hytterne"), in which, with an undercurrent of indignation, he revealed the injustices among the peasants in an age which boasted of democracy, humanitarianism and progress. In the stories entitled *Clouds* ("Skyer", 1890) Pontoppidan attacked with searing irony the lack of fighting spirit among the Danish farmers at a time when the highest interests of democracy were at stake, since the upper classes were trying to introduce political tyranny, completely disregarding the constitutional rights of the common people. In these stories Pontoppidan poured scorn on the farmers for contenting themselves with verbal protests, demonstrations and meetings, instead of proving their love of liberty by open revolution against their tyrants.

In several short novels, such as *Vigil* ("Nattevagt", 1894), *The Polar Bear* ("Isbjørnen", 1887), *Old Adam* ("Den gamle Adam", 1895), *Højsang* (1896), *Borgmester Hoeck og Hustru* (1905) and *Hans Kvast og Melusine* (1907), and in several stories, of which *The Royal Guest* ("Den kongelige Gæst", 1908) should be mentioned, Pontoppidan discussed the political, moral and religious problems of his day. He detested superficial lyricism, emotional intoxication, and the verbose embroidery of J. P. Jacobsen. His own style was sober, virile and objective. He states his artistic creed as a belief in "the clarity of thought and the masculine balance of mind."

But Pontoppidan's greatest contribution to Danish literature are his three long novel cycles, *The Promised Land* ("Det forjættede Land", in three volumes, 1891–95), *Lucky*

Per ("Lykke-Per", in eight volumes, 1898–1904) and *The Kingdom of the Dead* ("De Dødes Rige", in five volumes, 1912–16). They are all concerned with contemporary Denmark, and they are the most penetrating and convincing, but the least flattering, analyses of Danish national character in the entire literature, and his pessimism grows from cycle to cycle.

In *The Promised Land* the main character, Pastor Emmanuel Hansted, is a burning idealist, who attempts to do what Pontoppidan had attempted in his early youth, to identify himself with the peasant population among which he lives, to marry the daughter of a farmer and become one of them, but fails (as Pontoppidan did himself), because it is an artificial attempt. The idealistic visionary ends in a lunatic asylum. It is left to the reader to decide whether he was a Messiah or a Don Quixote. This important trilogy may be regarded as Pontoppidan's disillusioned commentary on Ibsen's *Brand* (see p. 141).

In *Lucky Per* Pontoppidan has portrayed a Danish equivalent of *Per Gynt,* called Per Sidenius. Like Pontoppidan he is the son of a parson and studies engineering. He is like the young eagle, brought up in a duckyard, and his wings have been clipped. He is portrayed as the national type, *the* Dane, lyrical and emotional, but without true passion, a man without power of action or moral courage, a Danish troll who hides in his hill, scared of the light. For the Danes are "a Lilliputian race, with large intellectual brains, but with the powerless limbs of an infant." In contrast to the tamed and frustrated Per, Pontoppidan has drawn Jacobe Salomon, a young Jewess who feels the passion, both in love and hate, which Per lacks.

The Kingdom of the Dead is a desperate warning to a nation which appears to be heading for doom and destruction. Pontoppidan presents a horrifying picture of a Denmark where men and women have become sterile in a frame of "progress" and "democracy". Lyrical emotions are plentiful, but the ability to love is lacking. That is the fundamental rottenness in the state of Denmark. Pontoppidan is a moralist, but not an evangelist: unlike Paludan-Müller, who holds the Ten Commandments in his uplifted hand. He is more like a doctor who diagnoses the patient's illness and tells him the unvarnished truth, without attempting to soften the blow by prescribing patent medicines. Anyone who wants to understand the Danes, should read Pontoppidan's works, including his memoirs, entitled *On the Way to Myself* ("Undervejs til mig selv"). From these one realises that although he wrote only *about* the Danes and *to* the Danes, Pontoppidan holds high rank among the men who have devoted their lives to the liberation of the human spirit. – In 1917 he was awarded the Nobel prize.

"We suffer ourselves, and make other people suffer as well – that is all we know." That, in a nutshell, is the gospel of disillusionment preached by Pontoppidan's contemporary, HERMAN BANG (1857–1912). As a novelist he cultivated the small things: insignificant people, the grey and lonely and miserable men and women who are normally overlooked, because nothing ever seems to happen in the monotonous drabness of their undramatic lives. Herman Bang felt their fate to be tragic, but at the same time he could look at them humorously, and he showed that sometimes something did happen in their lives, after all. In several novels and short stories – his so-called tragic idylls – he identified himself with the insignificant and unimportant people, the *Silent Beings* ("Stille Existenser", 1886) who lived *Under the Yoke* ("Under Aaget", 1890). In his books we meet the elderly spinster, who had once dreamed of becoming a great ballerina, but is now forced to earn her living as an itinerant dancing instructress of clumsy peasant children; the music lover, who had once

believed that he would become a great singer, but who
became instead an underpaid schoolmaster in the unbear-
able drabness of a middle-class slum; and the nice young
girl from the small provincial town whose romantic dreams
and longing for tenderness were stifled in a tedious marriage
with a respectable station-master. Bang shows how cruelly
life has treated these people, the step-children of life; he
felt one of them himself: life had shattered his own dreams
and illusions.

In some of Bang's novels there is a sickly and degenerate
fin de siècle atmosphere and a sophisticated manner; this
is especially so in his first novel, *Hopeless Generations*
("Haabløse Slægter", 1880). Some of his later works are
complete failures, because outside his own particular field
he had little or no talent; this is shown very clearly in
his two ambitious novels *Mikaël* and *Those without a
Fatherland* ("De uden Fædreland").

Bang's style was greatly influenced by that of Hans Andersen, but even more by that of Jonas Lie, whose use of
the impressionistic style he imitated and carried to perfection. He is a master of indirect characterization; the
sensitivity of his writing is such that a pause may be more
important than a word, a comma alter the meaning of a
whole sentence. His best novels are *By the Wayside* ("Ved
Vejen", 1886), *Tine* (1889) and *Ludvigsbakke* (1896); *The
White House* ("Det hvide Hus", 1898) and *The Grey House*
("Det graa Hus", 1901) — in which he has largely drawn
on memories of his own childhood — are two other fine
examples of his psychological penetration.

KARL GJELLERUP (1857–1919) had for a time a certain
European reputation, for which, surprisingly enough to us
now, in 1917 he was awarded the Nobel prize. He began
as a disciple of Brandes, a fanatic Radical who attacked the
theologians violently in his first novel, entitled *The Disciple
of the Germans* ("Germanernes Lærling", 1882). His

enthusiasm for German abstract philosophy, however, severed him from Brandes, and later he bitterly opposed the movement to which he himself had belonged for a time. The metaphysical idealism in his later novels has made most of them unreadable today. The only exceptions are *Minna* (1889) and *The Mill* ("Møllen", 1896), which have survived because of their poetic beauty. Gjellerup lived mostly in Germany and gradually became more German than Danish.

*

In the 'nineties a Neo-Romantic poetic revival took place: emotions and fantasy were reinstated. This was a demonstration against the idea that literature should debate problems, and the worship of beauty took the place of the worship of truth. The lyric poets of the 'nineties called themselves "Symbolists", because they stated that their object was "to express the inexpressible in symbolic form." They had learned from Baudelaire, Huysmans, Mallarmé and Verlaine, and from the Flemish poet Maeterlinck. Shelley was another of their favourites (cf. Sophus Claussen's masterly translation of *The Sensitive Plant*). A rediscovery of the poet's soul took place, and instead of expressing social criticism, or discussing contemporary political, ideological or moral problems, their poetry described mental processes and religious and mystic experiences.

Their leader was JOHANNES JØRGENSEN (born 1866), who was also the editor of their magazine, *The Tower*. His early poems reflect a desperate longing for a religious creed, which he found ultimately in Roman Catholicism, and since his conversion all his writing has been tendentious: his poems, his *Parables* ("Lignelser") and stories, his many books of travel, his *Autobiography* ("Mit Livs Legende", in seven volumes, 1916–28) and his biographies of saints (especially of *St. Francis* and of *St. Catherine of Siena*).

VIGGO STUCKENBERG (1863–1905) was a close personal friend of Johannes Jørgensen, but refused to become a convert to the Roman Catholic faith. His stories and tales are mostly forgotten now, but his poems have a subtle, pale beauty, and there is an intimate tenderness in their expressions of sad resignation.

SOPHUS CLAUSSEN (1865–1931) has none of Stuckenberg's paleness. He is the satyr among the Symbolists, a lustful and sensual lover of female beauty, a Pantheistic lover of nature, and a sophisticated and capricious aesthete, whose poems are often obscure riddles, in which all manifestations of nature have symbolic significance. His poetry is frequently diabolical and cynical in its humour, but can be tender and subdued. His taste is often Gallic, rather than Danish, but he loved the Danish countryside. He can mock the ludicrous meaninglessness of life, but he can also cry out in agony a warning against its meaningless destruction, as in his prophetic poem *The Revolt of the Atoms* ("Atomernes Oprør"). He is the most difficult poet of his generation to understand, but his poetry is greater and more significant than that of any of the others.

HELGE RODE (1870–1937) was a playwright, a critic, and a poet. In his dramas and his criticism he attacked modern intellectualism, especially the agnosticism of Brandes and the Darwinism of Johannes V. Jensen. As a poet he was a Neo-Romantic and a religious mystic. He writes with a strange ethereal beauty: like Ariel playing on the Aeolian harp.

LUDVIG HOLSTEIN (1864–1943) is another lyric poet, whose poetry is less abstract than that of Rode. He is a fastidious artist who never tires of watching the ever-recurring miracle of growing, budding, and blossoming. The fine delicacy of his description, for instance of the beauty of an apple orchard, is characteristic of the sober clarity of his expression: his religion is entirely Pantheistic. As a poet he is more akin to Goethe and Oehlenschläger than to his own generation of Symbolists. Other important Neo-Romantic poets of the same period are SOPHUS MICHAËLIS, THOR LANGE and NIELS MØLLER. Among the writers of the 'nineties there is only one prose writer of true distinction, GUSTAV WIED (1858—1914), one of Denmark's greatest humorists. His wit is cynical and bitter; his laughter that of a disillusioned man who watches with a pitying smile the human race performing on the stage of the puppet theatre called life. His philosophy is a caricature of that of J. P. Jacobsen: "We should feed our carp, make our whisky stronger, and leave the rest to the Lord!" His two best novels, *Livsens Ondskab* and *Knagsted,* are masterpieces of malicious wit, but there is an underlying tenderness and a feeling of solitude which he cannot entirely suppress. His humour may sometimes recall Dickens, and his pessimism Strindberg, but he has none of the emotion and intensity of Dickens, and none of the mysticism of Strindberg. Among his best and wittiest comedies are $2 \times 2 = 5$, several small one-act plays, and his so-called satyr-plays, such as *Nobility, Clergy, Burghers and Peasants* ("Adel, Gejstlighed, Borgere og Bønder"), *The Weaker Sex* ("Det svage Køn"), and *Dancing Mice* ("Dansemus"), which is a grotesque picture of contemporary Denmark. In it appear some white mice in their tread-mill; their futile running has a symbolic significance: "They do not appear to be amused by the dance, but they cannot stop it — *Soli deo gloria!*" Wied is the wittiest Danish playwright since Holberg and Wessel.

Several other good, and some excellent, writers belong to the period 1870—1900. Among novelists, the most distinguished is KARL LARSEN (1860—1930), who caught the atmosphere of Copenhagen and drew a picture of Danish "Cockneys" with fine linguistic precision. Among dramatists, the most noteworthy are SVEN LANGE (1868—1930),

Einar Christiansen (1861—1939) and Henri Nathansen (1869—1944).

During this period several women made important contributions to Danish literature, especially Gyrithe Lemche (1866—1945), whose novel *Edwardsgave* (in five volumes, 1901—12) is the story of a family. Her trilogy *Guardians of the Temple* ("Tempelvogtere", 1926—28) is a novel concerned with the emancipation of women. Agnes Henningsen (born 1868) is a brilliant writer whose novels — among which *Love's Seasons* ("Kærlighedens Aarstider") is the most important — are concerned almost entirely with the erotic experiences of the emancipated woman. Her candid and charming *Memoirs* (of which five volumes have been published so far) may also be regarded as an important literary work. Karin Michaëlis (1872—1949) is a fine psychologist. Her novel *The Dangerous Age* ("Den farlige Alder", 1910), concerning the problems of woman at the climacteric, has been translated into many languages and made her a great name. Other important novels of hers are *The Tree of Good and Evil* ("Træet paa godt og ondt"), *Mother* ("Mor") and *The Girl with the Glass Splinters* ("Pigen med Glasskaarene").

(b) *1900—1920.*

Among 20th century Danish writers two men stand out as world famous. They are Martin Andersen Nexø and Johannes V. Jensen.

Martin Andersen Nexø was born in 1869 in the slums of Copenhagen, but spent most of his childhood on the island of Bornholm in the Baltic. He was first a shepherd's boy, then an apprentice to a shoemaker, and eventually a bricklayer, until he came in contact with Socialist ideas and with Danish trade unionism. From then on he devoted his life and literary talents to the cause of the working classes, first as a Social Democrat, but after the Russian Revolution as a convinced and uncompromising Communist.

Nexø's fame is based almost entirely on his two novels, *Pelle the Conqueror* ("Pelle Erobreren", in four volumes, 1906—10) and *Ditte: Daughter of Man* ("Ditte Menneskebarn", in five volumes, 1917—21). *Pelle the Conqueror* has been described as the great epic of the proletariat; its hero represents all the best and most valuable qualities of the working classes, and becomes a leader at a time when the workers were only slowly beginning to liberate themselves. The novel is a great work of art, written by a man who knows poverty and hunger from personal experience, and the first volume in particular is unforgettable, with its description of Pelle's childhood on Bornholm, for which Nexø has largely drawn on his own recollections. There is a warmth and humour in this book, and an optimistic belief in the fundamental goodness and kindness of primitive man. Its influence has been very great on millions of readers, not only in Scandinavia, but in many other countries all over the world, particularly Germany and the Soviet Union.

In *Ditte: Daughter of Man* we follow the fate of a proletarian girl from the cradle to the grave. The human warmth in this novel is even greater than in *Pelle the Conqueror;* the illegitimately born Ditte, whom life treats so miserably, is a moving symbol of true human greatness: she gives with both hands, although she receives so little. There are no cheap panegyrics in the description of Ditte, either, but the author inspires belief in the fundamental unselfishness and tenderness of a young working-class girl.

Among Nexø's other books *Midt i en Jærntid* (English title: *In God's Land*) should be mentioned. It is a bitter attack on the egoism of Danish farmers, but it lacks the warmth and humour of the two novels just mentioned.

11*

Several of his short stories are of high literary quality, and like all his other works they are about poor people. His collection of stories entitled *The Passengers of the Empty Seats* ("De tomme Pladsers Passagerer", 1921) was dedicated to the Russian people, and Nexø's impressions of his many visits to the Soviet Union are recorded in several travel books which show his enthusiasm for the Russian Revolution and for Soviet Communism.

A sequel to *Pelle the Conqueror,* published since the war and called *Morten the Red* ("Morten hin Røde"), is a mixture of memoirs and fiction, and reflects Nexø's views on the development of the Danish working class movement in this century, his despair and disgust at seeing the Socialist leaders becoming reformists instead of revolutionaries, bureaucrats instead of fighters, and dropping Socialism for Social Reform.

Nexø's *Memoirs,* published in four volumes during the 'thirties, rank among the finest in Danish literature. Like Hans Christian Andersen, Nexø came from the lowest class of society; but, unlike Andersen, he never tried to escape by seeking refuge in another social class. Andersen's *Story of My Life* was a fascinating, but sentimental, autobiography, which all the time seeks to arouse the reader's sympathy. Nexø does not ask for pity; his memoirs are wholesome and virile, human and warm-hearted.

JOHANNES V. JENSEN (1873–1950) is a North Jutlander, from the district called Himmerland, the scenery and people of which he has described so wonderfully in his *Himmerland Tales* ("Himmerlandshistorier", 1898–1910). They are revelations of primitive minds and instincts, made by a great artist who knows the secrets of those silent and shy peasants. *The Thundercalf* ("Tordenkalven") may be taken as an example; it is the story of a well known Himmerland character who had been a strong young man, but fell from a horse and was crippled and bent double for the rest of his life. "One of his legs was too short, but his gigantic strength was in him still. He looked like the history of Denmark." He is described in these words: —

> The Thundercalf was like a landscape, or an old countryside, with his nobbly hat that looked like a tumulus, and his eyes that shone like sun-baked window panes in an old house. His beard and hair were like hoary shrubs; his back was hunch'ed like a hill, and his ears were like gravel pits. Each corner of his mouth was like a puddle; the backs of his hands were furrowed like a fallow-field. And the harsh and sullen weather showed in his features — rain and sunshine, the onrushing wind, and the sullen mists.

Jensen's *Himmerland Tales* show us an unknown world, a world of primitive selfishness and kind helpfulness, a world beautiful and ugly, of unhappy, irresolute people who dare not believe in themselves, of incompetent fools whose fantastic conceit offers them compensation for their social degradation, and of people whose sole moral code is never to reveal their true feeling, and whose language is that of understatement or complete silence. It is a *Heimat* literature of high quality, and can be compared with John Steinbeck at his best.

Johannes V. Jensen's first important novel, *The Fall of the King* ("Kongens Fald"), was published in 1901. It is one of the most remarkable works of fiction in Danish, a bitter book revealing what Jensen considers to be the Danish national character, but at the same time containing the most charming descriptions of Denmark and the Danes. Irresolution and lack of spontaneity, a tendency to make life exclusively an intellectual or emotional affair, these are the qualities which, according to Jensen, have made Denmark so small and insignificant a country. Selma Lagerlöf described *The Fall of the King* as written "partly by a weird, wild spirit of nature, partly by a monastic chronicle-writer, partly by a poetic buffoon."

After a journey round the world Johannes V. Jensen wrote a charming travel book, *The Forests* ("Skovene", 1904), and a collection of *Exotic Short Stories* ("Eksotiske Noveller", 1907—15). The two novels, *Madame d'Ora* (1904) and *The Wheel* ("Hjulet", 1905), are based on Goethe's *Faust:* Faust, Gretchen and Mephisto transplanted into 20th century New York and Chicago.

Jensen's most important work of fiction is *The Long Journey* ("Den lange Rejse", in six volumes, 1908—22). Darwinism is the Alpha and Omega in this book, for the journey he describes is the long journey of humanity, from the baboon stage of man in pre-glacial times to the time of Christopher Columbus — a period of several million years. His ambitious purpose was to write a new Bible, a Darwinian Bible, based on scientific knowledge about the evolution of man, and the result is a Myth, full of poetry, in which he has used elements from the Old Testament, from Scandinavian and Greek mythology, from the Icelandic sagas, from Snorri and Saxo, and welded them together with knowledge derived from geology, anthropology, archaeology and ethnography. Into it are worked also recollections of his own childhood and impressions from his many travels. Swift and Defoe, Jack London, Kipling and H. G. Wells all have their share in this great work.

Between 1906 and 1940 Jensen published eight volumes of what he calls *Myths* ("Myter"). They are concentrated essays, or tales, of high poetic quality. The starting point is often a description of some everyday object, but a deeper perspective is introduced whereby, often by means of distant recollections and associations, and by ideas of evolution, the original object is transformed into something far more significant; it has gained a fourth dimension — the unimportant has become important. In Jensen's *Myths* is to be found some of the most varied and beautiful descriptive writing in Danish literature; it is an important innovation in literary form, which has so far not received the attention outside Denmark which it deserves. In this connexion, also, should be mentioned Jensen's many collections of *Essays*, especially *The Gothic Renaissance* ("Den gotiske Renaissance", 1901), *Introduction to Our Age* ("Introduktion til vor Tidsalder", 1915), *Aesthetics and Evolution* ("Æstetik og Udvikling", 1923), which is a commentary on *The Long Journey*, and *Evolution and Morals* ("Evolution og Moral", 1925). They all show his Darwinian philosophy.

Johannes V. Jensen is also a great and original lyric poet, influenced both by Heine and Walt Whitman. There is a masculine soberness in his poetry, and a sense of colour and composition which has left its mark on several poets of a later generation. — In 1944 Jensen was awarded the Nobel prize.

Like Jensen, JEPPE AAKJÆR (1866–1930) is a Jutlander. His parents were poor peasants on a small farm in the moor district. In Copenhagen he became an adherent of Brandes's Radical ideas, and in his early novels he expresses a violent condemnation of the exploitation of the farm labourer by the wealthy farmers.

Aakjær is great, however, not as a novelist, but as a lyric poet, a Danish Robert Burns, whose *Songs of the Rye* ("Rugens Sange") and many other volumes have become the property of all Danes, in a way which is very rare with poetry. In Denmark it is very unusual to meet anyone over the age of ten who does not know at least one or two of Aakjær's many poems, and the explanation lies in their wonderful musical quality: many of them have become the most popular songs in Denmark. There is no social propaganda whatsoever in Aakjær's poetry; in simple and

beautiful language he sings the praises of the Danish countryside and pays homage to the faithfully toiling peasant
population. There is no great depth in Aakjær's poetry;
its popularity lies in the fact that he paints a real Denmark
in such a simple and unsophisticated way that it is appreciated by both chilaren and grown-ups alike. Here is an
example, the first three stanzas of *Oats* ("Havren"):

I'm the oats. I've little bells on me;
more than twenty to a straw you'll see.
They are what the farmer calls my 'crop'.
God be good to him, that farmer chap.

I was sown while larks made happy song
over grassy hillocks all day long;
as the mumbling bumble bee-notes grew,
softly came a peewit's piping through . . .

Here's a thing cold reason would condemn —
I'm the skylark's song upon a stem;
lilting life, with summer pollen sprayed,
more than munching-stuff for beast and jade.

Jeg er Havren. Jeg har Bjælder paa,
mer end tyve, tror jeg, paa hvert Straa.
Bonden kalder dem for sine Fold.
Gud velsigne ham, den Bondeknold.

Jeg blev saa't, mens glade Lærker sang
over grønne Banker Dagen lang;
Humlen brumled dybt sin Melodi,
og et Rylefløjt gled ind deri . . .

Det kan kolde Hjerner ej forstaa:
Jeg er Lærkesangen paa et Straa,
Livets Rytme døbt i Sommerdræ,
mer en Gumlekost for Øg og Fæ.

Together with Aakjær should be mentioned two other Jutland poets, JOHAN SKJOLDBORG (1861–1936), who expresses, both in his poetry and in his novels, the sentiments of the Danish smallholder; and THØGER LARSEN (1875–1928), who cannot compete with Aakjær in the matter of popularity — with the exception of *The Danish Summer* ("Den danske Sommer"), a song in which he has captured all the atmosphere of the light summer nights; but the beauty, both in his earthy Jutland poems and of his cosmic poetry, is unique.

JAKOB KNUDSEN (1858–1917) is yet another representative of what has been called the "Jutland movement", but unlike Aakjær and Thøger Larsen he has mainly distinguished himself as a novelist. It is doubtful how far anyone unfamiliar with Denmark would understand Jakob Knudsen's books; they have as their background the Grundtvigian movement and the influence it has had on Danish farmers. His novels discuss Christian and moral, rather than social or political, questions. Jakob Knudsen is the Carlyle of Denmark, one who believes in the inequality of man and in the necessity of authority and obedience. He has little respect for so-called progress, and sees as its consequence only a generation without roots in the past. His views are often highly controversial; in *The Old Parson* ("Den gamle Præst", 1899) he advocates the right to destroy an evil man who has committed, from the legal point of view, no crime, and in *Lærer Urup* (1909) he vehemently attacks the overhumane treatment of criminals. Other important novels are *Progress* ("Fremskridt", 1907) and *Rooted* ("Rodfæstet", 1911), and *Fermentation* ("Gjæring", 1902) and its sequel *Clarification* ("Afklaring", 1902), in which two novels he contrasts the philosophies of Naturalism and Christianity, and in his novels *Fear* ("Angst", 1912) and *Courage* ("Mod", 1914) gives a personal interpretation of Luther, which reflects his own religious views.

In this connexion also three other authors deserve mention: MARIE BREGENDAHL (1867—1940), HARRY SØIBERG (born 1880) and THOMAS OLESEN LØKKEN (born 1877) — all three Jutlanders, who have won a place for themselves in Danish literature. Their works all contain faithful descriptions of the Jutland countryside and people.

HARALD KIDDE (1878—1918) follows the main tendencies of the lyric poets of the 'nineties. He is a solitary, introspective, and melancholy author, preaching a gospel of renunciation and humility. His chief works are the novels *Aage og Else* (in two volumes, 1902—03), *The Hero* ("Helten", 1912) and *Iron* ("Jærnet", 1918).

KNUD HJORTØ (1869—1932) is a keen and intelligent observer, whose novels, especially *Two Worlds* ("To Verdener"), *Dust and Stars* ("Støv og Stjerner"), and *Green Youth and Grey Souls* ("Grøn Ungdom og graa Sjæle"), are important in the development of the Danish psychological novel.

Two other lyric poets of this period should also be mentioned, the sensitive Naturalist KAJ HOFFMANN (1874—1949), and VALDEMAR RØRDAM (1872—1946). The latter is versatile, both as a poet and as a prose writer, and has learnt much from both Drachmann and Swinburne. His glorification of Denmark, his jingoism, and his *rôle* of patriotic moralist demanding sacrifices from his countrymen, had a certain effect, which was lost, however, when Rørdam praised Hitler and the Nazis during the Occupation of Denmark.

(c) 1920—1950.

The Danish novel has flourished in recent years, and a survey of the last three decades provides an interesting and many-coloured picture. In its manner it ranges from the dissector's knife, cutting mercilessly into the wounds of present conditions, to an individualistic escapism, art for art's sake! But of lasting value are a number of novels, contemporary or historical in their content, social or psychological, yet written by men and women who were deeply concerned with the future of their country;   and in much the same way as the shadow of the First World War lies over the novels of the 'twenties, so the shadow of Nazi Germany and the Second World War — the inevitability of which was seen by many — lies over the novels of the latter part of the 'thirties. And the period of the Occupation meant that all Danish authors discussing contemporary problems were gagged — or had to find new ways of expressing themselves, and in the latter half of the 'forties Danish novelists have been groping and experimenting, but it is too early yet to judge of results.

Characteristic of the first period are two Danish novelists who approach the problems of the unhealthy post-war period from almost opposite angles. They are Tom Kristensen and Jacob Paludan.

Tom Kristensen (born 1893), who is also known as a lyric poet and a critic, has written three novels, *Life's Arabesque* ("Livets Arabesk", 1921), *Somebody Else* ("En anden", 1923) and *Destruction* ("Hærværk", 1930), all reflecting the unhealthy atmosphere of the post-war period. In *Destruction* it is the gospel of 'destructionism' he preaches, and the drunkard-hero of this novel deliberately destroys himself in an anarchistic belief in the necessity of destroying everything — himself, first — before anything new can be achieved.

The chief novels of Jacob Paludan (born 1896) are *Birds Around the Light* ("Fugle omkring Fyret", 1925), *The Fields Ripen* ("Markerne modnes", 1927), and *Jørgen Stein* (1932 —33), in which he, also, deals with the post-war period, but explains the illness of contemporary Denmark in a different way. *Jørgen Stein*, especially, is a deeply pessimistic novel, in which he scourges his countrymen for their materialism, their wantonness, and their lack of morals. Curiously enough, they were both influenced by an English novelist: Tom Kristensen by D. H. Lawrence, and Paludan by Aldous Huxley. Tom Kristensen and Jacob Paludan — both great artists — were the most important representatives of "the generation that stumbled at the start", to quote an expression coined by Paludan to describe the people who had just grown up when the First World War broke out. Was that to be the fate of the Danish novel, to have to choose between the Scylla of destructive nihilism and the Charybdis of reactionary pessimism? Was there no road between?

There was. The novels of Hans Kirk, Knuth Becker and Harald Herdal — to mention three of the most outstanding social writers of this period — were of quite a different kind, and no less seriously concerned with the future of Denmark. HANS KIRK (born 1898) published his first novel, *The Fishermen* ("Fiskerne"), in 1928; it was followed by two others, *The Land Labourers* ("Daglejerne") and *The New Times* ("De nye Tider"). Kirk at one and the same time carries on the best traditions of the Danish novel and brings to it something completely new. In his work are elements of the Danish *Heimat* novels, and his descriptions are as faithful as a documentary. He is a Marxist and a Freudian, and his novels are the finest examples of social Realism in modern Danish literature.

KNUTH BECKER (born 1893) is a novelist, whose main work, the first volume of which was published in 1932, is still in progress. It is an autobiographical novel — about the boy Kai Gøtsche, an imaginative and sensitive child, who is driven to lies and crimes by the morbid morality of the grown-ups. It is a remarkable combination of social criticism and a penetrating analysis of a child's mind.

HARALD HERDAL (born 1900) is a Copenhagen proletarian

by birth and has followed in the footsteps of Andersen
Nexø. His novels are bitter and anti-capitalistic; he reveals mercilessly the rottenness, the filth, and the hypocrisy
of present society. He lacks Nexø's warmth and humour;
but the warmth and love which his novels lack are to be
found in his very fine poetry, which ranges from Socialist
agitation to personal love lyrics.

MOGENS KLITGAARD (1906–45) made his début in 1937
with a novel, entitled *A Man in a Tram* ("Der sidder en
Mand i en Sporvogn"), about the drab and dreary life of
a poor middle-class man; an important analysis of the
white collar proletariat. In all the six novels he wrote,
ordinary, unimportant people remained his favourite subject, even when, as in *The Red Feathers* ("De røde Fjer")
and *Hullabaloo in Nytorv* ("Ballade paa Nytorv") he delved
into history, which afforded a better outlet for his very
fine sense of humour. LECK FISCHER (born 1904) also
concerns himself in numerous novels, most of little artistic
value, with the problems of the Danish middle-classes. In
some of his plays he has shown a much finer artistic sense.

HANS MØLBJERG (born 1915) has attracted considerable
attention with his novel *The Farm* ("Gården", 1949), a
'collective novel', in which elements of the *Heimat* novel,
the social novel, and the psychological novel are beautifully
combined.

The novels of Jørgen Nielsen, Michael Tejn, Aage Dons
and H. C. Branner are pre-eminently psychological rather
than social. JØRGEN NIELSEN (1902–45) wrote five novels
and several outstanding stories between 1929 and 1944.
Most of them take place among Jutland peasants, and their
recurrent themes are suppressed feelings: hatred, sin and
fear. *The Depths* ("Dybet", 1940) is his most remarkable
work, a tragically intense story of silent hate and of the
desperate fight between a boy and his father.

Similar problems, but in a different social class, are the

subjects of the novels of MICHAEL TEJN (born 1911). *Dream and Reality* ("Drømmen og Virkeligheden", 1942) is his best, but it is still too early to decide what his capabilities are.

AAGE DONS (born 1903) is a sensitive and intelligent psychologist, among whose novels *The Soldiers' Well* ("Soldaterbrønden", 1936) and *The Rain on the Window Panes* ("Regnen paa Ruderne", 1948) are the best. Dons is absolutely devoid of any political and social tendencies whatsoever; he concentrates on feeling and penetrating analyses of the depths and conflicts of the human soul.

H. C. BRANNER (born 1903) has written five novels and several volumes of short stories. He is undoubtedly the most important psychologist in his generation, and his books deal with the loneliness of men, the dangers of fear, and the dangers of power. *The Dream about a Woman* ("Drømmen om en Kvinde", 1941) takes place in Denmark immediately before the war and is marked by the fear of what is to come. *The Story of Børge* ("Historien om Børge", 1942) is a novel which demonstrates Branner's unusual ability to reproduce, in artistic form, the thoughts and feelings of a child. His latest book, *The Horseman* ("Rytteren", 1949), is his finest, so far; in its penetrating psychology it is of even greater intensity than any of his previous books. As a short story-writer H. C. Branner is superb, undoubtedly the best among modern Danish writers, especially in his subtle understanding of children.

Apart from Branner the most important contemporary Danish novelist is probably MARTIN A. HANSEN (born 1909). After what appeared to be two social *Heimat* novels in 1935—37 he wrote a grotesque social satire, entitled *Jonathan's Journey* ("Jonathans Rejse", 1940), and an historical novel, *Happy Christopher* ("Lykkelige Kristoffer", 1945). His collection of short stories, *The Thorn Bush* ("Tornebusken", 1946), was written during the Occupation and deals with the conflict between illusion and reality. *The Partridge* ("Agerhønen", 1948) is another collection of short stories, written with an eminently artistic sensibility, and his collection of essays entitled *Thoughts in a Chimney* ("Tanker i en Skorsten", 1949) shows how seriously he is concerned with the functions of literature. In his early books he may sometimes recall Johannes V. Jensen, but of recent years he has shown a tendency towards an anti-intellectual mysticism, related to that of the youngest generation of Danish poets.

KNUD SØNDERBY (born 1909) began as an intelligent pupil of Hemmingway. His first novel, *In a Jazz Age* ("Midt i en Jazztid", 1931), was a book about a young group of sophisticated bourgeois, living a life of sexual promiscuity, with jazz-music, films and sport as their main interests, but this is anti-sentimental make-up, and behind it they are sensitive and embarrassed. Sønderby's best novel, *A Woman Is Superfluous* ("En Kvinde er overflødig", 1936), deals with the complete lack of understanding between two generations. The dramatized version of this novel shows Sønderby's importance as a playwright.

HANS SCHERFIG (born 1905) is the elegant satirist among contemporary Danish novelists. Most of his novels, disguised as detective stories, are full of acid satire. *The Lost Spring* ("Det forsømte Foraar", 1940) is a witty attack on the stupidity of secondary-school education, and his last book, *Idealists* ("Idealister", 1945), ridicules the many idealistic sects, each with its own easy remedy for improving the world.

It remains to mention two great writers, each holding an isolated place in modern Danish literature. They are Nis Petersen and Isak Dinesen.

NIS PETERSEN (1897–1943) wrote in 1931 an extraordinary novel called *The Street of the Sandalmakers* ("Sandalmagernes Gade"), the scene of which is laid in ancient Rome. It is well-composed, and a beautifully written book in a rather casual style, full of deliberate anachronisms. His other novel, *Spilt Milk* ("Spildt Mælk", 1934) is about the Civil War in Ireland, and his many stories — comic or pathetic, well written and well composed — are mostly amusing and harmless caricatures of contemporary life.

ISAK DINESEN (the *nom de plume* of Baroness KAREN BLIXEN FINECKE, born 1885) wrote her two best known works, *Seven Gothic Tales* ("Syv fantastiske Fortællinger", 1934) and *My African Farm* ("Den afrikanske Farm", 1937) in English, and they were published in England and America before they appeared in Denmark. She is a refined, aristocratic writer with a subtle irony, with an unusual elegance and sensitivity, more English than Danish in her style. Her *Winter's Tales* ("Vintereventyr", 1942) have a strange, cool, fascinating beauty.

Two Faroese novelists have also made significant contributions to contemporary Danish literature: JØRGEN-FRANTZ JACOBSEN (1900—38) with his novel *Barbara* (1939), and WILLIAM HEINESEN (born 1900) with his novels *Windy Dawn* ("Blæsende Gry", 1934), *Noatun* (1938; English title *Niels Peter*), and *The Black Pot* ("Den sorte Gryde", 1949).

*

The Danish drama of this period has been remarkable for one thing: for the first time in history there have been no less than three important dramatists living at the same time.

KAJ MUNK (1898—1944) was a parson in a small parish on the western coast of Jutland; his first play was produced in 1928, and a few years later he was universally looked upon as Denmark's leading dramatist. An early sympathy with Fascist dictatorship vanished completely after the Germans occupied Denmark, and he became a daring and violent spokesman for the Resistance. Several of his books were banned, he was officially silenced, and in 1944 he was taken by the Germans and murdered in a ditch not far from his vicarage. It is, however, not only the halo of martyrdom to which Munk owes his reputation. He is a dramatist of unusual qualities, and some of his plays, such as *An Idealist* ("En Idealist") — about Herod the Great; *The Word* ("Ordet") — about the reality of miracles; *He Sits at the Melting-Pot* ("Han sidder ved Smeltediglen") — inspired by the persecution of the Jews; and the small one-act play *Before Cannae* ("Før Cannae") — about power *versus* humanism — are landmarks in the history of Danish drama. He was a religious agitator who used the stage as a pulpit from which he could preach to his people — and all his dramas are centred on the eternal problem of God and Man. He wrote in the style of the Shakespearean heroic drama, but he cultivated the shock-effect. He often writes about the most solemn things in colloquial and very unclerical slang; and the frivolousness and flippancy of his style may often be a deliberate effort to create a sensation. He has contributed to Danish literature in many fields: travel books, essays, short stories, sermons, nursery rhymes, poems, and a very readable autobiography, *Spring Comes So Gently* ("Foraaret saa sagte kommer", 1942).

KJELD ABELL (born 1901) as a playwright is quite different from Kaj Munk, both in his ideas, his technique, and his style, but the best among his plays are no less important. His first play, *The Melody That Got Lost* ("Melodien, der blev væk", 1935), was an intellectually elegant and amusing topical play about the dullness of the respectability in which habit, tradition and snobbery force so many people to live, and an appeal to revolt against the humdrum of such an existence. In its form, it was a complete break with Naturalistic drama, and so were several of his other plays, particularly *Eve* ("Eva aftjener sin Barnepligt", 1936),

an imaginative and witty argument against the right of
parents to treat their children as their property, and form
their minds according to their own wishes. *Anna Sophie
Hedvig* (1939; English title *Cousin Anna*) was Abell's
most important pre-war play, in which the great human
and political problems of right and wrong, of democratic
liberty and Nazi tyranny, were reflected in the individual
fate of an elderly Danish spinster. Since the war his plays
have increased in importance; in *Silkeborg* (1946), contemporary problems are treated in the light of the Occupation
period, and *Days on a Cloud* ("Dage paa en Sky", 1947) is
an important commentary on essential post-war problems.
There is always a deeper meaning underlying his remarkably witty dialogue, and Abell has a humour and a poetic
sense which are related to those of Hans Andersen.

C. E. SOYA (born 1896) wrote his first play, *The Parasites*
("Parasitterne"), a harsh social satire, in 1929, and in spite
of its dramatic force it passed almost unnoticed. For several
years he wrote radio plays, which were rarely used, and
plays which were published and occasionally produced, but
never had any success. Between 1940 and 1943, however,
Soya wrote a dramatic trilogy which had an immediate
success and proved him to be an unusually gifted playwright.
The two last plays in particular, *Two Threads* ("To Traa-
de") and *Thirty Years' Respite* ("Tredive Aars Henstand"),
are in their dramatic technique comparable to Ibsen's.
Like Ibsen, Soya puts the problems, without solving them.
His recent plays are less important. It is Soya's technique
and his dialogue which are so fascinating, very seldom his
ideas. He has also written one important psychological
novel, entitled *My Grandmother's House* ("Min Farmors
Hus").

*

And finally *the poets!* During the twenties Tom Kristensen (see pp. 171—72) and Otto Gelsted were — together with

EMIL BØNNELYCKE (born 1893) and HANS HARTVIG SEEDORFF PEDERSEN (born 1892) — characteristic exponents of their age, and Tom Kristensen has only rarely in recent years reached the intensity of his Expressionistic poetry of those early years.

OTTO GELSTED (born 1888) has, since the beginning of the 'twenties, when he wrote his poem *The Show Boat* ("Reklameskibet") — which, incidentally, recalls T. S. Eliot's *The Waste Land* — become a more and more outspoken ideological poet, and his strange mixture of classical education and revolutionary ideas has produced poems of extraordinary power and sensitiveness. This subdued Naturalist, this exquisite love-poet, sometimes turns into a violent defender of liberty and humanism, and sometimes into a sage whose message is important and eternal.

PAUL LA COUR (born 1902) is a pupil of the modern French intellectual school — often very difficult to understand, and although greatly gifted never a poet who will win — or seeks to win — popularity. He can be compared to such poets as Auden, Spender and MacNeice. NIS PETERSEN has been mentioned as a prose writer, but he is much more important as a poet, for in his poetry he reveals his own desperate self. His poems range from romantic ballads to epigrammatic stanzas with the clarity of crystal. Many of them are intensely personal, and the terrifying depths revealed make one tremble, as on the brink of the abyss. Others are tender as a mother's love and carry one away by their exquisite simplicity.

JENS AUGUST SCHADE (born 1903) is the *enfant terrible* of modern Danish poetry — and he is one of those rare individuals who is nothing but a poet, even when he writes prose. He baffles his readers constantly — when one thinks he is being deep and original, he may just be cheating, and when one thinks he is cheating, he may really be a deliberate and very clever artist. A few collections of pure poetry, and several collections of sheer nonsense, are Schade's contribution to Danish literature. ALEX GARFF (born 1904) is a versatile and original lyric Naturalist whose notes are always sober and in tune. HULDA LÜTKEN (1896—1948) has written several interesting novels, but she is greatest as a poet; her poetry is passionate and mystic, full of sorrow and suffering and loneliness — her poems are revelations of her own unhappy self. KAI FRIIS MØLLER (born 1888) is a distinguished literary critic, and also a fastidious poet, who has made some outstanding translations of French and English poetry (notably of Baudelaire, Kipling, T. S. Eliot and Christopher Fry).

TOVE DITLEVSEN (born 1918) is young and sensitive — also a fine novelist, by the way — the greatest poet among present-day women writers. Her poetry has a tender beauty, and some of her lyrics have the clarity of the Classics. MORTEN NIELSEN (1922—44), who lost his life during the war, was also a great poet of unusual intensity, as his *Posthumous Poems* ("Efterladte Digte", 1945) proved.

The very youngest generation of present-day poets, of whom the most interesting seem to be OLE SARVIG, OVE ABILDGAARD, OLE WIVEL and THORKILD BJØRNVIG, attempt in their fear of the "prostitution of words" to find new ways of expressing their emotions; some of them seek refuge in an abstract, Surrealist form, others in an anti-intellectual mysticism, reminiscent of the "Symbolists" of the 'nineties. They are dominated by fear, of the world, and of themselves. They are the lyric poets of an atomic age.

CHAPTER IX

SWEDISH LITERATURE 1870–1950

(a) 1870–1890

The works and personality of AUGUST STRINDBERG (1849–1912) dominate Swedish letters in the period which begins about 1870. Indeed, Strindberg's début as a writer really ushers in modern Swedish literature, and even to-day the echoes of his phrases can be distinguished in the babble of literary debate. For Strindberg is, alas, the one and only Swedish writer who, in literature as such, has noticeably affected the general development of European and even American writing! One reason for this is that he is not primarily a lyric poet, whereas, as we have already noted, it was in the genre of lyric poetry that, up to this time, Swedish writers had reaped the richest harvest — and since lyric poetry so often defies rendering into other languages, this harvest has been largely inaccessible to those people who have no knowledge of the Swedish tongue. But Strindberg, though eminent in almost every genre, for he is a remarkably gifted novelist, short story writer, and satirist, achieved fame and influence primarily through his prose dramas, and these it has been comparatively easy to translate into other languages. So, while, for example, the great lyric poet GUSTAV FRÖDING remains practically unknown in Europe at large, Strindberg's plays, acted as they have been all over the Western world, have made him universally renowned.

The Swedish theatre of the late '60's and '70's, into

which Strindberg plunged as a young, ambitious, and yet self-doubting reformer, had very little to offer in the way of stimulus. The Romantic Age had succeeded as little or less than the Gustavian Age in creating a native dramatic tradition, for its verse plays were unactable. The historic dramas of VON BESKOW and BÖRJESSON, which were acted and appreciated, were in great part imitations in verse of Schiller's interpretations of Shakespeare. The novelist AUGUST BLANCHE (see p. 124) turned out popular tragi-comedies and comedies, the "pseudonym poet" E. BÄCK-STRÖM (see p. 127) wrote elegant trifles or declamatory works à la Hugo. Yet, with the continued rise and increasing prosperity of the middle-classes in this age of unbroken neutrality and peace, interest in the theatre, in Sweden as elsewhere, was markedly developing. The good citizens wanted their shows. Strindberg, however, did not give them what they wanted, indeed, it would not be unfair to say that his literary motto was, with a difference, Molière's "épater le bourgeois"; on the other hand, he perpetually yearned for a private life of middle-class domestic bliss, a state of things to which he never attained, in spite of — or because of — his three marriages and five children.

Up to about 1890 Strindberg was above all concerned to fight for honest, realistic, discussion of social and psychological problems, and the application of scientific observation to man and milieu. For this reason he was, during these years, generally unpopular, and often went hungry, working for long periods as free-lance journalist and ill-paid scribe. He fought to get light and air let into the stuffy atmosphere of contemporary Sweden, to shake the apathy of his fellow-countrymen, who, after the constitutional reforms of 1866, complacently settled down to admire themselves: not unnaturally they bitterly resented his efforts. He had absorbed the ideas of John Stuart Mill and Darwin, Buckle, Bernard, and Kierkegaard, had been stimulated by

Georg Brandes and roused by Ibsen's *Brand* (see pp. 145–7 and p. 141), and so he set to work to create a drama of ideas. His first, immature, efforts (dating from about 1869) failed to win recognition, and he therefore cloaked his ideas in historical form. *Master Olof* ("Mäster Olof") of 1872, which deals with Olaus Petri, Gustav Vasa, and the Swedish Reformation, is his first important play; indeed, though it remained unrecognized as such for many years, it is the first genuine living Swedish drama. In a sense it is a rejoinder to *Brand*, embodying Strindberg's own inner conflicts and revealing much of the subjective element that is so prominent a feature of all his work. The vigorous and ruthless treatment of history, and the racy dialogue, couched in everyday terms, contribute especially to the vital dramatic Realism which is *Master Olof's* greatest merit.

Strindberg's first completed novel, *The Red Room* ("Röda rummet"), of 1879, had a *succès de scandale*. In it he showed up the 'rackets' of contemporary life in Stockholm, in the business world, the press, in Parliament and Church, by means of a series of vivid, grotesque, satiric episodes. As a novel this work is formless, but Strindberg's wit and mastery of language — for as prose stylist he is still unrivalled in Sweden — prevent it from flagging. Moreover, like Bellman before him, Strindberg had the power of evoking the charm in the atmosphere of his native city and its surroundings.

The attack on contemporary hypocrisies was renewed and extended in the satire *The New State* ("Det nya riket") of 1882, a work which aroused further and greater bitterness against its author, who, not long after, left the country, with his first wife, Siri von Essen, for a period of wandering on the Continent. During this more or less voluntary exile Strindberg plunged into the debate on female emancipation and the so-called "sedlighetsfejden" (see pp. 213–14) with his collection of short stories *Married* ("Giftas"), volume I, of

1884, in which he ridiculed the ideas expressed in Ibsen's *Doll's House*, and also attacked the conventionality of the contemporary view of marriage. Thereby he set the feminists and their supporters, as well as those whom he had already alienated, against him, and a passage in one of his stories actually led to his being prosecuted for blasphemy. After a trial for which he returned to Sweden, the charge was dismissed, but the incident was a great shock to his already unbalanced nervous system, and intensified his feeling of being persecuted. It also brought about a deterioration in his relationship to his wife, which was already perilously unsound. Strindberg hated women, partly because he was so dependent on their love and respect.

Married, volume II ("Giftas" II) shows Strindberg's obsession with the struggle between the sexes, which had already been reflected in some of his earlier plays and was to inspire his most powerful dramas after the *Giftas* case. His optimistic belief in Rousseauistic Socialism gave way to a professed scientific ruthlessness, coloured by Darwin's theories, and in the desire, which he shared with Zola, to produce scientific documents rather than literature, he refrained for a time from writing plays, and produced the four autobiographical volumes which he called *The Son of the Bondwoman* ("Tjänstekvinnans son", 1886–1887). This highly subjective work is indeed hardly scientific, but it provides fascinating material to show how this child of a serving-woman and a bankrupt steamship agent felt in himself the pull of different social classes, and how, during his unhappy and insecure childhood and adolescence, he had seen himself in relation to society and man. Thereafter, in ever-deepening pessimism, Strindberg turned more and more to psychological rather than social problems, and, taking up the drama again, wrote the masterpieces *The Father* ("Fadren") and *Lady Julia* ("Fröken Julie"), together with other plays such as *Creditors*

("Fordringsägare"), during 1887–1888. With these works Strindberg really created Naturalistic drama in Europe, and himself supplied much of the theory for it in the famous preface which he wrote to *Lady Julia*. As Zola had done in his novels, he applied the laws of heredity and environment to his characters, and produced on the stage an extremely concentrated form of action. In *The Father*, the hero, an officer, is deliberately goaded into madness by his self-willed wife, who, in order to get control over her daughter, makes him doubt whether he is her father. In *Lady Julia*, the heroine, the count's degenerate daughter, lets herself be seduced by her father's valet, steals from her father, and then, in order to escape disgrace, kills herself, or, more truly, is willed by the valet Jean to kill herself, as the curtain falls. These plays evoked much shocked criticism, but they laid the foundation of Strindberg's European reputation, largely because in naturalness of dialogue and boldness of theme he had outstripped not only the timid Realists at home but also the more daring experimenters on the Continent. It is to be noted, too, that Strindberg's special brand of Realism owes much to his interest in the medical aspects of morbid psychology.

It is characteristic of Strindberg's complex personality that in 1887, in the throes of emotional and economic distress, and living as he was in the mountains of Bavaria, he achieved his most successful novel, *The People of Hemsö* ("Hemsöborna"), a story of the Stockholm skerries, full of grim humour and impregnated with the scents and sounds of an island in the Baltic. His next novel, *In the Outer Skerries* ("I havsbandet"), had a similar setting, but Strindberg's point of view had changed. Under the influence of Nietzsche, some of whose works he had read while abroad, and the impact of his growing personal distresses (for his marriage with Siri von Essen was breaking up), he took refuge in an intensified aristocratic individualism, professing to believe in an intellectual superman, typified in the novel in question by the hero, Borg, and scorning the democratic Radicalism that he had formerly cherished. In fact, at the very time when he was writing his Naturalistic tragedies, he was already, under the influence of Edgar Allan Poe and of French writers such as Maupassant, moving towards a kind of Symbolism. But between *In the Outer Skerries* and the new style of more or less symbolic works of Strindberg's later period falls the epoch of his greatest emotional and mental turmoil, the so-called Inferno crisis of the 1890's; and before considering this and the works which followed it, it will be convenient to go back a little in time and consider the other Swedish writers of the '80's, commonly subsumed under the generic name "Åttiotalet".

*

In comparison with the robust vigour of Strindberg's work and the shifting subtlety of idea and characterisation which we find there, the rest of this decade's productions cut a rather insignificant figure. "Unga Sverige" (Young Sweden), as these writers are often called, actually formed no definite school, they had no literary organ of any permanence in which to express their views, but they all, in varying degree, looked to the scientific Radicalism of France and England and admired Strindberg, until he outraged their feelings. Schooled on Ibsen and Brandes, they were aware of the conflicting currents of their time, and wanted to debate issues such as social reform, female emancipation, the decline of religious faith, education, and so forth, but their laudable ambitions did not suffice to produce good literature. GUSTAF AF GEIJERSTAM (1858–1909), author of *Erik Grane* and a series of other novels and short stories, was ambitious to be their leader, but had not enough intellectual stamina to achieve his aim. FRU LEFFLER (1849–1892) in her stories entitled *From Life* ("Ur livet") satirized upper and middle-class conventions as they affected her own sex, but her tales of blighted débutantes now appear dated and timid. More accurate observation of life is apparent in the works of VICTORIA BENEDICTSSON (1850–1888), who wrote under the pseudonym ERNST AHLGREN. Her novels, *Money* ("Pengar", 1885), and *Fru Marianne* (1887), are concerned with marriage, her short stories often deal with life in her own province of Skåne, but neither novels nor short stories equal in interest her outspoken (and in part only recently published) diaries and letters. She committed suicide in Copenhagen at the age of 38.

Skåne produced two other notable writers at this time, the lyric poet A. BÅÅTH (1853–1912), and the poet, novelist, and critic OLA HANSSON (1860–1925), whose earlier verses celebrated the quiet beauty of the southern plains. Indeed it is in Skåne, which at this time looked to Copenhagen as its intellectual capital, not to Stockholm, that we now find the beginnings of regional literature, which becomes such a significant feature of the '90's.

Other writers such as TOR HEDBERG and OSCAR LEVERTIN made their first dutiful début in the literature of "Åttiotalet", but found much more congenial forms of expression later on. With all its apparent 'dimness' to the eyes of a modern reader, the work of the '80's served a very useful purpose — in consolidating Strindberg's conquests, in further clearing the air, in accustoming the steadily increasing reading public to the discussion of ideas.

(b) 1890–1910.

Before the arguments of the '80's had died away, other notes, a prelude to the melodies of the '90's, had been sounded. These were struck by the aristocratic VERNER VON HEIDENSTAM (1859–1940) in the book of verse called *Years of Pilgrimage and Wandering* ("Vallfart och van-

dringsår"), of 1888. Joy in life, colour, individualism, were
the slogans he proclaimed in these descriptions of the
Orient, rendered in the nonchalant rhythms that Strindberg had used — for other purposes — in his youthful
poetry; and it was "inbillningsnaturalism" (imaginative
Naturalism) as opposed to "skomakarrealism" (cobbler's
Realism) that Heidenstam and his ally OSCAR LEVERTIN
(1869—1906) were to champion in their satiric little mani-
festo *Pepita's Marriage* ("Pepitas Bröllop"), and, with greater
effect, in their creative work. The ambitious, posing,
spoilt, uncertain personality that was Heidenstam's had an
effect on his own generation out of all apparent proportion
to his talents. Condemned by the doctors to an early death
and to long sojourns abroad for his health's sake, he survived, ultimately as a senile old man, until the age of 81,
at his country house of Övralid by Lake Vättern, where he
lived in state and wealth as the aristocratic *magus* that he
liked to think himself, and received those younger poets
who came to pay homage to the author of *Poems* ("Dikter",
1895) and *New Poems* ("Nya dikter", 1915). For, though
Heidenstam wrote a number of prose works, for example
the novel *Hans Alienus* (1892), a sort of modern version
of the Faust theme, the short stories *King Charles' Men*
("Karolinerna"), and the novel-sequence *The Tree of the
Folkungs* ("Folkungaträdet"), and, in his treatment of
national history and his vivid admiration, *à la* Nietzsche, of
heroic personages and past glories, did much to stimulate
the revival of nationalism in Swedish literature and the
development of a "precious" style of prose, his abiding
achievements were in the sphere of lyric poetry, the cause
of which he had defended with such spirit. The short
contemplative lyrics, inspired by Goethe and Runeberg,
that are to be found in his three volumes of verse, and the
descriptions of Lake Vättern and its environs, his adopted
native heath, have the serenity and dignity that Heiden-

stam signally failed to achieve in his own life. He is in fact what Henry James might have called "a so beautiful example" of the national poet *manqué*. To be such a national poet was his ambition at the turn of the century, before the break with Norway: he even dabbled in politics, seeing himself as another Bjørnson. Like Snoilsky, he failed.

Heidenstam did not wish to found a school: it was the liberation of the individual's talents that he championed; and Levertin, his close personal friend, possessing less fluency and much less metrical virtuosity, finally found his own way. Levertin, far more cultured and better read than Heidenstam, and aware of French Symbolism and English Pre-Raphaelitism, as well as of Dante and Pre-Reformation art, often relies in his poems on aesthetic rather than emotional inspiration, as, for example, in *Legends and Songs* ("Legender och visor"). This he does, too, in his prose works, *Last Stories* ("Noveller") and *Rococo Stories* ("Rococonoveller"), and the novel *The Masters of Österås* ("Magistrarne i Österås"). Yet when this sensitive Jew was inspired by personal emotion, as by the death of his first and beloved wife, or by his ancestry, or by the beauty of Stockholm, which was his "region", as it was — so differently — Strindberg's, he wrote very moving poetry. The song-cycle *King Solomon and Morolf* ("Kung Salomo och Morolf"), written shortly before his premature death, shows Levertin at his best. Moreover, as literary critic in the newly-founded *Svenska Dagbladet,* which became in many ways the literary organ *par excellence* of the '90's, he exercised, with his elegant, well-informed articles, a considerable influence on the Sweden of his day.

In general, Levertin's judgment was admirably balanced, yet his lapses in regard to the later works of Strindberg (to whom I must shortly return), and those of GUSTAV FRÖ-DING (1860–1911), became notorious. Fröding, in spite of poverty, loneliness, and a heritage of mental sickness that finally drove him into a madhouse, became the national, popular poet, whom Heidenstam longed in vain to be. Popular in the sense that once he had succeeded in writing and publishing his verses, of which the first volume, *Guitar and Concertina* ("Guitarr och dragharmonika") appeared in 1891, he was widely read; popular also in that his own attitude was that of a Radical, intent on the struggles of the industrial working class which had attained political consciousness in the late '80's. The Swedish Social Democratic party, which, in this century, has so largely shaped the Swedish social fabric, was founded in 1889. It was typical of Fröding's political views and personal generosity that, when he once received a prize from the Swedish Academy, he immediately gave away the money to a fund in aid of universal franchise. In this interest in politics and social affairs Fröding, like others, carried on the tradition of the '80's, and showed that, however much the "New Romantic Nineties" appeared to reject the ideals of the preceding decade, they actually owed much to it, and not only to the Romantic Movement and to "Stormaktstiden", the writers of which they were prepared to acknowledge.

In this first volume of Fröding, the section called *Värmland Folksongs* ("Värmländska låtar") gained the most immediate recognition, the depths underlying his poetry taking longer for the public to sound. Fröding, a descendant of Värmland gentry, whilst sympathising with the urban worker, was much more closely in touch with the life of the country labourer. Here, in the Värmland songs, are the joys and sorrows, the petty squabbles and the jokes of his Värmland country-folk, seen through the tenderness and h u m o u r which are such integral parts of Fröding's work and personality. It was this "folklighet" that Levertin despised, ignoring the complexity of the poet, who was continually looking for a philosophical solution to the discords of life, and who often saw himself as the hired clown, struggling to make the populace laugh whilst in his own heart he weeps; or as a captive imprisoned behind the bars of his own temperament; or as a defiant and fallen Lucifer. In both humorous and serious verses — and the two strains, of course, constantly intermingle — Fröding displays a technical virtuosity, a gift for rhythm and phrase that both dazzles and entrances, not least because the subtlety is so often hidden under a superficial simplicity of treatment. In *New Poems* ("Nya dikter"), of 1894, and *Splashes and Rags* ("Stänk och flikar"), of 1896, he perfected this technique, which, whilst owing something to Byron, Heine, and Swedish predecessors, was above all intensely individual. *Splashes and Rags* contains such masterpieces as *Marquis de Moi-Même* and *Dreams in Hades* ("Drömmar i Hades"); it contains also the celebrated poem *Morning Dream* ("En morgondröm") which, with its outspoken and honest treatment of sexual love, led to Fröding being prosecuted for pornography. Like Strindberg before him, Fröding was acquitted, but for him too the case was a turningpoint in life. Tormented by self-doubt, he finally broke down, and the schizophrenia, which had already enforced periodic short sojourns in mental homes abroad, now necessitated a long period of confinement. Yet one further volume had been added in 1897 to his works, and then in 1898 came the cycle *Grail Splashes* ("Gralstänk"), which more particularly embodies Fröding's effort to express the philosophy of life to which he clung so passionately, that is, the belief that everything in the world, even what is ugly or evil, has a divine function.

Fröding's poetry has influenced and stimulated many subsequent Swedish writers, up to the present day. ERIK AXEL KARLFELDT (1864–1931) was the first to reflect the influence, in the volume with which he made his début in 1895. Yet just because he was not merely a disciple of

Fröding, he continued and enriched the lyrical tradition of his country, and, from that first volume until the last which was published in his lifetime, *Autumn Horns* ("Hösthorn"), he developed and refined his poetic gifts. A son of the province of Dalarna, who by force of personal circumstances was compelled for many years to live elsewhere, he sang with enhanced appreciation of its beauties, in spring and especially in autumn. His verses are full of the lore of a countryman, who, like Fridolin, the hero of his collections *Fridolin's Songs* ("Fridolins visor") and *Fridolin's Pleasure-Garden* ("Fridolins lustgård"), of 1898 and 1901 respectively, looks at his crops under the harvest moon and takes pleasure in the sight. Karlfeldt, like Fröding, handled metres with great skill: unlike his friend, however, he sometimes played about with them for the mere fun of doing so, clothing his themes in the slightly archaic language he had learnt from the Bible and from older Swedish literature. His themes are, or appear, slighter than Fröding's, and he is almost contemptuous of philosophical or political problems, yet beneath the beautifully decorative surface and the humour, which made his poetry attractive to the public, sound undertones of passionate eroticism:

> Sub luna amo.
> Dark is my bride,
> Veiled in the moonbeams, dancing
> In dusk of the eventide;
> Scented as lychnis
> Under a flash-lit sky;
> Cool as the dawn-dews — waxing,
> Waning, as moons go by.

> *Sub luna amo.*
> *Mörk är min brud,*
> *brinner i bruna kvällar,*

dansar i månglitterskrud,
doftar som nattglim
under en kornblixtsky,
svalkar som morgondaggen,
växlar som nedan och ny.

It was in the hands of SELMA LAGERLÖF (1858—1940) that the prose fiction of the '90's came alive, and earned for the authoress, especially outside Sweden, a popularity that came to eclipse Strindberg's. Selma Lagerlöf loved stories; as a child she listened to them, enraptured, at her home, Mårbacka in Värmland, and throughout her literary career, until she was an old woman, she told them. The special value and charm of her long series of novels and collections of short stories and autobiographical writings lie in the pleasure they gave to the story-teller herself. In her first published work, *Gösta Berling's Saga* (1891) she related the lives and adventures at Ekeby of a group of Värmland cavaliers at the time of the Napoleonic Wars. Facts, legends, superstitions, are interwoven in a richly textured tapestry, but the book turned into a series of episodes rather than a genuine novel, and the style too often reveals the rhetorical influence of Carlyle and the uncontrolled lyricism of the writer. Essentially, however, the work reveals Selma Lagerlöf herself, for whom Nature is always animated by living spirits, giants and elves, while human beings are always black or white, never grey: yet from evil they can be redeemed through suffering and renunciation, and ultimately saved. With all her imaginativeness and love of the fantastic and heroic, Selma Lagerlöf had some of the optimism of the Radicals of the 1880's, as she had their sense of justice and injustice and of the need for reform. These things lend weight to her writings, but do not always make them convincing, as for instance in *The Miracles of Antichrist* ("Antikrists mirakler"), of 1897. She is at her best

History of Scandinavian Literature   13

when she is inventing myths, as in the collection of stories *The Queens at Kungahälla* ("Drottningarna i Kungahälla"), or describing the reactions of simple country-folk in the first part of her long novel *Jerusalem* (1901—1902), where the peasants are men of Dalarna, under the spell of a revivalist sect. Selma Lagerlöf died full of honours, having, like Heidenstam and Karlfeldt, won the Nobel Prize for Literature, but having also quite lost touch with the modern world and the trends of recent Swedish thought.

PER HALLSTRÖM (born 1866) also did his best work before 1910, and quite definitely belongs to the '90's though he is, in some ways, more conscious of the claims of society, and more bitterly aware of the conclusions of pessimistic philosophy. Poet, novelist, and dramatist, he is chiefly appreciated for his many collections of short stories, for instance *The Diamond Ornament* ("Briljantsmycket"), of 1896, *Thanatos* (1900), and *The Four Elements* ("De fyra elementarna"), of 1906. ALBERT ENGSTRÖM (1867—1940) is one of the Swedish writers most beloved by his own countrymen, for his irrepressible though often grim humour, which he expressed in his drawings as well as his stories, very often at the expense of the people of Småland and Roslagen. He founded the humorous paper *Strix* in 1897, and was a faithful friend of Strindberg in the latter's old age.

*

Strindberg, as we have seen, had anticipated many of the ideas of the '90's, but, unwilling to follow where others led, turned his back on Heidenstam, with whom he had for some time associated while they were both living in Switzerland. Beset by increasing financial troubles, tormented by the divorce from Siri and the loss of his children, only temporarily consoled, during his renewed exile, by his second marriage, with the Austrian Frida Uhl, and the birth of their child, he found it difficult to create. At this juncture, indeed, science, and pseudo-science in the form of alchemy, absorbed his interest and employed his pen. In 1894 he had settled in Paris, after parting from Frida. Loneliness, disappointments — for the crucible, after all, turned out no gold, and he feared he could no longer write — ill-health, all these and other factors prepared the soil for the increasing influence of Swedenborg and for Strindberg's "conversion". During the years 1894—1897, the years of the so-called Inferno crisis, named after the title which he deliberately chose for the diary-chronicle he later wrote about his experiences, Strindberg's fortunes were at their lowest ebb. Without here discussing the spiritual elements, the genuineness, or the permanence, of his conversion, one may confidently say that from the point of view of literature Strindberg's sufferings during the crisis were extremely valuable, for it gave him new creative powers, kindled his imagination once more, and led to a new series of plays. He needed a God to believe in: even in his most defiant and atheistic period he had never given up searching for a faith, and to the end he was destined to go on trying to reshape his beliefs. His dynamic vitality, indeed, and his defiance never left him as long as he lived.

The first notable results of this creative revival were embodied, after Strindberg's return to Sweden, in the drama *To Damascus, parts I and II* ("Till Damaskus" I—II), of 1898, the third part of which was not completed until several years later. *To Damascus* is a symbolical, largely autobiographical, drama, in which The Stranger, representing Strindberg himself, meets The Lady, and enacts a sort of retrospective interpretation of his own experiences, that is to say, of his search for truth and the expiation of his transgressions. Various other characters represent aspects of The Stranger himself, and in the powerful Hospice-scene, the crux of Part I, he confronts these sinister or pathetic apparitions. In Part II the most effective scene is the Ban-

13*

quet, in which The Stranger is at first fêted as one who has succeeded in creating gold, surrounded by pomp and circumstance.   And then the banquet is invaded by riff-raff, the golden goblets turn into tin, and The Stranger is arrested by the police, as he cannot pay for the party.   At the end of Part II the conversion of The Stranger, punished by the "Powers", as Strindberg names his instruments of divine justice and revenge, is still not definitely accomplished.

Even from this brief synopsis it emerges how different from the technique of the Naturalist plays is that which Strindberg had now evolved.   Instead of the concentrated action, the economy of scene, there is a shifting but patterned framework and a mysterious atmosphere of dream or nightmare.   In The Dream Play ("Drömspelet") of 1901 this technique is even freer, appealing still more urgently to the imagination of the audience.   In this play the heroine, daughter of the god Indra, descends to earth, takes on human shape, and experiences the common, trivial sufferings of mankind, such as quarrels with her husband, the crying of her child, and the smells of human domesticity. The core of Realism remains, even in the most ethereal visions, and it is characteristic of Strindberg's complexity that, in the same period during which he wrote The Dream Play, he also wrote The Dance of Death ("Dödsdansen"), with its Realistic intensity of savage matrimonial conflict. One cannot, in fact, divide Strindberg's production up by lines denoting hard and fast classifications.   His love for the gifted young actress Harriet Bosse and his marriage to her stimulated him to further creative activity;   but in 1899, before he met her, he had embarked on his second series of historical plays, of which The Saga of the Folkungs ("Folkungasagan"), and more particularly Gustav Vasa and Eric XIV, are the most brilliant.   The firm construction of Gustav Vasa, the careful building up of character, especially that of the King, make it a play which is compellingly effective on the stage. These historical dramas were Strindberg's response to the nationalism which was so much in the air at the end of the '90's. Even now his inventive genius was not exhausted, in spite of further personal griefs, of which far the worst was the speedy break-up of his third marriage and the consequent loss of Harriet's and his daughter. His life in Stockholm became more and more solitary. His plays had at last conquered the Swedish stage, indeed he had even become a *popular* dramatist, but the appearance of his bitterest and most satirical novel, *Black Banners* ("Svarta fanor"), which was written in 1904 and published in 1907, temporarily destroyed all the popularity he had won, and he was again faced with the problem of how to get his plays performed. So he started up a small experimental theatre, in collaboration with the gifted young producer August Falck, and for this theatre, with its small stage and resources, he wrote the series of so-called Chamber Plays, of 1907. Of these, *The Ghost Sonata* ("Spöksonaten") is the most fantastically effective, *Storm* ("Oväder") the most attractive. In *The Ghost Sonata*, a mixture of scathing Realism and ultra-fantastic Symbolism, which anticipates the Surrealists, Strindberg attempts to strip all pretences and hypocrisies from society and individual, and in doing so he created yet another new dramatic form. It was particularly the Post-Inferno dramas and the Chamber Plays which influenced first the German, then other European, and American stages, but the effect of the so-called Naturalist works is also evident in these literatures, not least because the "Naturalism" of Strindberg's earlier periods is a Naturalism impregnated with other elements.

In *The Great Highway* ("Stora landsvägen"), of 1909, Strindberg, subjective to the last, bid farewell to the stage, but continued in the *Blue Books* ("Blå böckerna") to comment in aphoristic form on mice and men. A renewed spell of journalistic activity during these last years brought him into conflict with Heidenstam and the Conservatives, and he ended as the champion, once again, of Radicalism, and, this time, of the rising industrial classes.

In all, Strindberg's *Collected Works* occupy 55 volumes, and these include none of his vast correspondence, much of which is still unpublished. It is, therefore, not surprising that, in order to attempt this brief survey, much has had to be left out or treated more briefly than it is easy to justify. Strindberg cannot be summed up in a few words, but the qualities in him which are most striking, and often most difficult to seize, appear to be his intellectual and emotional intensity, his mastery of language, whatever literary form he is employing, and his almost preternatural energy.

*

Of the generation of the '90's, two writers remain who had links with both the Rationalism of the '80's and the aestheticism of Heidenstam and Levertin, but who nevertheless stood a little apart from the others, and yet, unlike many of this generation, kept their interest in modern trends. Like Strindberg, HJALMAR SÖDERBERG (1869—1941) and Bo BERGMAN (born 1869) were devotees of Stockholm. For Strindberg, both skerries and city were a source of abiding delight, and recur constantly in his works: with Söderberg and Bergman, it was the grey streets, swept by rain, the parks in spring, the boats shrouded in mist, and other aspects of the capital itself, that inspired verse and prose. Söderberg made his début with a novel in 1895, Bergman, at the age of 34, with poems entitled *The Marionettes* ("Marionetterna"), but both have written novels, short stories, and poetry. This does not mean that they lack their own individuality. Söderberg's novels *Martin Birck's Youth* ("Martin Bircks ungdom") and *Doctor Glas* show a capacity for discussing ideas as well as interpreting moods. Söderberg's pessimistic irony appears at its best in short stories, for instance *The Fur Coat* ("Pälsen"), and it is his elegant, simple prose style, modelled on that of Anatole France among others, that has given him influence among Swedish men of letters. Bo Bergman, who published his seventh collection of verse, *The Kingdom* ("Riket"), in 1944, and his second novel in 1948, is especially beloved on account of his poetry. Its limpidity conceals the erotic passions and mental anguish of a highly sophisticated modern man.

(c) *1910—1950.*

Neither the year 1900 nor the year 1910 is a definite milestone in Swedish literature. It is clear that, as the 20th century progresses, the continued development of Swedish industry, the revolution in national and international communications, and other changes, lead to a levelling out of the old social classes within the country, and permit foreign influences to exert themselves more and more speedily and effectively. Bergson, Freud, Sartre, are all quickly taken up in Sweden, and America leaves her imprint not only on factories and refrigerators but also on press and literature. The power of the press assumes formidable proportions, and shapes public opinion on politics and philosophy, on sociology and the arts, among ever-increasing circles of readers. The industrial proletariat gives birth to its own writers, who often approach literature by way of journalism. Not merely the readers, but the writers of literature, too, are multiplied, and there is an obvious rise in what one might call the "standard of efficiency" of Swedish letters. Clearly connected with this is the development of the novel — lyric poetry continues to attract both writers and readers — but there has been no

real successor to Strindberg as dramatist, in spite of some
notable work, especially by PÄR LAGERKVIST (born 1891).

It is difficult, as yet, to place some of the writers of the
most recent age, and many who deserve to be mentioned
will be crowded out of these pages for lack of space, as
their ranks thicken around us. The ambiguous VILHELM
EKELUND (1880–1949) is an example of one who cannot yet
be properly assessed. This son of Skåne appeared as early
as 1900 with a volume of poems, rather in the manner of
the young Ola Hansson, but his interpretations of moods,
in himself and in nature, reveal, in the following volumes, the
deepening influence of George, Nietzsche, Hölderlin, and
other classicistic Germans, shown in his idealization of the
antique and his adoption of ancient metres and unrhymed
verse. This beautiful dithyrambic poet, curiously im-
personal in his individualism, then turned away from
poetry. His last collection of verses, *The Star of the Sea*
("Havets stjärna"), appeared in 1906, and the first book
in his new style of aphoristic prose in 1909. Still pursuing
the cult of the antique, he published a series of similar
esoteric volumes, which have influenced other writers, but
are too difficult for the general public, and, in a sense,
remain outside the main stream of tradition. It is probable, however, that the effect of Ekelund will some day
manifest itself in works that have not yet been conceived.

ANDERS ÖSTERLING (born 1884), another native of Skåne,
began as a pupil of Ekelund in 1904, but after a time started
to write in a less mannered style. He is an essayist of
much charm, and his numerous poems express a kind of
poetic Realism, full of the appreciation of nature. In this,
KARL ASPLUND (born 1890) and GUNNAR MASCOLL SILFVER-
STOLPE (1893–1942) have followed him, with variations,
as they have followed Bo Bergman, whilst STEN SELANDER
(born 1891) has adapted this poetic Realism to the life of
town and press.

PÄR LAGERKVIST first appeared on the scene in 1913 with a pamphlet on aesthetics. His first volume of poems, *Anguish* ("Ångest"), of 1916, reflects the mental agonies of a sensitive youth overwhelmed by the chaos of the First World War. His "Anguish, anguish is my heritage" may stand as the motto of the *dépaysé* generation of that war: yet Lagerkvist matured notably, both as poet and prose-writer, during the '20's and '30's, and has indeed continued to develop up to the present day. He has been a potent influence, in respect of both form and content, especially on the generation of the '20's, and, for all his quiet and retiring personality, is perhaps the most dynamic and versatile Swedish writer of the period since 1910. His almost painfully intense search for a philosophy of life recalls that of Strindberg; and it was Strindberg's Post-Inferno dramas, and the German Expressionism partially dependent on them, that inspired such plays as *The Invisible Man* ("Den Osynlige"), 1923, and the, particularly beautiful, *The Man Who Was Allowed to Relive His Life* ("Han som fick leva om sitt liv"), of 1928. Here Lagerkvist already strikes a more subdued note. His sharp awareness of the powers of evil that were engulfing Europe in the '30's inspired apocalyptic satires such as *The Hangman* ("Bödeln"), 1933, and the historical novel *The Dwarf* ("Dvärgen"), 1944. In his lyrics this anti-bourgeois son of the lower-middle class, champion of a recurrently abstract Radicalism, has gone on to idyllic nature poetry.

*

The third outstanding literary personality who emerged during the first decades of the 20th century is HJALMAR BERGMAN (1883–1931), fascinating in his emotional complexity and his contradictoriness. Like his contemporaries GUSTAF HELLSTRÖM (born 1882), LUDVIG NORDSTRÖM (1882–1942), SIGFRID SIWERTZ (born 1882), and ELIN WÄGNER

(1882—1949), he developed Swedish prose as a medium for irony and the expression of ideas. By a brief characterization of the works of these writers one may perhaps seize on some of the differences that separate them from one another and from Hjalmar Bergman. Hellström's work as journalist took him to Europe and the U.S.A., and a long stay in England, especially, influenced his attitude and his writing: he learnt to appreciate humour and common sense, but retained some of the ironic scepticism of Söderberg, under the impact of the philosophy and politics of modern life. His best known novel, *Lacemaker Lekholm Gets an Idea* ("Snörmakare Lekholm får en idé", 1927), is a leisurely but amusing picture of life in a small Swedish town, an epitome of larger issues. Nordström, too, through his mother, had connexions with England, and his later work, very often formless and inartistic, reflects the optimistic Utopianism of H. G. Wells. It culminates in a kind of mystic belief in "totalitarianism" as applied to industry, in which Nordström's family had roots, and in the collective novel. Nordström's best work, however, is in his short stories about the life of fishermen and peasants in Norrland, his native Härnösand being perpetuated in his fictional Öbacka, for instance in *The People of Öbacka* ("Öbackabor", of 1921), and in other, earlier, collections. Nordström's unvarnished realism and broad humour here build upon Strindberg's novel *The People of Hemsö*.

Siwertz began as a romantic poet, then, after publishing various collections of short stories, and some novels, made his literary mark, influenced by Bergson and Freud, with the novel *Down Stream* ("Selambs"), 1920. Here he shows up the fraudulence and pettiness of a profiteering Stockholm family during the First World War. Siwertz handles both verse and prose with sober elegance: his novels and short stories, often concerned with life in Stockholm, keep close to reality, and he has become a favourite with the reading public.

Elin Wägner, feminist and pacifist, reacted with particular vehemence to the First World War. As wife of John Landquist, the first academic exponent in Sweden of Bergson, she was doubtless influenced by the French philosopher's affirmative attitude to life, but she was more moralist than philosopher, and in her novel *The Rise of the Jerneploog Family* ("Släkten Jerneploogs framgång", 1916), she gave vent to the disgust inspired in her by militarism. Elin Wägner is at her happiest in ironic short stories about the trials of modern women, and at her most powerful in the novel *Åsa-Hanna*, of 1918. Here her intimate knowledge of her native Småland is combined with a deep understanding of the peasant woman Hanna, who has unwittingly been lured into a life of crime, and who gradually redeems herself.

In comparison with the solid worth, the painstaking or sweeping realism, the "gentlemanly" ideals represented by the bulk of these writings, Hjalmar Bergman's often bizarre imagination and restlessly nervous energy seem more and more mysterious. He was the son of a wealthy banker at Örebro — or "Wadköping", the name under which it was to be immortalized in his later writings — and one might well have expected his life to pursue a conventional and comfortable course. But a fantastically lively imagination, and a certain timidity in face of the realities of life, set him apart even as a child. Then, in his twenties, he was threatened with the loss of his eyesight (which, fortunately, never quite came to pass), and his father actually lost his fortune, and these facts created new and difficult conditions for him. Much of the rest of his life was spent in foreign countries with his wife; and though so much of his work was inspired by memories of Örebro and its surroundings, his almost crazy restlessness, like a Fury, drove him from

place to place and from one work to another. He died
alone in a Berlin hotel.

Bergman started with gifted but dilettante pastiches after
Maeterlinck, Anatole France, and others, and made his
début with a play in 1905; his real production began after
1910, and there followed until his death a stream of novels,
plays, short stories, sketches. He wrote both for film and
radio. His view of life was fundamentally pessimistic, yet,
like Fröding, he sheds the redeeming light of humour on
the most sordid or miserable incidents: like Fröding, too,
he showed himself to the populace as a clown — this in his
last novel, *The Clown Jac* ("Clownen Jac"), 1930. This
macabre stylized Realism and agonized clarity of vision had
already marked the *Memoirs of a Dead Man* ("En döds me-
moarer"), of 1918, one of Bergman's most remarkable efforts.
His brilliant, serious, satire, *God's Orchid* ("Markurells i
Wadköping", 1919), was to prove the most popular of a
long series of narratives of Wadköping or Örebro. This
success was followed by others, and meanwhile his dramatic
work, especially *Swedenhielms* (1925), and *The Riff-raff*
("Patrasket", 1928) made him equally popular as playwright. Hjalmar Bergman is one of the few Swedish writers
who have ever composed genuine comedies. It is his ab-
sorption in psychology, in the failures as well as the suc-
cesses and strong personalities among humanity, that makes
him so interesting. See, for instance, *Thy Rod and Thy Staff*
("Farmor och Vår Herre"). For all types of men he has
the same understanding pity. No doubt his awareness of
the irrational impulses of mankind helped to make him
so fascinating, so invariably stimulating — a writer who is
never dull.
                              *

Meanwhile the so-called "proletarian" novel has been
developed, not always by working-class writers, and from
varying points of view, for example, by GUSTAV HEDENVIND-

ERIKSSON (born 1880), by FABIAN MÅNSSON (1872—1938), and by MARTIN KOCH (1882—1940). The latter's *Timmerdalen*, for instance, describes one of the big strikes which took place in Norrland in the '70's, his *God's Beautiful World* ("Guds vackra värld"), of 1916, is an honest and terrifying indictment of the Stockholm underworld and the apathy which permitted it to exist. RUDOLF VÄRNLUND (1900—1945), and IVAR LO-JOHANSSON (born 1901) have carried on this valuable and necessary criticism, the latter exposing the appalling conditions which prevailed among "statare", farm labourers, before the First World War. His massive "collective novels", such as *Good-Night, Earth* ("Godnatt, jord"), are less aesthetically effective than his short stories.

VILHELM MOBERG (born 1898) has used the historical novel to depict, sometimes too romantically, the recurring labours of the farmer's life, as in *The Rask Family* ("Raskens"). His anti-German, anti-neutrality best-seller *Ride To-Night* ("Rid i natt", 1941) also makes use of the historical form. MOA MARTINSON (born 1890) has given expression to the miseries of working-class women in a series of novels. Autobiographical experiences clearly underlie all these writings, and this genre becomes more and more popular in and after the '20's, not only among the so-called proletarians. Sharp contact with the harsh realities of working-class life has, for instance, inspired JAN FRIDEGÅRD's novel-sequence *Lars Hård* (1935—1936). Fridegård (born 1897) is probably the most effective of this generation of "indignationsförfattare", not least because of the directness of his style.

Both EYVIND JOHNSON (born 1900) and HARRY MARTINSON (born 1904) are proletarian, self-educated authors, yet they have followed quite different paths, and have experimented with various literary forms. Johnson's *The Novel of Olof* ("Romanen om Olof", 1934—1937), the story of his own experiences as an adolescent, as timber-floater and sawmill hand, describes with rare power his own personal fight for survival. Before writing it down he had travelled abroad, had read D. H. Lawrence and Joyce, and had published other works. His allegorical *Krilon* (1941—1943), *The Swell of the Shores* ("Strändernas svall", 1946), in which he takes up the Odyssey story, and his latest work, *Dreams of Roses and Fire* ("Drömmar om rosor och eld", 1949), a historical novel set in the France of Richelieu, all reveal his mastery of the art of writing and his interest in form, yet show, too, that he has retained his interest in people.

Harry Martinson's experiences as a sailor and stoker were embodied in *Cape Farewell* ("Kap Farväl!", 1933), prose sketches of life on the seven seas, written in an intensely individual style. His childhood contacts with poorhouse and misery inspired the moving novel *Flowering Nettle* ("Nässlorna blomma"), of 1935. Martinson has written a considerable number of prose works, of which the latest, *The Way to Klockrike* ("Vägen till Klockrike", 1949), a paean to vagabond life, is the best. He has also created new forms of lyrical poetry. He is the first proletarian writer who has won — as he has certainly deserved — a place in the Swedish Academy.

*

In following up some of the lines of development of the proletarian novel, we have left behind other forms of prose fiction since the '20's — and also certain lyric poets, such as DAN ANDERSSON (1888—1920), charcoal-burner from Dalarna. Andersson wrote both novels and short stories about the Swedish forests, but his most personal works are the poems in which he depicts his search for a faith. His cry of loneliness has been echoed by many of his successors in the Sweden between the two World Wars. The various beliefs, ideas, or idols adopted, such as psycho-analysis, Marxism, "primitivism", as enunciated by D. H. Lawrence and others, T. S. Eliot, the Oxford Group, and so on, have as a rule exercised only a transitory sway over their adherents: but the anguish of the search lends sincerity and depth to some of the work evolved under these stimuli. Other writers, again, have remained untouched — and individual.

BIRGER SJÖBERG (1885–1929), a shop assistant from Vänersborg, made his belated start in 1922 with *Frida's Book* ("Fridas bok"), a half-ironic, wholly charming, collection of lyrics about small town life, which he set to music. But his next collection of poems, *Crises and Garlands* ("Kriser och kransar"), betray his own dualism, his tense and religious awareness of death, and of the futility of the daily compromises of existence. ERIK LINDORM (1889–1941), though not by birth of the working class, began as a literary champion of their cause: his poetry often takes up motives from the poorer quarters of the capital, but the best of his later verses — he had by that time become a moderate Conservative — is intimately lyrical and in the nature of self-confession. RAGNAR JÄNDEL (1895–1929), poet and novelist, and ERIK BLOMBERG (born 1894), Marxist and follower of Freud, have both produced memorable poetry, influenced by Ekelund and Lagerkvist.

KARIN BOYE (born 1900), one of the most gifted of modern Swedish authors, killed herself in 1941, in deepening horror at the prospect before her. Her very able novel *Kallocain* (1940) had already expressed her fear of the Brave New World promised to human beings, and her largely theoretical faith, imbibed at Uppsala, in the extreme Left Wing, her interest in Surrealism and psycho-analysis, and in the intellectual *Waste Land* of T. S. Eliot, had by that time ceased to bear her up. Her work had matured constantly and surely from her first beginnings in 1922, and a series of collections of verses revealed that she was a lyric poet of quite unusual powers.

Another woman writer, AGNES VON KRUSENSTJERNA (1894 —1940) shows a similar *dépaysement*, emotional perhaps rather than intellectual. Her three novel cycles, which include *The Tony Books* ("Tonyböckerna", 1922—1926) and *The Misses von Pahlen* ("Fröknarna von Pahlen", 1930—1935), build on autobiographical experiences, and express with lucidity, and without any experimentation with form, her criticisms of the conventions of the aristocratic and upper middle-class circles whom she knew so well. But the main reason why these books have been so much discussed in Sweden lies in their outspoken treatment of sexual problems. Morbid eroticism and sexual perversions had not hitherto been treated with any marked psychological subtlety in Swedish literature, which, as we have seen, had never created that tradition of psychology that is so typical of the literature of France.

In sharp contrast to these glimpses of irrational fears and subconscious horrors stand the novels of OLLE HEDBERG (born 1899). These are witty, elegant pictures, in some ways rather irritating, satirizing upper middle-class life, where the author, however critical of his subjects, never loses his sense of proportion or his feeling for his best-seller public. A prose-writer of much greater originality is TAGE AURELL (born 1895), who achieved appreciation only in the '40's for his concision and the overtones in his works. See, for example, *Three Stories* ("Tre berättelser"). A more grossly fantastic view of life, coupled with considerable humour, is represented by such products of Lund as FRITHIOF NILS-SON-PIRATEN (born 1895) and by FRANS G. BENGTSSON (born 1894), the author of the historical novel *Red Orm* ("Röde Orm", 1941—1945).

Meanwhile, the sincerity and technical skill of the Swedish lyrical tradition have been sustained by the versatile and

attractive HJALMAR GULLBERG (born 1898), by JOHANNES
EDFELT (born 1904), by BERTIL MALMBERG, NILS FERLIN,
KARL RAGNAR GIEROW, and many others.

GUNNAR EKELÖF (born 1907) was one of the first Swedish
poets to reflect, among other influences, the doctrines of
the French Surrealists, in his lyrics of 1932; and his latest
collection of poems, dated 1945, *Non Serviam*, continues
to develop this illogical, fascinating medium. Of the so-
called "Fyrtiotalister" (poets of the '40's), whose general
mood, not uninfluenced by Kafka, is one of pessimism and
despair in face of the Second World War and its implications,
ERIK LINDEGREN too has been influenced by Surrealism, and
Ekelöf. KARL VENNBERG, another lyrical poet, the theorist
of the group, takes up T. S. Eliot, and deliberately makes
intellectual use of recondite associations. It is as yet far
too early to pick out among this youngest generation those
writers who possess any staying power, but STIG DAGERMAN
(born 1923) has already made his mark both as novelist,
with *Burnt Child* ("Bränt barn"), of 1948, and more especially as dramatist. *The Shadow of Mart* ("Skuggan av
Mart",1948), to mention nothing else, suggests that out of
the moods of introspective bitterness and, let us say, over-
intellectualized brooding of this generation, may emerge
works of lasting value.

CHAPTER X

NORWEGIAN LITERATURE 1870–1950

With the first authorship of Henrik Ibsen and Bjørnstjerne Bjørnson the period of National Romanticism in Norwegian literature may be said to have come to an end, although it was to manifest itself in later writers in a different form. In 1869, Ibsen's first social play *The League of Youth* ("De Unges Forbund"), which was to be the forerunner of a whole series of plays of similar nature, was published. Bjørnson, too, turned his attention to literature with a social purpose, and they were soon to be joined in the same field by the novelists Alexander Kielland and Jonas Lie. Ibsen, Bjørnson, Kielland and Lie are, in fact, the "big four" of 19th century Norwegian literature and the main props of the undoubted literary greatness of the country at this period.

The League of Youth has as its background the political situation of the time and the strife occasioned by the rise of the party system in Norwegian politics from which the Liberals were soon to emerge as the largest party. Its principal character, the disreputable political weathercock, Steensgaard, was received with howls of delight by the Conservatives who saw in him the type of their opponents and Ibsen as the Conservative poet *par excellence*. Neither assumption was correct, although the Liberals took offence at what they regarded as a caricature of themselves and in particular of their darling, Bjørnson, in the figure of Steensgaard. Ibsen soon made it clear that he was not to be reckoned amongst the assets of any political party and, as soon as the dust of political controversy had settled, it was seen that Steensgaard was simply the type of the political go-getter, irrespective of party label or colour. The sequence of social plays was interrupted by the publication in 1873 of the huge double-drama *Emperor and Galilean* ("Kejser og Galilæer"), a work which had been occupying Ibsen for some time. This is not a play the modern reader is likely to derive much satisfaction from; it is, it must be confessed, diffuse, and the author himself appears to have got tired of it before it was completed, although, it is said, he regarded it as his masterpiece. It deals with the attempt of Julian the Apostate to reintroduce paganism into the Roman Empire. In it Ibsen adumbrates, through the character of Maximos, the mystic, the idea of what he calls, "det tredje rige" (the third kingdom), which was to be a sort of synthesis of knowledge and revelation, indulgence and renunciation, the whole hinting at the concept of freedom with responsibility which was to occupy him in later plays.

The Danish literary critic, Georg Brandes, whose epochmaking work of literary criticism *Main Currents* began to appear in 1871, was greatly admired by Ibsen, and his dictum that writers should debate social problems in their works gave great impetus to the works of Ibsen which were to follow: *The Pillars of Society* ("Samfundets Støtter", 1877), *A Doll's House* ("Et Dukkehjem", 1879),*Ghosts* ("Gengangere", 1881) and *An Enemy of the People* ("En Folkefiende", 1882). The first, *The Pillars of Society*, is in some ways the corrective of *The League of Youth* and a cold douche for those Conservatives who had enthusiastically received that play as a testament of political faith. Here Ibsen takes a "pillar of society", the prosperous and respected shipping magnate, Consul Karsten

Bernick, who outwardly appears to be a model of public
and private virtue but who, in fact, is a very rocky support
of society, corrupted as he is by lies, dubious dealings and
the like. Ibsen removes his garments of respectability one
by one, but perhaps mindful of what Solveig had achieved
in the case of Per Gynt, allows a good angel, in the person
of Lona Hessel, to appear, before it is too late, to save the
Consul's soul from damnation by urging him to public
confession of his misdemeanours. *A Doll's House* was
the play that established Ibsen's European reputation. It
deals with the position of women in marriage. Nora, the
heroine, is married to the fatuously pompous and possessive
Helmer who also, in his small way, regards himself as a
pillar of society. A crisis is reached in their matrimonial
relations (and the play is largely occupied with the events
leading up to it) when Helmer discovers that years before
his wife had forged her father's name in order to obtain
money to provide for a health trip to Italy for *him,* Helmer. This revelation stuns Helmer, humbles his pride
and makes him tremble for his civic position. His shallow-
ness of character, which we had always suspected, is now
clear for all to see, whilst Nora displays a hitherto unre-
vealed firmness. It results in her leaving him, marking her
exit by a firm slamming of the front door, a manifestation
of feminine independence which shocked Ibsen's contemporaries and evoked angry protests. The commotion was
such that prudent theatre managers abroad presented the
play with a revised ending. *Ghosts,* which followed, was,
in a way, Ibsen's retort to the scandalized. Here we have
a woman, Mrs. Alving, who does everything (and more
besides) that the society of the day demanded in the way
of wifely duty. Even the death of her debauched libertine
husband does not put an end to her efforts in that respect.
In order that his name may be permanently revered she
has built an orphanage, sacred to his memory, which is soon

to be opened. Catastrophe is, however, not far off. Her son, who has been kept in careful ignorance of his father's real character, returns from Paris a physical and mental wreck, a victim of the sins of the father, and the orphanage is, appropriately enough, burnt down. This play was again regarded as an attack on the institution of marriage and the resultant clamour was even more violent than it had been in the case of *A Doll's House*. Ibsen was, in fact, dubbed an "enemy of the people", a description he used as the title of his next play, *An Enemy of the People*. Here, in the person of Dr. Stockman, the chief character, he is mildly satirizing himself. Stockman is a zealous medical officer who discovers that the baths which supply the town with its major item of revenue are polluted. When he informs his fellow-townsmen, instead of getting the gratitude he expected for pointing out this evil, he is showered with abuse and finally hounded out of the town as an "enemy of the people".

With *An Enemy of the People,* the social plays of Ibsen may be, strictly speaking, said to have come to an end, but here, as in other cases, hard and fast boundaries are dangerous, for other of the later plays have "social" elements in them. Before proceeding to them, however, we will take a look at what Bjørnson had been writing of a similar nature. Already in 1865 he had written a short comedy *The Newly-Married Couple* ("De Nygifte"), which whilst more of a novelette in dramatic form than a real work for the stage, is mildly social in purpose, dealing with the relationship of parents and children after the latter have married; but it was with the group of plays, *The Editor* ("Redaktøren", 1875), *A Bankrupt* ("En Fallit", 1875), *The King* ("Kongen", 1877), that Bjørnson really gave himself over to the dramatic presentation of contemporary social problems. The first two of these plays make a call for higher standards in journalism and business respectively;

judging from their appearances in literature newspaper editors in 19th century Norway could exercise an influence over the lives of private citizens, which to-day seems surprising, and in the person of Bjørnson's editor we have a particularly unpleasant specimen of the breed; bankruptcies also figure largely and seem to have been of frequent occurrence. *The King* appears to advocate a more democratic kind of monarchy and its appearance resulted in Bjørnson being attacked, on the grounds that he was a red-hot republican, which he was not. The play is a curious mixture of comedy, melodrama, poetry and social philosophy and is a good example of how deficient in artistic sense Bjørnson at times could be. There is always something interesting in Bjørnson's plays but it must be admitted that as a dramatist he is far inferior to Ibsen. Later followed *Leonarda* (1879); *The New System* ("Det ny System", 1879), and *A Gauntlet* ("En Handske", 1883). In the first we have the basic situation of a young man faced with the problem of choosing between two women, one a young girl and the other a mature woman, but in social tendency the play is a revolt against prejudice and exaggerated respect for, and unwarranted interference on the part of, established authority. In *The New System*, it is again established authority, bureaucracy and officialdom of all kinds that get the worst of it, although the theme of the play is the struggle over a new railway system. The last play in this group, *A Gauntlet*, is, in respect of its subject matter, the most celebrated of Bjørnson's plays and the subject of much controversy. It deals with masculine morality before and during marriage and comes down with a heavy hand on the existing tolerant conventions in that respect. Bjørnson felt so strongly on this issue that, in the years 1887—1888, he toured Scandinavia lecturing on *Monogamy and Polygamy* ("Engifte og Mangegifte"), in an effort to impress his views on his fellow Scandinavians.

It is convenient at this point to leave Bjørnson and return to Ibsen, for with *A Gauntlet* social questions ceased to be the predominating ones in Bjørnson's plays. In 1884 appeared *The Wild Duck* ("Vildanden"), perhaps the finest of all Ibsen's plays. Here are combined realism, poetry, tragedy, humour and the whole is marked, above all, by a wonderful warmth in characterization. Misconception has made this play a favourite with those who like to regard Ibsen as an apostle of gloom, and some of Ibsen's contemporaries were not pleased, accusing him of apostasy, in that in his earlier plays the sinner was always seen to be capable of conversion, a Bernick, a Per Gynt or even a Brand, and that the truth was the best healer for the ills of the soul. Here, in the character of Hjalmar Ekdal, we have a man for whom the truth is too much and for whom existence is dependent on the maintenance of what Ibsen calls the "life lie", in other words on an elaborate apparatus of self-deception. What so often seems to be overlooked in this play is that Hjalmar is largely a figure of fun, a tragic one, no doubt, the day-dreamer who is incapable of facing up to the realities of life and must deceive himself at every turn.

Rosmersholm (1886) has as its background the political situation after 1884, in which year the Liberals succeeded in getting the king, Oscar II, to acknowledge the principle of government by the largest party in the Storting. The conflict between the old and the new in politics enters into the life of the retiring, scholarly, former clergyman, Johannes Rosmer, the master of Rosmersholm and the last of a race of officers, clergymen and the like, and he is forced to declare himself for one or other party. Rosmer's belief, as it happens, in the way of life of his fathers, has already been seriously undermined, and when the storm breaks he is in the process of ridding himself of what he considers to be the dead-wood and encumbrances of family tradition.

Assisting in this process is the unscrupulous, vigorous Rebekka West, one of the most fascinating, yet at the same time most repulsive of Ibsen's female characters. The story of her relationship with Rosmer and the clash of loyalties, which brings about the final tragedy of their double suicide, has an elegiac note to which is added the symbolism of the "white horses of Rosmersholm" and the unseen yet palpable presence of Beate, Rosmer's dead wife.

The move towards the more positive use of symbolism to be noted in *Rosmersholm* becomes more apparent in *The Lady from the Sea* ("Fruen fra Havet", 1888), and it is further marked by that interest in abnormal psychology which was to be a characteristic of Ibsen's last plays. "The Lady from the Sea", a pampered doctor's wife, is under a curious spell cast by a man with "fish eyes", from which she only succeeds in freeing herself when allowed to make a free choice between him and her husband. The moral of the piece seems to be that freedom with responsibility (self-determination) is a prerequisite of human happiness, although this aspect of the play, whilst often emphasized, seems less important to me than the poetic quality which pervades it. What this comes of is difficult to say, perhaps the nature of the subject is partly responsible, but it is impossible not to be aware of the overtones, suggestive of remote keys, which the apparently most ordinary exchanges between the characters can evoke.

Hedda Gabler (1890) returns us to the reality of Christiania of the 1880's and concerns Hedda, the general's daughter, whom Ibsen calls by her maiden name to remind us that she is to be regarded as her father's daughter, although she has just been united, in a not very well assorted marriage, to Jørgen Tesman, a molly-coddled doctor of philosophy. Hedda is the degenerate society woman, whose personality and will to live have been vitiated, not by the degeneracy of vicious living, but by doing nothing. She has had leanings towards the Bohemian life which is currently fashionable, but lacks the courage to take the plunge and it seems unlikely that she will shoulder the obligations of married life. When she is later faced with a situation likely to place her in the power of someone else and restrict her freedom she chooses suicide as the way out. Hedda is, in fact, a person who wants freedom *without* responsibility. Of *Hedda Gabler* it has been said that it was the last play in which Ibsen deals with other people and there seems much (with the exception of *Little Eyolf*) to support the view that henceforth he was to deal largely with himself. All the plays that were to follow are, at all events, marked by a retrospection not found before, as if the ageing Ibsen found it incumbent on him to take stock. Soaring high above them all is *The Master Builder* ("Bygmester Solness", 1892), and there can be little doubt that much of it is autobiographical. It concerns the belated and unavailing regrets of the elderly master-builder Halvard Solness regarding the conduct of his life. Implicit is the problem of the creative artist, be he master-builder or poet, and his relationship to the other claims life imposes on him. The tone of the piece is predominantly poetic and there is a warmth in the characterization which was hardly to be captured again. Technically it is one of Ibsen's finest achievements, for in spite of containing much that is symbolic and fanciful it loses nothing in dramatic intensity.

The last three plays, *Little Eyolf* ("Lille Eyolf", 1894), *John Gabriel Borkman* (1896) and *When We Dead Awaken* ("Naar vi døde vaagner", 1899) are full of interest for the student of Ibsen, throwing, as they never fail to do, new and revealing light on the art and mind of that remarkable man, but it must be admitted that to the ordinary playgoer they are likely to be something of a disappointment. This, I think, is mainly due to the slackening of dramatic tension which is noticeable in them and a certain misanthropy that chills. *Little Eyolf* has, as its motive, what Ibsen calls *forvandlingens lov* (the law of change), as it applies to the affections of partners in marriage. Here, in the case of Alfred Almers and his wife Rita, this law does not function in what is probably its normal way, for whilst passion with Alfred Almers wanes it waxes in Rita. The death of their crippled son Eyolf by drowning causes them to take stock of their loveless life and finally to devote themselves to works of charity. *John Gabriel Borkman* and *When We Dead Awaken* both deal with men with a "call", the one an ex-convict financier, who has heard the iron – ore singing in the earth, calling out to be released, and has dreamt and still dreams that he is the man to release it and enrich his country; the other is the world-famous sculptor Rubek. Many of the problems from the *Master Builder* are raised again here. Both plays have a certain poignancy, but the sum of bitterness, which the almost exclusively elderly protagonists in them have saved up, makes sympathy for them difficult: it may be life but it is chilling. The reader who feels disposed to read Ibsen from cover to cover — a profitable proceeding — should not neglect his poems. The poetic qualities of many of the plays will be readily appreciated and there is much in his poems which throws light on the plays.

Whilst Ibsen had been thus engaged, Bjørnson had produced two of his most important plays: *Beyond Our Power I* ("Over Ævne", Part I, 1883) and *Paul Lange and Tora Parsberg* (1898). The former reflects the interest in abnormal psychology which we have already noted in certain of Ibsen's later plays. It deals with a religious faith-healer in Northern Norway called Pastor Sang, a lovable character with a faith in his powers, and in the power of religion that is not shaken until the very last. The moral of the piece, as with so much of Bjørnson's work, is the avoidance of fanaticism and extremes in all things. The play is marked by much lyric beauty and can be best appreciated when read. *Paul Lange and Tora Parsberg* is based to some extent on actual events; the political situation at the end of the 1880's and the suicide of the Norwegian government representative in Stockholm, Ole Richter, who is the Paul Lange of the play. Politics are, however, only the background of the play; its chief merit lies in the psychological penetration Bjørnson displays in the character of Paul Lange, a weak, sensitive man for whom conflicting political loyalties and his love for Tora Parsberg are too much. Between these two plays Bjørnson had written a comedy *Geography and Love* ("Geografi og Kjærlighed", 1885), concerning an eccentric professor of geography for whom nothing exists but his subject, and for this all other considerations take second place. It contains some matters of topical interest but was intended largely as a satire of himself. It is a pleasant piece of fun bordering at times on the serious but the end is rather boring. Together with *Beyond Our Power* it is the play of Bjørnson which has been most performed in recent years. After *Paul Lange and Tora Parsberg* Bjørnson wrote several plays, none particularly worthy of note except the last one *When the Vineyards Are in Blossom* ("Naar den ny Vin blomstrer", 1909), a sparkling comedy of family-life.

Bjørnson's literary production since his first tales of peasant life had not been confined to playwriting. Novels, short stories, poems both long and short, and much journalistic and polemical writing had flowed from his pen. Of the greatest permanent value is perhaps his lyric poetry, and most noteworthy of his novels, *Magnhild* (1877), the story of a peasant girl who has artistic aspirations. Here there is nothing idyllic in the descriptions of peasant life and its realism scandalized his contemporaries. The present-day reader would find much of the long novel *Flags Are Flying in Town and Port* ("Det flager i Byen og paa Havnen",

1884) boring, containing, as it does, much theorizing on the
question of the education and upbringing suitable for
young girls. Of particular interest, however, is the unusual
understanding Bjørnson shows of the psychology of girls
of adolescent age and some of the character-drawing is first-
rate. Particularly worthy of mention is the section called
"Generalstaben" (The General Staff) and the characterization of Fru Rendalen who is the central figure in the book.
Unfortunately it is also marked by appalling lapses in taste
and artistic sense of which the seduction of Tora is the
worst example.

The next member of the "big four", JONAS LIE (1833–
1908), took to the pen as a means of livelihood after a short
and disastrous career as a lawyer and speculator in timber
which ended in bankruptcy. He gained success straight
away with his novel from Northern Norway, *The Visionary*
("Den Fremsynte", 1870), and his subsequent production,
mainly in novel form, is considerable. Unlike many of his
contemporaries social problems are not of paramount importance to him; they are often implicit in what he wrote
but there is nothing of the propagandist in him. He has
often been called "hjemmenes dikter" (the writer of the
home) and it is, no doubt, Norwegian home-life he describes best. Lie's first important full-scale work was the
novel *The Pilot and his Wife* ("Lodsen og hans Hustru",
1874), the story of a marriage that is going to pieces through
misunderstandings. It contains excellent pictures of life
in a small Norwegian sea-port and realistic descriptions of
life at sea. His next novel of importance, *The Lifer* ("Livs-
slaven", 1883), bears marks of the tide of Naturalism which,
generally speaking, hardly washed the shores of literary
Norway at all. It is a piece of uncompromising Realism
from the back-streets of Christiania with Barbro, the un-
married mother, and her son Nikolai, as the central figures.
Social criticism is perhaps nearer the surface in the depict-

ing of these two unfortunates than anywhere else in Lie. Barbro is obliged to hire herself out as a wet-nurse whilst Nikolai is boarded-out, early to become the victim of prejudice, neglect and social injustice. He ends up as a convict with a life sentence after having murdered the arrogant Ludwig Wejergang whom his mother had suckled. In 1883 also appeared *The Family at Gilje* ("Familjen paa Gilje"), the most famous and beloved of all Lie's novels. Again home-life is the theme, this time the home of a country gentleman, an officer, and it is set in the district of Valdres around the 1840's. It is first-rate as a piece of social history and artistically it is on a high level. In tendency it has affinities with Camilla Collett's *The Sheriff's Daughters*, in that it depicts the position of women of the upper classes in the society of the day, and the same can be said of *The Commodore's Daughters* ("Kommandørens Døtre", 1886). In neither case, however, does this tendency obtrude, yet the sympathy we feel for the female characters has a persuasiveness that is more effective than all Fru Collett's fanaticism. Other novels of family life are, *Life Together* ("Et Samliv", 1887) and *Niobe* (1893). Lie was himself a great home-lover and regarded harmonious family life as of vital importance to the community. Perhaps it is because of this that he so often shows family life in a state of decay, and indicating the causes, often of a trivial and remedial nature, points the moral. Supernatural and psychic phenomena had always had a strong fascination for him. His first book, *The Visionary*, dealing with the clairvoyant David Holst indicates this, and this interest received further expression in his collection of tales called *Trolls* ("Trold", 1891–1892). In many of them he succesfully reproduces the style of the popular folk-tale whilst contriving to give them ethical import. In much of Lie's writing it is clear that the mysteries of the *trolls* of human nature and temperament, the unseen powers, appealed to the mystic in him. *Trolls* is the profoundest expression of this side of him. Lie's production also included plays and other novels, but none of outstanding merit.

ALEXANDER KIELLAND (1849–1906) was an aristocrat with a social conscience. The son of a wealthy Stavanger merchant he wrote only to draw attention to what he considered to be the social and moral evils of his day. He was not for that any dry-as-dust pamphleteer, his prose style is, in fact, regarded as the most elegant in the whole of modern Norwegian literature. His weapons were irony, wit and conscious exaggeration, all used with the greatest artistry: the artist in him not infrequently gets the better of the zeal of the social reformer.

Kielland's literary activity lasted no more than a matter of 12 years, and began in 1879 with a collection of *Novelletter*. They are amusing, moving, but the pill is always there, elegantly coated though it may be. Most famous are his novels from Stavanger, especially *Garman and Worse* (1880) and *Skipper Worse* (1882), which are largely based on personal recollection and family tradition. The decay of the Garman fortunes (his own family really) is depicted with a certain melancholy, and there is a lingering affection in his descriptions of the expansive, cultivated life at Sandsgaard, the Garman family seat, although his social conscience was active enough to prevent his forgetting the unfortunates who lived in that part of the town, called, ironically enough, "West End". In *Skipper Worse* we get an understanding, but nevertheless critical picture of the Hauge sect, a Pietist movement founded at the beginning of the 19th century by Hans Nielsen Hauge and in many ways comparable to the Quaker movement. In a trilogy of novels *Poison* ("Gift", 1882), *Fortuna* (1884) and *The Midsummer Fête* ("Sankt Hans Fest", 1887), humbug and murky dealings of various kinds in divers spheres receive the brunt of the attack, whilst the grammar-school education of the day and the State Church are badly mauled. *Workers* ("Arbeidsfolk", 1881) is a biting attack on the bureaucratic incompetence Kielland imagined prevailed in the Norwegian civil service; here, it must be admitted, that away from his home-ground of Stavanger, as is the case in this book, Kielland's touch and factual background are less sure. In *Else* (1881) are related the misfortunes of a young girl who has been seduced by a rich business-man and the author provides himself with the opportunity to express his uncomplimentary opinions regarding the activities of snobbish social welfare workers. With *Jacob* (1891) Kielland's creative work came to an end. There has been much speculation as to the reasons for its abrupt cessation. The subject of *Jacob,* a *parvenu* of peasant origin of the worst type, seems to indicate that Kielland's reforming zeal had brought him disappointments.

The use of New Norwegian as a literary language was to receive epoch-making impetus through the authorship of ARNE GARBORG (1851–1924), and, in it, were to be mirrored the problems attendant on the agrarian revolution of the century; a task, for which his keen intellect and peasant background fitted him admirably. Garborg was born in Jæren, in South-western Norway, and was brought up in a strict, pietistic home. He reached manhood at a time when the disintegration of the old peasant society had reached a critical phase. The days when Norwegian agriculture was mainly self-supplying were past and the new capitalist basis was a hard taskmaster, particularly as most farms had been heavily mortgaged to effect improvements of one sort or other; a precarious proceeding in days of financial uncertainty.

Peasant Students ("Bondestudentar", 1883) was Garborg's first important work and it has become his most famous. It deals with the career of a peasant lad who aspires to become a parson, an ambition, which, after many trials and tribulations and discarding of early idealism, he finally achieves. Besides being a piece of psychological writing of quality it gives a first-class picture of prevailing social conditions, particularly in the contemporary student milieu of Christiania, and reflects the current trends in the political and religious life of the Norwegian capital, at the same time giving enlightening portraits of many of the leading personalities of the period.

The next work by Garborg of which we need take note is *Peace* ("Fred", 1892), largely reminiscent of his own childhood and with its chief character, Enok Hòve, clearly modelled on his own father, whose sickly pietistic habits of life led him eventually to self-destruction. It is the melancholy saga of the peasant struggling to wrest a meagre living from an ungenerous soil, afflicted by economic misfortune and a prey to a cheerless Pietism in an effort to find a firm rock in a world of shifting values. It should not be thought from this that the book is merely harrowing; the whole is invested with a sombre beauty and artistry which are deeply impressive.

As if to show, in contrast to *Fred,* the peasant life of an earlier period with its customs, beliefs, superstitions and way of life still firmly rooted in paganism and Pre-Reformation Catholicism, Garborg wrote his cycle of poems called *Haugtussa* (1895). It contains some poems of rare beauty and is a perfect demonstration of the wonderfully evocative quality of the New Norwegian language, but most of all it gives a clear insight into peasant psychology and makes for understanding of what consequences the impact of modern economy and industry on such a society, for Norwegian rural society retained much of its medieval character right up to the 19th century, must have been.

In his early years as schoolmaster, journalist and student Garborg was much influenced by the current Bohemian, anti-religious tendencies of the Norwegian capital's intellectual life, much of which is reflected in his early works. He abandoned Christianity but later came to an independent religious philosophy where the influence of Tolstoy is clearly discernible. The fruits of his speculations are embodied in the play *The Teacher* ("Læraren", 1896) and in *The Lost Father* ("Den burtkomne Faderen", 1899), and *The Returned Son* ("Heimkomin Son", 1908). Besides the works mentioned, Garborg wrote much in letter form, *Kolbotnbrev* and *Knudaheibrev*, which contain descriptions of nature and recollections and reflections on many subjects, particularly on peasant life.

A somewhat isolated position in Norwegian literature is occupied by AMALIE SKRAM (1846–1905), in that she was the only thorough-going Naturalist the country produced. Her Naturalism is one of matter and not of style and has its background in her own unhappy life to which marriage at the age of 18 formed the prelude. In a number of books she depicts women afflicted as she was herself, with a frigidity, which turns marriage into a torment of Hell for them and yet who are filled with a deep longing for, what for them must be, the unattainable.

Most unpleasant of these novels is *Betrayed* ("Forraadt", 1892), which by the nature of its subject — a young girl who marries a sea-captain — must be largely autobiographical. More considerable and to be regarded as her chief work is the series of novels in four volumes, *The People of Hellemyr* ("Hellemyrsfolket") which appeared from 1887 to 1898. It is the story of a family inexorably ground, generation after generation, by the wheels of an unkind fate. It is monumental in its pessimism yet impressive in its search for truth as the authoress conceived it.

The epoch of social writing in Norway did not last very long. Even amongst the writers of the older generation the presentation and debating of problems ceased to be of prime importance, as, for example, with Ibsen in his last plays where the symbolic and poetic elements become more and more pronounced, or in Jonas Lie's *Trolls* and Garborg's *Haugtussa*. In the 1890's a New Romanticism, as it was called, set in, partly under the influence of literary movements abroad, particularly in France with the Symbolist lyric poets Baudelaire, Verlaine, Rimbaud and Mallarmé and in Sweden in the figures of Heidenstam and Levertin. In Norway the young Knut Hamsun poured scorn on the literary ideals of the writers then current.

The extreme features of the new movement are represented almost exclusively in Norway by SIGBJØRN OBSTFELDER (1866—1900), whose lyric poetry embodies the elements of evocative language, Symbolism, and a certain morbid glorification of the sordid which were characteristics of the French school. Particularly typical in this respect is his poem *Nameless* ("Navnløs"). His production included a play *The Red Drops* ("De røde Draaber", 1897) where the chief character is a creature entirely at variance with the realities of life, filled with a sickly longing for the infinite and imbued with a fantastic mysticism which causes him to renounce all earthly advantage and gain. Similar ideas are to be found in his unfinished *A Parson's Journal* ("En Præsts Dagbog", 1900), which whilst throwing much light on Obstfelder's curious personality is evidence that hard thinking was not his line of country. Apart from his poems his best work are *To Novelletter* (1895) and *The Cross — A Love Story* ("Korset — En Kjærlighedshistorie", 1896).

A "New Romantic" poet seeking inspiration at home in the idyllic and sequestered charm of Sørland (South-western Norway) with its rocky and skerry-wreathed coast is VILHELM KRAG (1871—1933). In his many poems he evokes the atmosphere of that part of the country to perfection. Best known of them is *O, Sørland, Thou My Native Land* ("O, Sørland, Du min Moderjord"). Southern Norway also provided him with material for novels and plays and

here the reader would find amusement and a delightful
introduction to the idiosyncrasies of the folk of those parts
in his *Major von Knarren* (1906) and the play *Baldevin's
Wedding* ("Baldevins Bryllup", 1900).

NILS COLLETT VOGT (1864–1937), his contemporary, was
a poet made of sterner stuff, radical and rebellious in outlook, but often expressive in his poems of a longing and
love for his native land.

Norwegian drama, after Bjørnson and Ibsen had completed their best labours, tended to languish but received
some sustenance from the hand of GUNNAR HEIBERG (1857–
1929). He was no respecter of institutions or persons and
he gave his disapproval sharp, sarcastic, and often bitter
expression in his plays. His first play *Aunt Ulrikke* ("Tante
Ulrikke", 1884) has its background in the political situation
around this time and contains much that is unflattering to
the Conservatives; Aunt Ulrikke herself is modelled on the
champion of women's rights in Norway Aasta Hansteen.
King Midas ("Kong Midas", 1890) is an attack on hypocrisy
and was considered as being mainly directed against Bjørnson. *I Will Defend My Country* ("Jeg vil værge mit Land",
1918) scorns the settlement made with Sweden in 1905, and
The Catafalque ("Paradesengen", 1913), his last play, has as
its subject "small sons of great fathers". It led to uproar
when performed at the National Theatre in Oslo in 1924.

The pre-occupation of many of his contemporaries in the
1880's with love, marriage and associated problems led
him in his two plays *The Balcony* ("Balkonen", 1894) and
Love's Tragedy ("Kjærlighedens Tragedie", 1904) to probe
into the nature of sex and sexual relationship. In these
plays he depicts it as an all-consuming anti-social force not
to be reconciled with the claims of a working life; a
conception which owes much to those current at the time.

From the turn of the century the novel was to dominate
the literary scene in Norway and in particular the novel

having a certain regional background; psychological interest as opposed to the predominantly social interest of the
earlier writers was also a general characteristic of the new
school.

KNUT HAMSUN (born 1859) made his début in 1888 with
Hunger ("Sult"), a novel illustrative of the ravages starvation
can work in the sensitive mind of a young artist.   Here, at
once, something new is to be detected, for whilst the subject
was appropriate to the period and had been treated before
(in Garborg's *Peasant Students,* for example), Hamsun is
not a bit interested in the social or even Naturalistic implications of starvation.   He is only concerned with its effects
on the psychology of its victim. The newness of his approach
and his original handling of the language make this novel
a mile-stone in Norwegian literature.   In some ways Hamsun is a curious mixture.   On the one hand, in novels like
Mysteries ("Mysterier", 1892), *Pan* (1894), *August* and many
others, he appears to extoll the joys of the life of the
wanderer;   in others, notably, *The Growth of the Soil*
("Markens Grøde", 1917), his most famous book, for which
he was awarded the Nobel Prize for literature, he praises
the settled life of the tiller of the soil;   in fact, the whole
book can be regarded as a call of "back to the land".   All
these works, however, are marked by a sort of nature-
mysticism and very often by an expressed detestation of
town-life and all its manifestations.   In *The Growth of the
Soil,* we are introduced on the first page to Isak making
his way northward in search of land and at once a casement
is opened on to a primitive society and a primitive land.
Isak has the soil and his hands and nothing else and we
watch him build until a whole thriving community has
grown up in "Ødemarken" (The waste land) and Isak bears
the title of "Markgreven" (Count of the prairie).   There can
of course be much that is irritating in Hamsun's yearnings
for the solitude of Nature, his optimism as to the agricultural

possibilities of undeveloped Norway, and his enthusiasm for illiterates, but it is impossible to deny the majestic sweep of this work and its high poetic qualities. In other of his books, *Children of the Age* ("Børn av Tiden", 1913) and *Segelfoss Town* ("Segelfoss By", 1915), he depicts life in a Nordland trading post, not without considerable irony, particularly when contrasting the old established landowning classes with the new rich, whom he detests. In his later novels, *The Women at the Pump* ("Konerne ved Vandposten", 1928) and *Last Chapter* ("Sisste Kapitel", 1923), much to the disappointment of those who had admired *The Growth of the Soil*, he evinces a misanthropy which is only matched by the repulsiveness of his characters. His trilogy of novels, *Tramps* ("Landstrykere", 1927), *August* (1930) and *But Life Remains* ("Men Livet lever", 1933), marks a return to his former good humour and ideals with an insistence on the virtues of settled life. August, the tramp, the chief character, is a sort of Per Gynt figure, Norwegian but universal, likeable but the bearer of the vices of his race, as Hamsun saw them. In the use of the Norwegian language Hamsun has affected nothing short of a revolution and his influence on younger contemporaries has been considerable if not always beneficial. Besides the large number of novels he wrote, his production also includes plays and a collection of poems *The Wild Choir* ("Det vilde Kor", 1904), which puts Hamsun amongst the foremost Norwegian lyric poets of this century.

HANS E. KINCK (1865–1926) is one of the most considerable of the many Norwegian writers who have taken upon themselves, through the medium of imaginative writing, the task of delving into the characteristics of the Norwegian peasant and exploring his peculiarities in the light of geographical and historical circumstance. The clash of the "to kulturer" (the two cultures) — the peasant culture and the imported culture of the upper, civil-service class — is also a favourite theme with him. The novels *Herman Ek* (1923) and *The Avalanche* ("Sneskavlen brast", 1918–1919) are noteworthy in this respect. Kinck is not an easy writer, his style is his own and tends to turbidity. Particularly difficult is his verse of which the most important is the dramatic poem *The Drover* ("Driftekaren", 1908). Here, in the person of Vraal, the chief character, who is a combination of horse-dealer, poet, philosopher, he depicts a type which is to be met with over and over again in Norwegian literature; the peasant who in a way is a sort of genius, "bygdegeni" (the parish genius), as the Norwegians say.

Mention might be made before passing on to the next outstanding figure in Norwegian literature of several minor writers. Tryggve Andersen (1866–1920) is beloved for his *In the Days of the Cancelliraad* ("I Cancelliraadens dage", 1897) descriptive of life centred on the administrative ("embets") class in a country district of eastern Norway at the beginning of the 19th century. Andersen has a prose style that is a delight and we get in this book a piece of social history with an authentic ring which includes a vivid picture of the consequences of the blockade of Norway during the Napoleonic wars.

Niels Kjær (1870–1924) is noted as the author of *Epistles* ("Epistler", 1908, 1912, 1924), ironical, witty, sometimes sombre reflections on a wide variety of topics. As a playwright he achieved great success with his play *The Happy Election* ("Det lykkelige Valg", 1914), a delightful comedy poking fun at the stupidities and follies of political life.

Among the many minor writers who selected peasant life as their field Hans Aanrud (born 1863) is perhaps most worthy of mention. His stories from his native Vestre Gausdal have much of the character of the popular folktale in them, are generally idyllic, and are marked by great humour and optimism.

Gabriel Scott (born 1874) is a writer with special affilia-

tions to Sørland, who had his first real success with the
novels *Ordeal by Fire*. *The Story of Jan Vibe* ("Jernbyr-
den, Historien om Jan Vibe", 1915) and *Enok Ruben's Life*
("Enok Rubens Levnedsløb", 1917). They are partly historical from the period around 1770 and set in the area
of Kristiansand, and partly (written as they were during
the 1914–1918 war) intended as an object lesson, in the
persons of the chief protagonists, in courage and endurance
in the face of persistent misfortune. They are also marked
by a warm patriotism of the kind Hamsun manifests in
The Growth of the Soil. On a high level is his *The Source*
("Kilden", 1918), the story of a simple fisherman who has
a clear understanding of the real values in life and the
sources of human happiness.

In OLAV DUUN (1876–1939), the New Norwegian novel
was to get its most distinguished exponent so far. His
mature style is a wonder of subtlety and quiet art, and
particularly to be admired is his mastery in reproducing in
all its freshness, pithiness and whimsicality the oral style
of the peasant which, as the popular folk-tales show, has
high artistic qualities, indicative of the great importance
attached to oral communication by the peasantry. In
addition to this Duun's descriptions of nature are particularly fine. His production, all in novel form, fills twelve
medium-sized volumes; most of them are set in Duun's native
region of North Trøndelag. Of these *The People of Juvik*
("Juvikfolke", 1918–1923), in six parts, is to be reckoned
as his chief work. It gives a broad picture of rural life and
change from about the beginning of the 19th century up
to the 1920's. In *The People of Juvik*, as elsewhere in
Duun, the clash of personalities, often symbolic of conflicting codes and principles of life, plays a dominating part
and here this is particularly illustrative of the changing
ethos of a society which, at the beginning of the 19th century,
was still largely medieval in way of life, custom and outlook.

Of Duun's other works perhaps *The Present Time* ("Samtid", 1936) and *Man and the Powers* ("Menneske og Maktene", 1938), should be singled out for mention. There is no doubt that these novels were intended as portraits of the contemporary world and prophetic of the calamity that was soon to come.

JOHAN BOJER (born 1872) is a prolific novelist setting his books often in the province of Trøndelag, but best known for his novel *The Last of the Vikings* ("Den siste Viking", 1921) telling of the fishing in Lofoten in the old days.

PETER EGGE (born 1869), also from Trøndelag, has written many novels of a Realistic kind from his native regions. Most successful was his *Hansine Solstad* (1925), the story of a woman who as a young girl was suspected of having committed a theft, a suspicion which, although she was innocent, attached to her for almost the rest of her life. In her refusal to allow this to undermine either her character or her will to live she achieves heroic proportions.

Outstanding for his series of 10 novels *The Dance through the Land of Shadows* ("Dansen gjenom skuggeheimen", 1911 —1924) is KRISTOFER UPPDAL (born 1878). Here, the emergence of a new industrial proletariat from the peasantry, occasioned by the rapid development of hydro-electric power and extension of communications at the beginning of this century, is the theme. Through the medium of a wide range of characters we witness the birth of this class, watch its growth and organisation and, in the process, the whole tragedy and saga of the peasant uprooted from the soil is made plain. Uppdal's almost exact contemporary, JOHAN FALKBERGET (born 1879), has also concerned himself with the problem industrial worker and peasant and has devoted himself to depicting the milieu he was born and brought up in, the mining district of Røros. In his chief work *Christianus Sextus* (1927—1935), he gives a broad social historic picture of the Røros region from the beginning of the 18th century.

SIGRID UNDSET (1882–1949) shares with Knut Hamsun the distinction of being the Norwegian writer of this century who has attracted most attention in the world at large. She was awarded the Nobel Prize in 1928. Her first books are marked by Naturalistic tendencies and are particularly concerned with the women of the Oslo middle-classes and their problems: most distinguished of her novels from this period is *Jenny* (1911). In the years 1920 –22 appeared the three volumes of her weighty historical novel from the Norway of the first part of the 14th century, *Kristin Lavransdatter*, which is the chief support of her literary fame and indicative in its content of a vast change in the writer's views on life since *Jenny*, for which conversion to Roman Catholicism was largely responsible. Similar in its religious and ethical purpose is *Olav Audunssøn i Hestviken* (1925) and *Olav Audunssøn and His Children* ("Olav Audunssøn og hans børn", 1927) which deal roughly with the same historical period as *Kristin Lavransdatter*. The wealth of historical detail and convincing atmosphere of these novels bear witness to the writer's profound knowledge of and insight into the Norwegian late Middle Ages: equally remarkable is her presentation and understanding of the religious and erotic problems of her characters. In her later novels Sigrid Undset again uses a contemporary setting: *Gymnadenia* (1929) and its continuation, *The Burning Bush* ("Den brændende Busk", 1930) relate, in terms often hostile to Protestantism, the *via dolorosa* of a young man which ends at the communion rail of the Catholic Church. *Ida Elisabeth* (1932) and *The Faithful Wife* ("Den trofaste Hustru", 1936), are two modern Realistic novels, and in *Eleven Years* ("Elleve Aar", 1934), largely autobiographical, and *Happy Times in Nor-*

way (1942), (written in U.S.A.), she shows a remarkable insight into the mind of young children.

A final assessment of Sigrid Undset's younger contemporaries is, of course, hardly possible yet. In the novels of SIGURD CHRISTIANSEN (1891—1947) moral and ethical problems are largely to the fore. In his best-known book *Two Living and One Dead* ("To levende og en død", 1931) he depicts an armed attack on a post-office; one assistant resists and is shot dead, another also resists and is wounded, but a third, who has time to reflect, hands over his till to the bandits without resistance. The book is then concerned with the subsequent relations of the two survivors and the attitude of the outside world to them. It gives the author the chance to display his powers as casuist and psychologist.

RONALD FANGEN (1895—1946) is also a novelist with marked ethical and religious purpose, whose most considerable work is the two-volume novel *Duell* (1932): it is a psychological investigation into the duel-like nature of a friendship between two persons of quite different type. In *Some Young People* ("Nogen unge mennesker", 1929) we are presented with a group of young people of different types and listen to their conversations on the various problems life has for them; from this group one of them emerges to become the chief character in the sequel *Erik* (1931). In this we get much criticism of the materialism and cynicism of contemporary life. Of a completely different type to Christiansen and Fangen are, SIGURD HOEL (born 1890) and HELGE KROG (born 1889). Hoel has been a much discussed figure in modern Norwegian literature. He is an extremely competent writer, greatly interested in modern psychology and often accused of being a rank materialist. Most discussed of his books were *One Day in October* ("En dag i oktober", 1931) and *Sinners in the Summer Sun* ("Syndere i sommersol", 1927). In the latter he depicts a group of students, full of modern ideas, disciples of Freud and quite sure of themselves. With delightful irony Hoel shows how they make the same mistakes as the older generation, whom they despise, made. His best book so far is perhaps *The Way to the End of the World* ("Vejen til verdens ende", 1933), remarkable for its understanding of the psychology of children. Helge Krog has in many ways been the *enfant terrible* of contemporary Norwegian literary life. As a critic he has been admired for his acuteness and for his detestation of all that smacks of sham and, above all, for his highly polished prose style, but his fearlessness and lack, sometimes, of chivalry towards opponents has also made him detested by others. His best work in the field of criticism is collected together in his *Opinions* ("Meninger", 1929 and 1933) which also represent modern Norwegian *riksmål* at its best. As a dramatist Krog has concerned himself with social problems, but he has been most successful in his light, erotically tinged, comedies where he often seems playfully to pay court to that social class, the Oslo upper-classes, which he elsewhere subjects to much violent criticism.

Norwegian lyric poetry has been particularly rich in this century with perhaps its major representatives amongst the New Norwegian writers. One of the most remarkable (and most difficult) of them is OLAV AUKRUST (1883–1929). His works are marked by a strong religious-patriotic sentiment of which *Himmelvarden* (1916), *Hamar i Hellom* (1926) and *Sunrise* ("Solrenning", 1930) are the most remarkable.

Another poet of dimensions who writes in New Norwegian is TORE ØRJASÆTER (born 1886). His chief work is *Gudbrand Langleite* (1913–1927) a long narrative poem of peasant life.

OLAF BULL (1883–1933) is one of the most distinguished amongst modern *riksmål* poets and is a strong individualist.

ARNULF ØVERLAND (born 1889) is a prominent *riksmål*

poet who combines Radical tendencies with a high degree
of artistic refinement; he has been active in politics and,
in recent years, as an ardent opponent of further language
reform. Amongst his best work are the collections of poems
Hustavler (1929) and *Thine is the Kingdom* ("Riket er ditt",
1934). During the war he became particularly well-known
for his poems designed to provide spiritual support for his
oppressed countrymen. Celebrated also for his war-time
poems is NORDAHL GRIEG (1902–1943) who met his death
whilst serving with the Norwegian forces. His literary
production was considerable and varied, including many
plays which together with his lyric poetry represent his
most important work. He was widely travelled, and this is
reflected in much of his poetry of which the cycle of poems,
Norway in our Hearts ("Norge i våre hjerter", 1929), is
the most famous. In his plays he usually deals with some
aspect of modern life of which he disapproves, but he is
not so partisan as Hoel or Fangen. Particularly to be re-
commended are, *Our Honour and Our Power* ("Vår ære
og vår makt", 1935), and *The Defeat* ("Nederlaget", 1937).

One of the most popular of the modern lyric poets is
HERMAN WILDENVEY (born 1886). His light-footed, elegant
and melodious verse has a charm few can resist. OLAV
NYGARD (1884–1924) left several collections of verse of a
serious nature which rank high amongst New Norwegian
poetry. Another poet who died young is RUDOLF NILSEN
(1901–1929). He took as his field the East End of Oslo
and prided himself on being a proletarian poet. His three
collections of poems show that he had the makings of a
lyric poet of distinction. GUNNAR REISS-ANDERSEN (born
1896) is a poet whose fluency has often been a menace to
him, but who, all the same, always has something interesting
to say. HANS-HENRIK HOLM (born 1896) attracted much
attention with his lengthy poem *Midsummer Night* ("Jon-
soknatt", 1933), a huge patch-work of peasant life, aiming

at expressing the ethos of the rural communities. INGEBORG REFLING HAGEN (born 1895) is also a writer for whom the "national" is something of a cult, with strong affiliations in language and choice of subject with the province of Hedmark in Eastern Norway. Much of what she has written shows a predilection for the fantastic and fearful. Belonging to the same nationally-minded school is INGE KROKANN (born 1893) who in his novels *I Dovre-sno* (1929), *Gjenom Fonna* (1931) and others shows a deep understanding of the Norwegian Middle Ages. TARJEI VESAAS (born 1897) is one of the most considerable of the more recent New Norwegian writers and unlike some of his fellow-writers in this field he contrives to give his novels of rural life a wider and more universal perspective.

Most popular of current *riksmål* writers is perhaps the prolific AKSEL SANDEMOSE (born 1899), who, although born a Dane, has become one of the most stylish of present-day Norwegian novelists. CORA SANDEL (born 1880) is noted for her novels from Northern Norway, particularly the so-called "Alberte" novels. Amongst the writers of the youngest generation to be dealt with here, the novelists GUNNAR LARSEN (born 1900) and JOHAN BORGEN (born 1902) are most worthy of attention.

INDEX

(The Scandinavian letters *å*, *æ/ä* and *ø/ö* are treated as the last letters of the alphabet, in that order.)

DATE

DEC 2 1 '73	
GAYLORD	